WARRIOR
IN THE RING

The Life of Marvin Camel,
American Indian World Champion Boxer

BRIAN D'AMBROSIO

RIVERBEND
PUBLISHING

Warrior in the Ring:
The Life of Marvin Camel, American Indian World Champion Boxer
Copyright © 2015 by Brian D'Ambosio

Published by Riverbend Publishing, Helena, Montana

ISBN: 978-1-60639-077-1

Printed in the United States of America.

3 4 5 6 7 8 9 0 FN 22 21 20

Cataloging-in-Publication data is on file at the Library of Congress.

Cover and text design by Sarah Cauble, sarahcauble.com

Front cover illustration by Robert Rath, courtesy of *Distinctly Montana.*

Riverbend Publishing
P.O. Box 5833
Helena, MT 59604
406-449-0200
riverbendpublishing.com

To my family and friends.

*To the hands and hearts of the boxers who,
to paraphrase Woody Guthrie,
came like the dust and were gone with the wind.*

CONTENTS

PROLOGUE

"Marvin Camel Day"

February 2, 1980, Flathead Reservation, Montana

SNOW CAME DOWN IN THE BIG, SHIMMERY CLUMPS TYPICAL OF western Montana's February squalls. Emerging from houses, doorways, and alleys—and thriving boldly in the elements—several hundred smiling fans held signs and cheered, a fluid mass of joy expressing its appreciation of the Flathead Indian Reservation's hero.

Bundled in hats and winter clothes, men, women, and children lined the roads of the small town of St. Ignatius on the edge of the reservation. They blocked traffic, forming long human processions weaving through the streets, shouting themselves hoarse as they cheered for one of their own: Marvin Camel, Montana's favorite boxer and sports personality. "As far as we are concerned, you are the champion," read one placard.

The crowd spotted Camel and his family and cheered even louder. In his dark sunglasses and light blue and white athletic jacket, Camel worked his lean jaw on one conversation after the next, paying attention to each person. He looked right and left with an expression of thanks.

Camel was something special—a great eagle heart, a great bear heart, a great twisting wind—and a fighter, a deliverer, a source of pride. With his soul burning with a flame of longing, Camel was thriving in the crazy world of boxing.

Two months earlier, on December 8, 1979, Camel had fought in boxing's first cruiserweight title match. Camel was the top-ranked contender for the new division and Mate Parlov of Yugoslavia was second.

The contest was in Split, Yugoslavia, and Camel had to brave the blood cry of thousands of Croatians screaming for their brother. The twenty-eight-year-old American, three years younger than Parlov and about an inch taller, had a five-inch-longer arm reach, and was five pounds lighter.

Parlov sent Camel tottering slightly backward in the first round and had an edge in the final round. Parlov also scored points midway through the bout. But Camel was more agile. He danced around the flat-footed, back-stepping European, scoring points. At bout's end, Parlov showed signs of fatigue.

The referee gave Camel a five-point advantage (a significant margin in a boxing match) but the two judges called it a draw. By rule, the majority consensus prevails. The match was a draw.

This outcome stunned the boxing public—and Camel. "It was highway robbery," declared an outraged Camel as he left the ring. In his heart he knew he had beaten Parlov in Parlov's backyard.

What was unmistakable was that Camel had brought the thrill of boxing to Montana and with it the buzz of success, the likes of which the state had not seen since Jack Dempsey fought Tommy Gibbons under the Big Sky in 1923.

Boxing is customarily credited with changing the lives of disadvantaged youths. Camel fit this paradigm. The young man had set some lofty, long-term goals for himself, including winning a world championship. His drive to the top wasn't easy. It included a brief jail sentence and a struggle to escape the stifling atmosphere of an Indian reservation. At this point in his career, Camel boxed because he enjoyed it. It was a job with prospects for wealth and glory, certainly better than most of the ill-paid jobs the unprivileged class do to stay alive. Boxing was his ticket out of the reservation quicksand.

The reservation had watched him grow into a champion: AAU (Amateur Athletic Union) Champ five times; Montana state champion four times; Junior National Inland Empire Champ; State Male Athlete of the Year for 1972. Traveling the expanse of Montana (no small feat in the fourth-largest state), he was the state amateur champion from 1964 to 1972 in various weight classes from 105 to 165 pounds. Before turning pro, he fought Marvin Johnson and beat Sugar Ray Seales (both were future boxing hall of famers).

The half-day salute—"Marvin Camel Day" was sponsored by the Flathead Culture Committee and Salish Tribal Council to honor Marvin and the Camel clan for their various "noteworthy achievements in athletics." The chatty, amiable Marvin was received with respect. A calm, good-looking man with a fresh face, quick smile, dark eyes, and an air of confidence, Camel looked antithetical to boxing's crooked-nose pug living on the fringes of civilization. He spoke articulately to friends and played the part of boxing's sympathetic spokesperson, talking ever so highly of a sport so alien to most others. His silly, eye-rolling sense of humor counteracted the usual melodrama of boxing.

Camel answered all the inevitable questions. He discussed the real threat of being throttled and torn to pieces every time he went to work. "Marvin, what's it like in there?" "Marvin, do those three-minute rounds feel like an eternity?" "What does it feel like to land one of those jolting right uppercuts on another man's chin?" "How about a white man's chin?"

"There is more to it than a mouthful of blood and just fighting," Camel answered. "It's boxing, not fighting. Fighting is out in the bars. That's what they do there. I'm a boxer."

Soon a large feast provided the crowd with an array of delicious options, and a full slate of approximately a dozen speeches commenced: two of Marvin's high school coaches, Joe McDonald and Larry Anderson; Tribal Councilmen Noel Pichette and Thomas "Bearhead" Swaney; three tribal spiritual leaders; a Spokane tribal leader from Washington, Hy Neh; a student of Indian culture, Michael Joseph; and noted pow-wow activist Octave Finley.

Joseph said Camel was like "a returning warrior of old, bringing honor to his people and being honored by them." Former Confederated Salish and Kootenai Tribal secretary Doug Allard praised Camel for his example.

"Thank you, Marvin for being courteous, a good businessman and a good Indian." Those words came from Walt McDonald, the man who had "been supporting Marvin the longest." McDonald added, "Marvin has fought some of the best boxers in the world and has shown his mettle. It is time that he is recognized as a great fighter in his own right."

During the ceremony Camel was given an Indian name: "Yosh-Ilimi Nenemay the First," meaning "Strong Leader." His wife, Sherry, became "Cho-we," or "Long Hair." Their two sons, "Livewire" Louis and newborn Marvin, Jr., became "Strong Leader, the Second" and "Little Fox Nenemay." The naming was carried out by prayer leader and language instructor Johnny Arlee.

When the last speaker concluded, Joseph and Arlee gave Camel a war staff: a bearskin-wrapped spear with thirty-nine feathers, one for each of Camel's professional fights. Arlee said there was space on the staff for one more feather, "which we hope will be a winning feather."

After the last words of praise and thanks, there was a general migration to the St. Ignatius Community Center where Indian dancers performed a pow-wow. The Native people respected Marvin and the years he had spent boxing, working at the local lumber mill, fixing pinball machines, and, in sum, surviving. They knew it took a special person to spend decades in a sport known for solitary discipline, isolation, and effort.

Indeed, this was no ordinary occasion and no ordinary place.

This celebration took place on an ancient land where the pure exhilaration of fighting was culturally understood. And the man they were here to praise, well, he took what mattered most to them and attached it to boxing: pride, despair, conflict, duality. He represented them when he battled in the ring, when he gave—and received—painful lessons, when he showcased his style and skills. He represented them when his face was cut, bleeding, grotesquely swollen, when his body was covered with his own blood, and he kept fighting.

Marvin Camel's relationship with his people, his family, and himself had suffered from a combination of distractions, the most prominent of which was Marvin's relentless pursuit of a pulsating sign pointing to better times ahead. Indeed, the epic journey of a man's desire to be free is never without personal demons. Nevertheless, the mood on this day was marked by visible, palpable expressions of triumph and friendship. With faces to the big sky, Flathead Indians (and non–tribal-members) filled their lungs with air and let out a scream of joy that seemed as if it would never end, and a scream that seemed to come from untold reserves of strength. They rejoiced with all their might.

Marvin Camel had touched the soul of Montanans, making them cheer, dream, and wonder. One man inspired an entire reservation—and state.

In the first half of the twentieth century, people all over the world listened to radio broadcasts of important boxing matches or watched them on flickering televisions. When Marvin Camel entered the world in 1950, boxing held a high place in the pecking order of sports. There was media space to devote to boxers and more reason for allotting it, since public interest in characters such as Camel was strong. Indeed, Camel's name is a throwback to the days when morning newspapers carried lengthy stories of last night's fights.

Nowadays, boxing stands on sports' outer reaches, battered and sagging, lumped with lacrosse, rowing, horse racing, cricket, sailing, soccer, and the WNBA in the "Other" section of newspapers' sports pages. No current sports magazine has a full-time boxing writer.

Camel's name has been lost on Montana's wider cultural history. Perhaps even worse, young boxers know nothing about the man who, in 1999, *Sports Illustrated* listed as Montana's eighteenth greatest sports figure. From Croatia to Denmark, Germany and Italy, to Las Vegas and Billings, Montana, in dimly lit gyms and large, sold-out arenas, Marvin Camel represented himself, his reservation, and his home state. In this great undertaking, Camel mostly had to depend on himself.

Just a few weeks after Marvin Camel Day, in the heat and sweat of Las Vegas, Camel brawled his way to a unanimous decision over Parlov in their rematch. With his right eye nearly closed and blood streaming from his left temple from the fifth round on, Camel showed more valor than style as he fought his heart out to beat Parlov. Camel was a bloody mess and not very pretty, but he fought one hell of a fight and became the World Boxing Council's first champion in the newly minted cruiserweight division.

At last, the fierce young warrior from a rural Indian reservation was a world champion. But nothing in boxing—or life, really—comes without a thick set of complications. At present, few reminders of boxing, or of Marvin Camel's accomplishments, or that special day decades ago exist outside of a sporadic dinner conversation and a faded poster on the wall of a St. Ignatius recreation center. Camel himself lives thousands of miles away from the reservation, in humble circumstances.

But all was joyful on that special day long ago when Camel felt the love of his people, their mood and judgment, their support and strength. It was a feeling of oneness, of unity.

Your Path

Everything is laid out for you,
Your path is straight ahead of you.
Sometimes it's invisible but it's there.
You may not know where it's going,
but you have to follow that path.
It's the path to the Creator.
It's the only path there is.

Chief Leon Shenandoah (1990)

01

BOXING'S UNDERBELLY

IN THE BOXING RING, EQUATIONS OF LIFE AND SPORT ARE INVERTED. It's a place where one needs to move with and transmit anger, violence, and prejudice to succeed. Amazing feats are accomplished in this sanctioned warfare, and there are no peace treaties, no philosophical discussions, just mutually destructive conflict. The slightest signal of neutrality or reluctance can spell demise. Everyone senses the danger. But boxing is not about drawing wisdom from sanity–it's about the common sense of survival.

Everyone in boxing faces fears and demons that most people don't accept or even see coming. Boxers know that isolative feeling of survival and intimidation bound up in boxing's bluster. Boxing is a dark journey. Its darkness explains why writers–particularly American ones—have always been intrigued by what happens between the ropes—the primal contest—juxtaposed with the wild carnival atmosphere outside. From musty gyms to glitzy casinos, writers have chronicled determination and dissipation, great champions and punch-drunk has-beens, colorful entourages and outrageous promoters. They have written incisively about race, rage, class, self-preservation, and spectacle.

Still, the fighter's endemic willingness to endure violence, with his own demise always imminent, remains ancient drama, difficult to explain. The moves, the speed, the power, the pain—they are all a part of the boxing mystique.

Blending raw power, brute courage, and trained skill, the "Sweet

Science" incites a wider range of emotions than any other sport. It reveals most of the hopes and tensions that make humanity stir.

Marvin Camel discovered that boxing was an absolute experience. It produced an extreme intensity that was difficult to find or duplicate in daily life. Boxing absorbed Camel whole, subsumed him into its underbelly.

In 250 amateur and professional fights, Camel was never knocked out. He may have had his lights turned off and his clock cleaned, and he may have been stopped by officials because of ugly cuts, bruises, and bleeding, but he was never knocked unconscious, and he never quit. His encounters were gnarly in detail, variously noted for their savagery, artistry, controversy, rivalry, or pure spectacle.

Camel was part of boxing's golden age when the sport was one of the most publicized forms of entertainment in the world. He tangled with personalities such as Matthew Saad Muhammad, one of the greatest Philadelphia fighters. Abandoned as a child along a busy parkway, Saad Muhammad lost just three bouts in his first 18 fights and in 1979 fought for the WBC world title, knocking out Marvin Johnson. But when the glory faded, "Miracle Matthew" kept fighting, and he was frequently battered and overmatched.

In 1980 Camel fought on the same card as the infamous "no mas" fight which saw Sugar Ray Leonard defeat Roberto Duran in one of the most shocking endings in boxing history. Having fought previously, with Duran winning a decision, the rematch was an inglorious embarrassment for Duran, a monster of a man said to have broken a policeman's jaw with his "hands of stone" as a twelve-year-old in the ghettos of Panama City, Panama. Ray out-boxed and out-maneuvered Duran so effectively that at two minutes and 44 seconds into the eighth round, the "savage warrior" quit. The ringside broadcaster thought he heard two words that would haunt Duran forever: "No mas, no mas." *No more, no more.* Duran actually said, "No quiero pelear con el payaso." *I do not want to fight with this clown.* Duran slunk to his corner, head hung low, a desperate, beaten figure of failure.

Camel sparred with men such as Ron Lyle, the son of a preacher father and missionary mother, who brawled with the best of boxing's heavyweights. The sinister-looking convicted murderer had been, by his own admission, "to hell and back."

Camel fought men whose stories could have been torn from pulp fiction. One was Bash Ali, an articulate, Nigerian-born political science major who thought boxing was "stupid." One day the college kid walked into a gym in Oakland, California, and without any boxing experience, declared that he could whip any man in the ring. He whipped many men in his subsequent career.

There was Willie "The Cannon" Shannon, who, while in prison, morphed from a scrawny teenager into a 6-foot-5, 185-pound accumulation of muscles. He took up pro boxing in small Florida arenas, often against opponents who outweighed him by thirty pounds or more because Shannon chose to fight as a heavyweight—they earned bigger paychecks. Even by boxing's sordid standards, Shannon's fall was precipitous and ugly. Months before he matched up against Camel for the Nevada State Cruiserweight Championship, Shannon murdered a woman in retaliation for a financial dispute. He was charged decades later.

There was Bill Sharkey, a former gang leader from Queens, who fought Camel in Missoula, Montana, for the first significant cruiserweight title fight in 1979. Nine years earlier, Sharkey and another man allegedly drove to a home in Queens and shot and killed a man. Charged with murder, the jury convicted him of manslaughter. Sentenced to 10 years, he was released in three. While in prison, Sharkey had a two-word expletive tattooed on the inside of his lower lip. In 1998, Sharkey's body was found burning deep in the woods in Pennsylvania. He had been shot, stuffed in the trunk of the old New York City police car he tooled around in, and then set on fire—several miles from a log cabin he had built with his own hands.

There were others. Camel's career intersected with some of the most memorable boxing luminaries of the modern era, including promoter Don King, trainer Eddie Futch, light heavyweight great Bob Foster, and the brash Muhammad Ali.

In 1980, boxing launched the cruiserweight division—a weight bracket from 176 to 190 pounds that was the answer for men too big for the light heavyweight class and not hefty enough to throw leather with the true heavyweights. Camel was the first cruiserweight champ with the World Boxing Council (WBC) in 1980 and the International Boxing Federation (IBF) in 1984.

Camel defied simple categorization as a fighter and as a person. For a pugilist, Camel was exquisitely handsome, tall and commanding, with a charming and a warm personality. Mild-mannered, easy-going, possessing a keen sense of humor and wisdom, he was the antithesis of the brash thug or tiresome showboat who provoked fisticuffs at weigh-ins, talked uneducated drivel, or stared down opponents with exaggerated machismo. Camel would personify your average mild-mannered gentleman, which he had been all his life, except for the fury unleashed from a wellspring of unexplored emotions when he laced up his gloves.

Camel was a solid defensive boxer who favored strategy over slugging. The fact that he was a lefthander—a fairly rare commodity in the boxing world and a trait that caused opposing fighters to change their styles—hampered his opportunities for big fights. His charging, awkward style—baffling to opponents—also made it difficult to find matches.

At times Camel felt as if he were the perennial underdog, a guy that no one gives a damn about. On occasion, he was pessimistic about his chosen profession—"legalized murder" he called it—and whether or not he should have dedicated his entire existence to something that received so little respect. At other times, he embarked on personal public relations campaigns on behalf of professional boxing.

Marvin Camel reached high plateaus in his professional life and made tremendous sacrifices in his personal life, which included a divorce from the woman who frequently worked as his trainer.

Told that he was risking his sight in one eye by continuing to box, he kept fighting until nearly age forty.

Ultimately, Camel made sacrifices to be exceptional. He proved that we are stronger the wider we open our perceptions. People such as Marvin Camel are the only ones who can create a climate for the American dream to survive another generation. "If the American dream is to come true and to abide with us," historian James Truslow Adams wrote in *The Epic of America*, "it will, at bottom, depend on the people themselves."

Life was there for the taking. Marvin Camel proved that.

02

CENTURIES IN THE MAKING

*"No other reservation can say they have a world champion,
except maybe Jim Thorpe's."*

—*Lincoln Billedeaux, Flathead Indian Reservation*

As a young man, Marvin Camel had many dreams, and those dreams guided the course of his future. But his course—his dreams—could not be set apart from the historical context of the American Indian.

On the Flathead Reservation of northwestern Montana, the story of Marvin's people is shared and experienced against the backdrop of sacred landscape. Here the skyline is drawn not by the architectural achievements of man, but by the jagged profile of the Mission Mountains. Snow-capped peaks loom above the mile-high Flathead Valley with its clear waters and eye-ravishing vistas. Wilderness is all around; elk, deer, and grizzly bears are present.

Most of the valley is not Indian land. From June until September, much of the traffic passing through the Flathead Valley on two-lane U.S. Highways 2 and 93 is going to and from Glacier National Park. Thirty-seven-mile-long Flathead Lake is the largest natural body of fresh water within a single state west of the Mississippi River. The lake's 135 miles of shoreline supports small towns, state parks, marinas, fledgling vineyards, and cherry orchards. Orchards and fruit stands sprout up along the shore. The lake boasts sailing and fishing tournaments.

The Flathead Indian Reservation occupies approximately 1,243,000 acres on the western slope of the Continental Divide, with exterior boundaries of the reservation spanning portions of four counties—Flathead, Lake, Missoula, and Sanders.

The National Bison Range is on its southern border. Highway 93 goes through it, and the town of Ronan lies within it.

Ronan—Marvin's birthplace, with a population of less than 1,500 at the time—was first called Spring Creek, a reference to the local warm springs flowing into nearby Flathead River. Residents adopted the name Ronan Springs in 1893 as a tribute to U.S. Army Maj. Peter Ronan, who "served the tribes with honesty and compassion" as the Flathead Indian Reservation agent from the 1870s until his death in 1892.

The three tribes of the Flathead Indian Reservation are the Salish, Pend d'Oreille, and Kootenai. Seliñ is the proper name for the Salish, who refer to themselves as Sqélio̊—the People.

There are 6,961 enrolled members of the Confederated Salish and Kootenai Tribes. Of this population, 4,244 live on the reservation. Many Indians still speak their indigenous languages, and ancestral storytelling is the bedrock of tribal art, music, and dance.

The Flathead Valley was home to bands of Plateau and Basin tribes for at least twelve to fifteen thousand years. The earliest tribes were nomadic and had seasonal camping spots, which form the basis of many Salish stories. They lived off the land, and the land could be stingy and capricious.

In the words of Salish elder and storyteller Kenny Camel—Marvin's younger brother—"The Salish People hunted buffalo, elk, deer, mountain goats and harvested the bounty of the grains, berries and camas plants. The water was also a provider. They fished for sturgeon and harvested abalone shells to make jewelry and use for trading. They followed yearly migration routes that started in northwestern Montana, into Idaho, part of Washington and up into Canada. Some of the world's most beautiful and resource rich lands are located here in Flathead."

From 1778 to 1871, as white Americans inched westward, the U.S government brokered—and often broke—treaties with American Indian nations. The 1855 Hellgate Treaty allowed for creation of the Flathead Reservation. In return, Salish tribal leaders reluctantly ceded more than 22 million acres elsewhere in western Montana to the United States government.

In 1870, the Bitterroot Salish Indians—falsely called "Flatheads" by the original white explorers—were a small tribe living in and around the Bitterroot Valley of southwestern Montana Territory. "The Salish are often been referred to as "Flatheads," said Robert McDonald, Tribal Communications Director of the Confederated Salish and Kootenai Tribes. "But this name is a misnomer and, in actuality, there are no Flatheads. There are three stories about the false origin. One is that since the foot of [Flathead] lake is flat, the early trappers got confused. The other is that a hand signal for the tribe was to put your palm facing your forehead, gesturing as if smacking above the forehead. Another suggestion is that we simply somehow got confused with the coastal Salish, who were known for flattening the heads of their babies. We never did that here, or had anything to do with that."

In 1891, the economically impoverished Salish accepted government promises of assistance and retreated to the Flathead Reservation, more than sixty miles north of their homeland.

The Dawes Severalty Act of 1887 was applied to the Flathead Reservation in April 1904, leading to enrollment, then allotment, and finally the opening of the reservation to a random drawing of 3,000 prospective homesteaders. Theodore Roosevelt described the legislation as "a mighty pulverizing agent to break up the tribal mass." One hundred sixty acres of reservation land were allotted to each family head, with half the amount given to orphans and single persons over eighteen years of age. Those Indians judged "competent" were allowed to acquire immediate ownership of their land, which meant they were free to sell it to whites.

After allotment of reservation land to Indian adults and exempting some land for such things as "town sites, a bison range, and power installations," the remaining lands were to be sold with the money used for tribal benefit. In effect, much of the reservation was opened to settlement by non-Indians.

Tribal rhythms were downright disrupted. Oral histories of Indians routinely include the phrases "before allotment" or "after allotment." Many tribes began to succumb to afflictions such as pneumonia, malaria, and meningitis. Open-range grazing of the Indians' livestock ended, pushing many families into hardship. On July 4, 1907, Secretary of the Interior James Garfield's train was met by nearly 500 mounted Flatheads who voiced their opposition to opening the reservation to homesteading.

Within a few years, however, an excited land grab ensued when unclaimed homestead lots were opened to entry and the Interior Department issued orders to sell two- to five-acre tracts of reservation land on Flathead Lake for cottages and vacation homes. The plan was to make the scenic lake front "bloom like a rose."

The 1.2-million-acre reservation, guaranteed in perpetuity less than a quarter century before, ceased to exist. By 1935 only 30 percent of the original reservation land remained in Indian ownership. Today, of the total population living on the reservation, only twenty-five percent are Native Americans.

The trajectory of the Flathead Indian Reservation was repeated all over the West, and perhaps the force behind it was as inevitable as it was irresistible. "Go West, young man, go West and grow up with the country," Horace Greeley intoned.

The myth of the West was the myth of America: a nameless person could set out for the Territory and build a prosperous new life. The belief in the individual's capacity to make his way—to cross oceans and mountains—only grew stronger as America grew older. Witness, for instance, Henry Williams Campbell, an African American born May 24, 1924, in Monroe, North Carolina. When he was 16, Campbell fled the prejudices of the Jim Crow South by joining the Navy.

Part of the Great Migration, Henry was one of more than 1.5 million blacks who moved from the South to the Northeast, Midwest, and West between 1915 and 1940. The move was Henry's way of distancing himself from the ugliness of segregation, escaping economic hardship, and following the dream of a better life. Around this time, as further repudiation of his former self, he abbreviated his last name to "Camel."

While stationed in Astoria, Oregon, the Navy Petty Officer, cook, and club boxer met Alice Nenemay, a full-blood Pend d'Oreille who had left the Flathead Reservation at fifteen and later found work welding U.S. Navy ships in Washington shipyards.

Alice was born to Alex and Elaine Nenemay on January 16, 1920, at their home near Dixon, Montana. Years earlier, Alex had moved to the lower Flathead River country, where he met Elaine. They married and settled near the river, raising cantaloupes, watermelon, and potatoes, and harvesting apples in the area's many orchards. Alice's grandmother, Josette, was an only child and said to be the "belle of the Mission Valley." Her grandfather, John Eneas, was a tall, handsome man. After falling in love with Josette, John built their log home on the river.

Alice, one of nine children, was a peppy young girl "who ran like the wind," said her daughter Patricia. Alice purportedly "outran her family's horses." She covered great distances cross-country and herded cattle on foot, "running all the way." She was said to have "chased the horses down when the family had no fences." The family tells a story about Alice when she was a child not yet in her teens. Her mother and father got on the buckboard to go to Dixon about six miles away. "You stay home," they told her. Instead, Alice took off running and beat the buckboard to town.

Alice and her siblings walked the cliffs and hills, roamed the openness playing games, worked in their great big garden, lassoed horses, and swam almost every day, according to Alice's written memoirs.

By fifteen, Alice was hopping trains to Washington, visiting family and working. She stayed on the Kalispel Reservation in eastern Washington with her brother, Frank, and his family, for about three years, working as a motel maid and waitress. She also lived on the eastern edge of the Yakima Reservation in Toppenish, Washington.

During World War II, Alice and her friend, Aggie, were part of a voluntary Relocation Program for war work which took them to Vancouver, Washington. Alice worked at a shipyard for the unionized Kaiser Company, Inc. Donning the welder's hood and a big leather apron, she worked on a ship's hull, unaware of even the vessel's name or destination. At the end of the war she was working in Portland.

A new segment of Alice's life began when she attended a USO dance across the Columbia River in Astoria. She described the encounter with Henry Camel as "love at first sight."

In 1944, after dating for six months, Alice and Henry married in Portland. They eventually moved to an 80-acre home site in Ronan, Montana, down a rutted dirt road slicing straight to the heart of the Mission Mountains. Alice happily brought her new husband—one of the few, if not the only, African Americans that locals had ever seen—home to the reservation.

Alice and Henry reared 14 children: Cathy, born in 1947, followed by Henry, Jr., Charles, Tom, Helen, Pat, Marvin, Frank (who died as an infant of pneumonia), Paula, Florine, Ken, Terry, Bob, and Renee. (Marvin and other siblings state that the first two Camel children, Cathy and Henry Junior, are full-bloodied Indians and definitely not Henry's. "That's the way it is on the reservation," said one family member.)

Life on the reservation had a lovely, rather magical side, as well as a bitter, Draconian one. The family worked hard, clearing the woods and building a home on Alice's trust land. Henry found employment as a ranch hand for successful Missoula businessman Harry Oscar "H.O." Bell. "Henry used nothing but physical force in his job," Marvin said later. "He had to. No stump grinders. No log splitters. No automated boilers or rakers. No luxuries. It was all physical."

Bell's Bar Lazy B ranch produced two cuttings of alfalfa hay a year and plentiful crops of oats, barley, and garden vegetables. Mary Ellen Rae, H.O. Bell's granddaughter, recalled Henry in a 1991 biography of H.O. Bell: "We had a man named Henry Camel (boxer Marvin Camel's father), who was with us for 24 years. He and Harry would get into these arguments. Henry would say, 'Mr. Bell, you're entirely wrong on that' or, 'That isn't the way you should do such and such.' They would have words about a lot of different things, but they always remained good friends. Harry was always interested in Henry because he felt he had a lot to offer."

Marvin Louis Camel was born December 24, 1950, a cloudy, foggy, Christmas Eve Sunday in the foothills of the Mission Mountains. His middle name was bestowed in honor of boxing legend Joe Louis. (Marvin's younger brother Robert Liston Camel received his middle name from boxer Sonny Liston.)

If there is one defining characteristic of Marvin Camel, it is supreme confidence in everything he does. The trait arises naturally from an iron will, steely nerves, and a fierce determination. Where these qualities came from is not difficult to discern. They were forged in the fiery furnace of environment and upbringing

The Camel family was caught in a cycle of poverty that often haunts those who live on Indian reservations. The growing family lived in a house with four bedrooms, one of which used to be the living room. Food and money were scarce. Keeping the kids washed, cleanly dressed, and getting them to school took most of Alice's time. Henry's work day on the cattle ranch started early and ended late.

Alice recalled her life as a never-ending cycle of washing, wood-splitting, cooking, canning meat, harvesting vegetables from the garden and preserving them, and, of course, refereeing the inevitable quarrels between her growing sons and daughters. "We lived day by day," she wrote in her journals. "Too much work. We didn't have the automatic washer, the dryer. We had to haul water, hang the clothes up outside. We just lived from scratch, I guess. You never sat and thought about how poor you were."

As soon as the Camel kids were old enough to walk, they were expected to contribute; they hauled water, cut firewood, washed laundry, tended garden, and canned vegetables. For food, they killed, butchered, and preserved the deer and bear flanking their property. When washday came, it was just that—a whole day of hauling and heating the water, filling the washer by hand, hanging the clothes outside to dry. In the winter, even before a blizzard stopped howling, they tugged on boots and trudged out to shovel the snow. After school, into the darkness of night, the Camel children worked.

Henry's philosophy was simple and unambiguous: if the kids knew how to put on their shoes and clothes, they could work, too. He could be stern, and the belt was his favored mode of punishment.

Henry's influence on the outlook and aspirations of his children was pervasive, and thanks to him, Marvin saw himself as someone special—someone set apart, not subject to the limitations holding others back. In the fifth grade Marvin scribbled an essay in which he declared, "I want to be the champ of the world." Marvin's dreams not only revealed the future. They controlled it.

Ruthlessly masculine, Henry Camel had been drawn at an early age to the primal survivalist drama of boxing and had boxed as an amateur. Familiar with the hard stares and the cross insults of racial disdain, Henry insisted that his sons Charles, Tom, Marvin, and Kenneth learn boxing as a form of physical and mental preparation. If they could handle themselves with their fists, they would earn respect and the space to live that most families take for granted.

To teach his sons and others, Henry started the Desert Horse Boxing Club in nearby Polson. Still working full-time, Henry taught boxing in his spare time. Polson resident and later Camel family friend Don Albert said that Henry was the best trainer he ever had. "Henry taught me more in five minutes than all I learned from any other trainer," Albert said.

Amateur boxer Allan Burland developed true boxing skills thanks to Henry, whom he called "a great, smart man." More than four decades later, Burland remembered Henry's lean, well-distributed physique as his most memorable trait. "He had a hard, smooth body type, no flab," Burland said.

Dean Kromarek, 64, remembered watching Henry in an unsanctioned boxing match one time in Great Falls. Kromarek was 16 and he had already boxed Marvin three times in the amateurs. He said that Henry's "peaceful practices" in the ring helped sear his image into memory.

"Henry was very smooth in the ring," said Kromarek. "He almost seemed to have too gentle of a heart in the ring, too cordial. He could've tore guys apart, but he didn't have that killer instinct. He enjoyed the sport more than the hostility—at least that is how it appeared to me at the time. Henry coached at the local job corps. It seemed like he boxed mostly to encourage the kids at the young corps and boxed more to show them—and his own kids—how to get out of—and stay out of—trouble."

Family friend Larry Anderson recalled once watching Henry Camel lose a fight to a younger boxer. "Henry just finished milking cows for old Bell," said Anderson. "After work, he fought a young kid from Kalispell. The kid beat Henry. [Later] I saw the rematch in Kalispell, and Henry beat him real quick." Anderson said he considered Henry Camel a friend who "may not have been real compassionate," and that he often sensed it was "difficult for the boys to be around Henry."

Joe McDonald considered Henry Camel a friend, too. While he said that Henry was a man known to "take good care of his children" and was "a real gentleman," he added that Henry had "a mid-life crisis" in which he went on "a wild drinking streak chasing young women."

While Henry was the dominant parent, Alice was strong-willed, forever telling her huge brood they could achieve whatever they wanted if they put their minds to it. "I loved my mother and I always skipped school to do things for her," Marvin said. Uninterested and truant, Marvin was forced to repeat the first and fifth grades. "I was my mom's messenger," Marvin explained. "I was always running errands and delivering messages and missing school. I was an outspoken little guy. If they wanted me to say something to somebody, I'd go say it. If you wanted something done, I'd do it. I missed a lot of school because of that."

Ken Camel recalled that his earliest years were spent playing outdoors and consuming the best elements of mountain living. Racism, however, was ubiquitous, even on the reservation, perhaps especially on the reservation. Ken recalled being told that he was "too dark" and his hair "too curly."

"Up until I was eleven-years-old, I heard the 'n' word," Marvin said. "Native Americans were the most racist people you'd ever want to meet. The white people were half-assed and talked bullshit. You hear the negative all day long and see your brothers getting into fights."

Helen Camel has done a lot of reflecting on her mixed racial heritage. "We didn't associate out in the community very much," she said. "Back then I wondered if this was some way my mom was protecting us. We were pretty well accepted, but in some ways the racial thing did help develop—I don't know—a sense of family and a sense of pride that we kids kind of clung to."

"The Camel family faced racism from the Indian community for being African American," said Robert McDonald. "That's true. There was a lot of conflict, and not just Indian-white, but Indian-black, and Indian versus Indian, and are you Indian enough? That's part of the historical trauma, and the life of a people who are uncertain about what's right in making even the smallest decisions. But there was no shortage of self-love in the Camel family."

In a place where a different physical appearance made people targets of hostility and indifference, the Camel kids sought protection—and vindication for being different—in athletics.

Ken turned to boxing because he "hated people." The steady stream of racial taunts made him "angry" and "unwhole." Yet Ken equally hated the brutality of boxing, the bone-jarring and head-snapping savagery. He remembered his father pushing him under the ropes into the ring as a scared six-year-old. When Henry would tell him it was time to practice, Ken would hide behind the woodshed. With his mom's help, Ken quit—for what would not be the last time—at age eight, after two fights.

Marvin's older brother Tom, fourth in the Camel birth order, recalled the racism. When Tom was about 10 years old, the owner of a Ronan café asked the family to leave because some customers did not want to eat in the same room as their father. Tom said he and his brothers were routinely on the receiving end of racial slurs from both whites and Native Americans.

Henry told his sons that boxing was their counterpunch against such affronts. "He said, 'If anybody calls you names, you fight back,'" said Tom. "He taught us that we had a responsibility to defend ourselves."

Tom began boxing at age twelve and fought in 78 matches before his twentieth birthday. He traveled with the Desert Horse team to tournaments across Montana and qualified for the national Golden Gloves tournament, where he reached the semifinals.

"Boxing gave me some control and self-esteem in a place that took away your self-esteem," Tom said. "It also gave my family self-esteem when they would come to watch me box."

Tom had a reputation as a hard-hitting slugger. "Tom had an overhand right that could knock your eyeballs out," Marvin remembered. Larry Anderson recalled Tom's toughness quite clearly: "One night he fought this kid from the Seeley Lake who was 26, while Tommy was just a teen. Tommy did a number on him."

Facing the military draft at age 21, Tom willingly enlisted. While in the Army, he boxed at every opportunity. A newspaper clipping from 1969 details Tom and his Fort Bragg Army boxing team beating up Camp Lejeune's Marine team.

Tom saw combat in Vietnam. He was so badly wounded by rifle fire that he had to have his right leg amputated. Marvin suspected fratricide. "It was not by the Vietcong," Marvin said. "It was one of our own guys in the barracks. It was a guy in his own platoon, I think. I never did ask him about it. He returned [from Vietnam] a full-fledged alcoholic."

"The story was that Tommy was with a white soldier," said Renee Camel. "The story was that some black soldiers started razzing the white soldier. Tom intervened on the white soldier's behalf and the black soldiers began firing."

When Marvin was twelve-years-old, he had gone with his father to watch Tom box at the Polson VFW. He took in all the sights of boxing, all the preparation for battle. He saw kids putting on their headgear, mouthpieces, and leather gloves, their hands enveloped in cotton. He saw their nostrils and brows slathered with sweat. The bells rang. Fighters sized up each other. Two youngsters shuffled and pawed with their jabs. Shouts of advice and the slap of gloves rang in Marvin's ears. Even with his unlearned eyes, Marvin sensed that boxers trained in order to throw punches fast, hard, and in number. Soon, he was yanked into the ring.

"Henry just put me in the ring without any training or anything," Marvin said. "My dad said someone was looking for a fight and asked me how much I weighed. I said 106 pounds, then Dad turned away and told the guy, 'I've got someone for you.' It was either get in the ring or face the belt."

Marvin did not want to fight, not yet, not that night. But he had no choice. He got in the ring and lost to an experienced 14-year-old named Allan Burland. "I had a few fights by then and had age and experience on my side," Burland said. "We ended up fighting, I think, five times. There is no such thing as a natural athlete. But Marvin was as close to it as you could be. You couldn't compare to his speed. I wasn't the least bit surprised that he went on to win the championship."

In that first fight, Marvin got his introduction to the haziness of absorbing blows and taking a punch. *Hook, cross, down, right, left. It seems to last forever. The rounds are a blur. Marvin is outclassed and outweighed. He is resigned and weary, yet during one of these flurries, a realization hits him: I can't quit. No damn way am I quitting. I'll learn this goddamn sport before I quit it. I'll show Henry my intention.*

In that contest, Marvin did not show an excess of talent. He did not display any remarkable skills. But he did get up. He finished on his feet. He lost, but he did not quit.

Even today, Marvin says that his first loss to Burland will stay with him for the rest of his life. "That's good for a lot of people, to just give up," Camel said. "But I didn't feel that way. I felt that I had got to keep moving forward. I had to keep advancing."

Even in defeat, the rhythms and postures of boxing felt natural to Marvin, as if defined through ancient muscle memory. "After that first loss, I knew I needed to change," says Camel. "I worked my butt off for the next bout. I stayed with it. Boxing was not a chore then, it was easy, second nature."

Second nature or not, Marvin knew he'd better put in his best effort if he wanted to avoid conflict with his father. "The best motivation with me growing up was the two-inch belt around his waist," Marvin said. "He had the belt and he knew how to use it. That was a training ritual on his part. The belt was my conditioning coach."

A widespread stereotype about boxing is that it is a relatively simple thing to do if one is simple or uneducated enough to do it. Marvin learned early that boxing was anything but an easy matter of putting on padded gloves and swinging to glory. He learned that people play baseball, basketball, football, tennis, and golf, but no one plays boxing—there is nothing dilettantish about it. He learned that boxing is brutal and unforgiving, and it takes a certain aptitude, both physical and mental, to endure a painful fight.

Marvin began training in earnest, sparring with his brothers in their yard. Within a few months, he knew how to throw a jab and avoid a left hook. He understood that the sport possessed brutality and ferocity that could harm him. Yet he knew there was so much more to it: instinct, bravery, skill, artistry, smarts, and aptitude. Above all, Marvin felt his own power, the sense that he was in control instead of being a victim. For the first time Marvin felt he could conquer any force. In the ring, where men are scored on their ability to harm one another, Marvin felt the safest he had ever felt.

Marvin provided Henry with a reflection of what his father hoped was his own masculinity and imagined prowess when it came to out-toughing other males and letting them have it. Marvin discovered a bloodlust that belied his normally sensitive disposition. The only thing that felt better than belting an opponent with a straight left jab was belting him again.

Before long, as Marvin's reputation as a boxer spread, the racial aggression directed at him abated. Marvin walked the halls of Ronan schools with a newfound sense of self-assurance, a swagger which told fellow students that he could "clean their clocks." Whenever any of his siblings was bothered or set upon by troublemakers older and bigger, Marvin warned the bullies to leave his family alone or face the consequences. When the warnings failed, Camel used his fists. From that point on, nobody dared call him "nigger." "We weren't accepted by the tribe or white community," Marvin said, but now he and his siblings were no longer constant targets.

Despite feeling unaccepted by the tribe, Marvin embraced his Native American heritage. "I've always wanted to be noted as Native American," said Marvin. "I wanted to be noted just like my mother and my kids. People always look at me and they think, 'What is he?' Only problem I had was from my own tribe when I was growing up. After I won the title, the Native Americans called me 'chief of the reservation.' But off the reservation, they say I have an accent.

"I'm not black if you look hard enough. I don't go to functions where black people congregate because I have nothing in common with them. When I was boxing in Los Angeles in the 1980s, I worked out where there was nobody but blacks, and I was accepted. But that's as close to it as I've ever gotten to them. The word 'nigger' was used a lot in my earlier years. After I entered the gym, I wasn't Marvin the nigger, but Marvin my friend."

Florine Camel, Marvin's sister, agreed: "We were never around or comfortable with black people. We grew up in a white man's world."

"They were something of an in-between family," said Joe Mc-Donald, a former Ronan school teacher who saw many Camel kids pass through. "They weren't familiar with black culture—and they couldn't be. Because they were part black, they didn't really get involved in Indian things, Indian music, or food, or dance."

After Marvin had won the first of his two world boxing titles, Salish Kootenai elders presented him with a war bonnet and made him an honorary tribal chief.

"They finally accepted me as a true brother," said Marvin. "I was not a boxer, I was not a half black, I was a true member. But we didn't feel that love growing up."

As part of training, Marvin began to run. On those long forays on slick, cold roads, he felt a philosophical sense of purpose. *With a large bird above me, I am running in the sky. I entrust myself to one wind. My feather sailing on the breeze. Honoring brave elders who came before me. Believing in myself. Believing in the warrior.*

In his early teens Marvin traveled across the region for amateur boxing competitions. Then he interrupted his boxing for three years to participate in high school sports. He was all-conference in football and basketball. He ran the 440-yard dash and the half-mile on the track team.

Larry Anderson was Camel's football, basketball, and track coach at Ronan High School. He remembered Marvin as a serious, dedicated youngster. "He seemed like he was on a mission and stayed with it. Like all the Camel kids, he paid attention, was polite, neat, and well-mannered. He was not outgoing as a kid, but reserved. He responded well to people around him, young and old. From early on, Marvin was a standout, with exceptional hand-eye coordination skills."

McDonald, who later became president of Salish Kootenai College, was the Ronan High School principal and a football coach when Marvin was there. McDonald coached Marvin through his sophomore and junior football seasons.

"Marvin played on defensive and offensive side of the ball," McDonald said. "He never missed a practice. He was not afraid of contact." McDonald remembered one incident that was indicative of Marvin's lifelong determination. At a track meet Marvin was severely spiked in the back of his calf. A doctor rushed down from the bleachers, black bag in hand. "It was a bad cut and the doctor stitched him up on the track. The doctor advised him to rest a couple of days. But a few minutes later, Marvin was running one leg of the mile relay."

There may be a fighting gene, a pugilistic predisposition carried in the blood, but boxers are both born and made. Many fighters, Marvin among them, were tethered to a pure dysfunction somewhere in their family. References to the whipping belt abound in the history of many fighters. Heavyweight champion Sonny Liston suffered vicious abuse at the hands of his father. St. Louis trainer Johnny Tocco once noticed something akin to bird tracks on Liston's back. He asked Liston about the scars, and Liston said, "I had dealings with my father." At other times Liston remarked, "The only thing my old man ever gave me was a beating."

As Marvin's athletic skills increased, things at home grew more tense. Finally Marvin stood up to his aggressive father. "One day, he took off the belt and the almighty blows came down with the strap," Marvin said. "I put my foot up to block the belt—not to fight with him, but to stop him. That was the last time he laid a hand on me."

Then tragedy struck the Camel clan. Henry Junior, age twenty, came home one night following a fight with his Missoula girlfriend. She didn't want to see him anymore, and he was distraught. As the other Camel children played cards and talked, Junior stormed to the back bedroom, grabbed a 30-30 hunting rifle off the wall, and disappeared outside. The sound of a gun blast pulled the children outside to investigate. They found their sibling on the ground, bleeding profusely from a gunshot wound through the stomach.

With no phones available, Henry and Alice drove Junior to St. Luke's Hospital in Ronan. The following day, Marvin and Helen visited Junior.

"Henry and Alice were out test-driving a new car," Marvin said. "Helen and I stayed at St. Luke's. I was in the room, and Junior pulled out the hose that had been filling up his stomach. He wasn't hooked up to a monitor. I went to tell the nurse that something was wrong. They were working on him. I saw Henry and Alice coming up the stairway. At that point, Junior passed away."

Marvin never knew if the gunshot was accidental or self-inflicted.

Shortly after his brother's death, Marvin's parents divorced. "Things got worse and worse with Henry and my mother," Marvin said. "Soon he was heading out the door."

Henry moved to Idaho with a Native American woman named Mildred Conko, whom he had met in a Ronan bar. "Mildred Conko was a young one," Marvin said. "At least ten or fifteen years younger than Henry."

Henry had four children with Conko, and two of their three sons became boxers. As with Marvin and his brothers, Henry and Mildred's sons Zach and J.R. said that boxing allowed them to cross the cultural divide at their heavily Mormon school.

"Without boxing, which gave me all the confidence and all the strength I got, I wouldn't have made it through," Zach said. J.R. agreed: "Dad was always in our corner for boxing and for everything else. He was always in our corner."

The same thing could not be said of Henry and his first family. He never came to any of Marvin's fights. He never came looking to make amends with his successful son. Sporadic phone calls were the extent of their relationship. "I should have been smart enough to have reached out to Henry's other kids," Marvin said. "I wanted Henry to come to me. I was too self-centered and I think about that every day. There is a void there I can never fill."

Henry and Mildred eventually parted ways, but when Henry was dying of esophageal cancer, Mildred moved him back to Ronan to stay at her home so both of Henry's families could be close to him. When Henry died in 1996, Marvin chose not to pay his respects. "I couldn't say anything to him in the casket," Marvin said. "I think about him periodically. I guess he got us through our lives. We were told what, when, and why to do things, and we all turned out well because of that, and because he was who he was."

Marvin's sister, Renee, ten years his junior, decided not to attend her father's funeral, either. "People, a lot of older people, remember Henry," said Renee. "Many of the people remember him as a nice guy, or tell me he was a nice guy. But what I remember of him is much different than that."

Abandonment rarely makes sense to anyone but the desperate people driven to it. Those left behind never fully understand. After Henry's exit, one thing that Alice and the kids did understand was that their lives were undoubtedly more difficult. Alice was left to raise eleven children who were still living at home.

Alice worked as a housekeeper and a cook in the cafeteria at Ronan High School. Money and resources were scarce. Space in the three-room household was non-existent. Clothes were recycled and passed down until the threads disintegrated. Meals consisted of one helping; there was no possibility of seconds or leftovers.

In large part due to domestic strife and his parents' separation, Camel stopped advancing during his final year in high school. Because of two flunked grades in math and science, the all-around athlete was ineligible for interscholastic competition. He only attended half of his senior year. "By going half a year, I got enough credits to graduate," Camel said. "On the day of graduation, everyone got their diplomas. But I had no cap, tassel, or gown. I jumped up and shadow boxed, waved, and walked on out."

Camel had walked the proverbial straight and narrow all his life. But now, without the firm guidance of his father or the rigors of sports, he went astray. Athletics were replaced by carousing, good times, and beer.

As a senior, he landed in jail for fourteen days after breaking a bar window and stealing a six-pack of beer with his friend, Rick Laslo. It almost cost him his life. On the joyride after the break-in, Laslo rolled the car into a ditch; the crash was severe. Paramedics pronounced Marvin dead at the scene.

Sherry Clairmont, Marvin's first wife, later said, "The paramedics and ambulance people didn't even lift him off the ground or pick him up, because they thought he was dead."

Fortunately, hospital medical technicians sought to find any signal of life and, somehow, Marvin provided it. "He moved his hand a bit so they didn't send him to the morgue," Clairmont said. Marvin spent two weeks in the hospital and after release he was slapped with a two-week jail sentence and three years probation.

"My history teacher, Mr. Muller, would drive me back and forth from Ronan High School to the Polson County jail," said Camel. "I was partying with my friend Rick and we ran out of hooch. Eventually the charges were dropped before I completed probation."

During his senior year, Camel had worked in Jim Kerwin's lumber mill at night. The drudgery of the manual labor made him anxious, and once more he thought of a career in professional boxing. He began training again. Mill paychecks financed trips to national amateur tournaments. Camel began to see other cities, other ways of life, and he wanted what he saw.

Marvin relished every aspect of training, from the long runs in the dark and cold, to the jabs he threw from one end of the gym room to the other, to the consistent pounding of the speed and heavy bags. After school, he couldn't wait to get to the gym to see if he was sharper with his punches or quicker with his footwork. Instead of taking the bus to school, he ran.

Other kids assumed he was crazy, but he believed—he needed to believe—the extra effort would pay off someday. More than once he came home from the recreation center with a black eye or a busted lip, much to the dismay of his mother. But the next day he always went back for more. During those intense months, Marvin knew, somehow, that something profound was changing in his body as well as his mind.

Upon graduating from high school, Marvin showed no desire to attend college. His family was upset by his lack of interest in education and his preoccupation with boxing. Alice hoped he would earn his livelihood with a college degree, which, she thought, would help him find dignity and his way against the hard current of hopelessness.

"Marvin, what are you going to do now?" Alice would ask.

"I'm going to be world champion," Marvin would respond.

"When are you going to quit those ideas?"

"I'll quit when I get a world title."

"You should get educated or a career."

"I'll quit when I get a world title."

At nineteen, a defiantly independent Camel participated in several AAU (Amateur Athletic Union) tournaments and "smokers"—unsanctioned boxing matches that do not count on a fighter's professional record. In fact, Camel estimates that approximately one-fourth of his 250 amateur bouts were "smokers." Even though boxing was legal in Montana in the 1970s, the public often held matches in private facilities, away from any legal or state oversight. Church halls, foreign legion groups, and Knights of Columbus clubs were popular venues for the generally all-male smokers, whose crowds were usually an eclectic blend of neighborhood politicians, businessmen, shopkeepers, factory workers, and blue-collar toughs. Here, Camel had an outlet for the rage of his disenfranchised youth. Here he had a privileged, consuming, and concerning look inside one of the most insular experiences on earth.

In a milieu reeking of sweat, liniment, Vaseline, cigar smoke, and blood, most spectators, seated on either folding chairs or bleachers, made wagers with one another on bouts involving fighters they had seen before; this way they had an inkling of whether their boy actually could fight, which many could not. Bouts generally ranged from three to eight rounds, and the ones that stirred the most excitement, betting, noise, and smoke were those involving ethnic fighters and those from rival parts of the state.

Boxing coach Jim Anderson of Polson, Montana, a man who Camel later said "took the place of my father," recalled Marvin as "a good kid" who was "devoted" to boxing at an early age. "Marvin was always an athlete," Anderson said. "He had no vices. For a kid in these parts, that's rare. When he was a kid he would box upstairs at the VFW in Polson. Marvin would get dropped off in Pablo and run to the VFW before the fight (approximately 12 miles). He would bounce up and down the stairs and jump rope. He was in extremely good shape."

Montana resident Larry Richards grew up boxing, even forming a friendship with the great Carlos Palomino, a boxing teammate in the Army. Two years older than Marvin, he remembers fighting Camel at least twice. "Very tough," Richard recalled. "He was very, very determined. That was at a time when boxing was big in Polson, Ronan, and St. Ignatius. It gave some kids an avenue to do something, mostly kids from low socioeconomic levels. It's not the same anymore."

The lack of opportunity on the reservation stifled Camel, as it does many Indian youths. He felt he had learned to box in captivity, so to speak. Now he needed to be let loose.

Still nineteen, Camel ran into a promoter from Alaska and considered moving there to begin his career. "He told me what he could do for me and all this, and it sounded pretty good," Camel said. But then Camel met an ex-Tribal Council Chairman who realized Camel's potential and worked to keep Marvin in Montana.

Walter "Little Beaver" McDonald didn't need much of an introduction to Marvin or his people of the Flathead Reservation. McDonald had served for more than twenty years as Tribal Council Chairman and was the first editor of the Indian-run *Char-Koosta* newspaper. McDonald had been a major force in the development of reservation events and policies. He had a lot to say to Marvin. In the 1930s, boxing insider Paddy Flood testified before Congress, "Let me tell you about boxing. It's the most treacherous, dirtiest, vicious, cheatingest game in the world.... That's the nature of the business. It's a terrible business."

Then and now, bad financial dealings, double-crosses, and shifting alliances characterized the sport, and McDonald was well aware of this. He warned Camel of the "leeches" in the boxing game, its disreputable dealings and heavy influence of criminals and extortionists. McDonald's warning discouraged Camel from acting on the Alaskan offer. Instead, McDonald drove forty miles to Missoula and sought advice from a boxing promoter named Elmer Boyce. According to McDonald, Boyce liked what he heard about Marvin's talents and asked McDonald to have Marvin come see him.

Boyce, unlike many managers, knew boxing. Shrewd and gregarious, Boyce acquainted himself with promoters, trainers, and scores of local sportswriters. Boyce even had some success in the business—most notably promoting Roger Rouse, whom he put in the position to compete for a world title three times.

Born in 1934, Roger Rouse started boxing at age nine when his father gave him a pair of gloves for Christmas. A football standout in high school at Anaconda, Montana, and later at the University of Montana, Rouse won a Golden Gloves title in 1954 in Chicago and accepted a boxing scholarship at Idaho State. Eventually he fought for the light heavyweight championship of the world three times, losing once to Dick Tiger and twice to Bob Foster. He retired from boxing in 1972 and worked at the Anaconda Company Smelter until it closed in 1980. "Roger Rouse was built like a Montana-raised person," Camel recalled. "He was short, strong, and well-built, but with no real reach or height to allow him to make it over the hump in boxing."

"Boyce was a really funny guy," said Richard Jackson, 67, a veteran boxing trainer who was a young man when he met Boyce. 'Remember the Burgess Meredith character from [the movie] *Rocky*? That was Boyce. "Rocky" was all bullshit, except Meredith was real, old-world stuff. Boyce was like that—a fight guy."

Camel met Boyce at the Oxford Café, the "Ox," a venerable— some might say "seedy"—Missoula institution established in 1883. The distinctly Montana-flavored diner was adorned with beer signage and memorabilia, a long, greasy bar that doubled as a breakfast counter, signs advertising its distinctive cow brains and eggs special, and a 24-hour nonstop hustle of roughnecks, felons, cowboys, Indians, bikers, drifters, and hung-over college kids.

"I didn't want anything to do with him," said Boyce. "He was on parole, he'd been involved in a robbery. But Walt McDonald kept saying, 'Talk to the kid.' So I said bring him down. We met in the back room. We even had the parole officer there."

Boyce looked up at the handsome young man. Small talk swiftly turned serious. Boyce, who owned the "Ox" at the time, tried to convince Marvin not to come into boxing. He said it would be too tough.

"If you're willing to be a lonely man, I can give you a career," said Boyce.

"I am," answered Marvin.

"This is not a sport where one can wimp out or be cautious," said Boyce. "You always have to fight with your instincts. Not reason. Instincts."

"I'm serious about any opportunity you can give," responded Marvin.

"It's a full commitment."

"I understand, Mr. Boyce."

"Nothing to take lightly."

"Never, Mr. Boyce."

Elmer took a piece of paper from his pocket and unfolded it. It read Elmer Boyce in big black letters.

"Let's talk tomorrow."

The next day, Boyce said, "I put him up in a hotel room and gave him a job. When he showed up he had no clothes, just a backseat full of trophies. I felt so sorry for him I went out and got him a TV, so he wouldn't be so darn lonely."

INSTINCTS—THE INSTINCT TO FIGHT INSTEAD OF FLEE, THE instinct to save yourself by hurting the other person more than he hurts you, the instinct to keep fighting when you can't breathe from being hit so hard—are not often encountered in civilian life. In fact, they are encountered almost exclusively in war, in which people's lives, rather than simply their livelihoods, are at stake. Boxing is replete with military symbolism, not to mention military pretensions. But the stark reality of life and death instincts are what makes boxing more than football, more than wrestling, more than an action movie, more than a combat video game. The legalized unleashing of deadly instincts is what makes boxing a blood sport.

BOYCE BECAME CAMEL'S MANAGER, AND FROM HERE ON, BOYCE had power over Camel's future. On July 6, 1971, Camel moved to Missoula when Boyce offered him a day job, room and board, a gym, help with boxing, friendship, and too little money to get in trouble. Taking into consideration the lack of training facilities on the Flathead Reservation, this move was the most pragmatic option. Camel began working for Elmer Boyce's Montana Music Rentals, which provided him with a glimpse into the consequences of slacking off from boxing or retreating from it.

"I must have traveled to 250 locations fixing pinball machines, and ninety percent of them were bars," Camel said. "I got a chance to see what was happening to kids and people. Ninety percent of the people I saw were staring at their beer cans with no place to go. They were waiting for life to start. At 19, 20, 21, I felt that there was more out there for Marvin Camel."

Though he rarely discussed them, Camel still faced several strong cultural obstacles. "In the 1970s and 1980s, things were still incredibly hostile for Indians in Missoula and Kalispell," said Robert McDonald. "There was an invisible line and they didn't want us to cross. In Missoula, I can remember college kids yelling, 'Hey, chief, go home.' One of the pressures is that the Indian finds success in staying where he is and sticking around at home. And sometimes if you leave and get some success, people [back home] will think you are too good for the reservation. And that's the poisonous perfect storm. If you go become a success and come back, some will take shots at you and say, 'Do you think you are better than me?' A return can be a mixture of welcoming and attack. Marvin must have known and felt that."

In Marvin's earliest days, his father dished out the discipline. But now he came to recognize that "self-discipline" was something very different. It was the skill of seeing through the hollow shouting of his own impulses. It was the skill of not allowing urges to scream and bluster at him; the skill of not giving in out of habit. Marvin felt that if he looked within and saw all the feelings bubbling up—restlessness, anxiety, impatience, pain—if he saw those potential obstacles but didn't allow them to fester, they would simply go away. Negative thoughts arose, and they passed away. Simple as that. Camel found another word for self-discipline. It was patience. *Be patient. It will all happen.*

The most important and often the most influential figure in a professional boxer's career is his manager. It is the manager's task to look after the physical and financial well-being of a fighter, to negotiate his fight contracts, and to oversee his training and preparation for a bout. Often flamboyant and extroverted, some managers become almost as famous as their charges. As a general rule, a manager receives one-third of a boxer's purse, but some of the more unscrupulous ones convince or trick their fighters into much more usurious terms.

Short, bald, looking much like "the caricature of Elmer Fudd," said Kenny Camel, Boyce was a persnickety, old-school trainer who cherry-picked fighters who took their work seriously. In return, he provided structure and teaching, and the periodic pat on the back.

"He treated me like a human being," Camel once said of Boyce. "I guess that's all the influence I needed."

Fearing the likelihood of losing a decision to hometown bias, no amateurs wanted to fight Camel on his own turf. Sparring partners were scarce, so Marvin educated his younger brother Kenny in the boxing craft and Kenny began to serve as his work-out and sparring partner.

The move sparked an emotional growth spurt in both brothers. "I was taken out of the society of being black and being Indian and not having anything to look forward to but work in the mill," Ken said. And during those long cold jogs along the railroad tracks, Marvin's thoughts crystallized. *There is no opportunity on the reservation, just stagnation. Thank you, dad, for the discipline. The isolation of athletic training is the best resistance to the disease of alcohol and drug dependence.*

By the time he was twenty years old, Marvin Camel knew how to put in a rugged day. He was up at 5:30 A.M. every day for a six-mile run, usually alone, but sometimes with friend and boxing savant Joe Phelps, a friend of Elmer Boyce. Phelps was the first trainer Marvin affiliated with as a professional boxer. "Phelps was a big, heavyset guy," said Marvin. "He was at least 300 pounds, and he was a man who knew what boxing was all about. He liked to drink and tell stories at the Ox."

After a couple of hours' rest, Camel put in a regular shift at Montana Music Rentals fixing gaming machines. From 8 to 10 P.M., Camel sharpened his boxing skills at his training headquarters. In fact, the two places were one in the same. Boyce built Marvin a small personal gym—a cubicle, really—in the back warehouse of the business. He cleared out the pinball machines, jukeboxes, and pool tables to give his protégé a space to shadow box his fifteen daily rounds. Camel's makeshift training site "had all the makings of a kitchen cabinet," said one visitor.

When he had finished his day job, Marvin walked through the warehouse to the training center. With barely enough room for light and heavy bags, he loosened up with a variety of exercises and did some shadow boxing. Then he jumped rope and sometimes more shadow boxing, bobbing and weaving. Then he tackled the heavy bag and worked out on the speed bag. Even if someone had been available, the room was too minuscule to have a sparring session.

During his daily training sessions, Camel used the rock tempos of Credence Clearwater Revival to keep and maintain a finely tuned beat to carry him through a rigorous two-hour workout. *It ain't me, it ain't me, I ain't no millionaire's son, no. It ain't me, it ain't me; I ain't no fortunate one, no.*

Phelps, who'd been around boxing for two decades, said Camel was the best fighter he had ever worked with. "He's the best in all respects," Phelps said. "He's the hardest worker I've ever had and he never quits. He has all the natural ability and learns quickly." Phelps didn't stay around long enough to watch Camel develop that ability.

"What happened was that I had no sparring partners, and Joe wanted to spar," said Marvin. "Joe really wanted to spar one day, and he came at me, grunting away. He couldn't uncork fast enough. I hit him in the eye with a light left jab and I gave him a blood blister on his eye. He didn't put his hands up fast enough. *Maybe I shouldn't have done it because of his age and weight. He thought he still had it, but he didn't.* Joe had a son named Buddy, who fought more in the bars than inside the ring. Buddy came down and he wanted to fight me. Joe understood why I popped him, but his son didn't. Joe eventually packed up and left. One day he quit coming. Maybe it was because of that."

For a middleweight Camel had an abundance of versatility: he was quick, had exceptional balance, and could hit with power from either hand, although he was primarily a southpaw. Boyce now told anyone who would listen that Camel had all the tools to fight professionally. "He has desire, ambition, and confidence. We've been working on polishing and refining some minor things. We're training him under professional conditions because the top amateurs on the East Coast train this way."

During the next few months Boyce began to reshape Camel's ring technique. He started with proper footwork, working on getting Camel to keep his weight balanced and his feet planted so that he would be in a position to throw a power punch at any time. He worked on Camel's left and on getting his weight behind his punches. He taught Camel how to slip punches, roll with punches, and block hits—all the details of being a professional. The fighters who have the longest, most successful careers are the ones who absorb the fewest solid blows.

Camel learned quickly. He paid attention, took criticism well, and trained diligently. Camel had two sparring sessions with former light-heavyweight contender Roger Rouse. After the second four-round session, Rouse told Boyce that Camel had moves he had never seen. Rouse was impressed with Camel's ability to hit with either hand.

This kid's got potential, thought Boyce. *This kid works his ass off. Damn, he's ambitious.*

03

BEAUTIFUL BRUTALITY

CAMEL DID HIS ROADWORK IN THE HILLY TERRAIN AROUND Missoula. He ran along highways and back roads and rutted dirt paths. Every few miles he would allow himself a few seconds to inhale the sweet scent of wildflowers. But only for a few seconds.

In the tiny, makeshift gym, Camel's routine was predictable: no conversation, nothing but silence and free weights, floor stretches, twisting and rotating in front of wall mirrors, loosening the arms and back, ducking, bending, skipping rope. Skipping rope for balance, for coordination, and to raise energy for the workout to come. Medicine balls and treadmills.

As his muscles did their work, he had time to wonder whether the fury he sometimes displayed in the ring—a fury uncharacteristic of his true nature—might be traced to incidents of fear and inadequacy as he was growing up, and to the stress of the intense fighting between his parents. He did not know. He was not a psychiatrist. He did know he was in a lot of mental pain as he chased his immediate goal of winning important amateur boxing tournaments, particularly in Golden Gloves circuit, the principal amateur boxing competition in the country. State success earns a fighter regional matches, then, if successful, a chance at the nationals, and perhaps onward to international amateur competition, leading to the Olympics.

In December 1971 at Missoula's St. Anthony's Gym, Camel beat an eventual Olympic gold medal winner, Sugar Ray Seales, in an informal "boxing night" put together by Boyce.

"At that time, I couldn't find anyone else to get a hold of to box," Camel said. "Seales wanted to fight, but I made him accept five rounds. Seales was trained to go three, and three only. I trained for 10, even though I wasn't a pro. He started to tire in the fourth, and, in the fifth, I pulled it out of the fire. I was not worried about winning or losing, but putting on a big show."

Seales was ahead in the early rounds, but Camel caught Seales with solid punches in the fourth and scored a decisive victory in the fifth. Seales fought out of a Tacoma, Washington, boxing club, and later Boyce allowed Camel a two-week furlough to train with the Tacoma club.

"They kicked my ass from one corner post to another," Camel recalled. "It was the roughest two weeks of my life. I made trips like that to other states to get in the best shape I could. In my mind, I still felt inside of me that I wasn't in quite good enough shape. If I got up in the morning and I was still tired, I didn't think I was in good shape. Excursions like that one to Tacoma paid off in the end."

Seales went on to win the only gold medal for an American boxer at the 1972 Olympics in Munich, Germany, and he became a contender for the middleweight title during the late 1970s and early 1980s. In his two most memorable fights, he lost a narrow decision to future middleweight champion Marvin Hagler in July 1974 and then drew Hagler in a rematch three months later. After losing to European champion Alan Minter in 1976, Seales remained on the outskirts of contention until a first-round TKO at the hands of Hagler effectively ended his title hopes. In 1980 Seales injured his eye in a fight and retired. He was subsequently declared legally blind, and during the 1980s, he pushed for an outright ban of boxing.

In the spring of 1972, Camel lost a split decision to Marvin Johnson in the National Golden Gloves tournament in Minneapolis. Johnson, the NAAU Middleweight Champion, went on to win a bronze medal for the U.S in the Munich games. (In his professional career, Marvin "Pops" Johnson became the first boxer to win the 175-pound championship three times, retiring with a 43—6 ledger, winning 35 fights by KO. Three of his opponents, Matthew Saad Muhammad, Victor Galindez, and Michael Spinks are in the International Boxing Hall Of Fame.

"Marvin (Camel) took (Marvin) Johnson down to the wire," said family friend Larry Anderson, who witnessed the fight. "It was a hell of a fight. Johnson had one helluva knockout record. Marvin (Camel) popped him with hard right jabs and struck Johnson with a left-right in the chops I'll never forget. I thought that a draw would've been more fair. But Johnson was extremely popular on the amateur circuit. Marvin was screwed out of some close decisions."

"When I fought Marvin Johnson," said Camel, "he was very experienced on the combinations that he could throw. He trained with right-handers only, and not with left-handers. And with me, you never drop your hands. He was a banger, but he carried his hands down. He wasn't the toughest I ever fought, but Johnson was a good boxer."

Perhaps Camel's biggest achievement was finishing third in the 1972 national AAU tournament at Boston. He won three fights in the tournament, losing only to eventual champion D.C. Barker of Denver.

Shortly before the 1972 Olympics, Camel stated that he did not qualify because the lack of sparring partners impeded his progress. He also felt he was handicapped by his location. "Missoula fighters couldn't get to the better tournaments," he said. "Seales' Tacoma club was in the loop and a team that went to the Olympic trials. Of all the boxers going for gold medals at the 1972 Olympics, there were four kids from that Tacoma team."

Learning the nuts and bolts of boxing doesn't come easily. There is nothing inborn about closing the distance on an opponent so that you can sock him. At that distance he can punch you as well. There's no way to fake the kind of aggression that is necessary to keep attacking while risking being hurt. It takes discipline combined with experience. All boxers, even the greatest, get hit repeatedly in training and in fights.

Some of the sport's tenets seem counterintuitive. For example, most boxers throw more punches with their weaker hand. A left-handed boxer leads with his right, sets up an opponent with his right, and separates himself from less talented fighters by his ability to effectively score with his right. A good boxer is almost like a switch hitter in baseball, and the talent is developed over years of practice.

Camel was still young and developing rapidly. He was also learning that despite boasting an impressive record as an amateur, fights were almost impossible to schedule in Montana. Camel craved ring experience. He needed it. No matter how hard work he worked at repairing flashy game machines, there was no future in that. Sure, Boyce had confidence in the young man and talked to him about expanding his workload to include regional duties. But, honestly, where would that take him? To a few hundred more desolate bars in a few hundred more lonely towns full of rusty combines and wet hay bales?

If one were gambling, the odds of young Marvin Camel becoming successful, of finding good fortune, of becoming the best in his field, seemed small. To him. To others. Camel could have simply remained stagnant. He could have let all of his dreams slip away. But he worked too damn hard and was too damn ambitious.

On the Flathead Reservation, most of the Native population was powerless to escape, but there was a nascent sense that Marvin was going places. Maybe he could represent them to the world.

04

SURVIVALIST DRAMA

BOXING IN MONTANA HAS DEEP ROOTS. IN HIS 1985 BOOK *Gladiators of the Glittering Gulches,* Frank Bell traced the first announcement of a Montana prize fight to August 27, 1864, when the *Montana Post,* the first (and, at the time, only) newspaper in the newly established Montana Territory, chronicled a fight between a pair of tough miners. A few decades later, one of the sport's greatest battlers called Montana his home.

Estimated by some boxing historians to be the best fighter in the history of the middleweight division, Stanley Ketchel stirred emotions as few men in boxing ever had. His real name was Stanislaus Kiecal and he was born September 14, 1886, in Grand Rapids, Michigan, of mixed German and Polish ancestry. He dodged school, falling in with a gang of street kids and often frequently losing his temper in fist fights.

In his mid-teens Ketchel became a hobo. In 1902, according to *Men of Steel: The Lives and Times of Boxing's Middleweight Champions,* "he wandered, penniless and hungry, into the town of Butte, high in the Montana Rockies." At the time, Butte was a rip-roaring mining town, the largest copper mining operation in the world and the biggest city between Minneapolis and Seattle. Ketchel found employment as a hotel bellhop "at a dive called the Copper Queen" and later as a bouncer in a gambling joint. This profession led to many scraps that established his reputation as the best fist fighter in town.

Soon sixteen-year-old Stanley was mixing it up in backroom boxing matches with older locals for twenty dollars a week. After being taken under the wing of promoter Freddie Bogan, Ketchel began traveling throughout Montana, offering to take on any man anywhere. Cowboys, miners, and loggers provided ample fodder for fisticuffs.

Ketchel started boxing professionally in 1903 in Butte. In his first fight, Ketchel knocked out Kid Tracy in the first round. In his second fight, he was beaten by decision in six rounds. He boxed his first forty-one bouts in Montana, recording thirty-six wins, two losses, and three draws.

Understanding that sporting horizons were limited in Montana, Ketchel moved his campaign to California in 1907. Ketchel twice won the world middleweight championship. He KO'd "Twin" Sullivan in the first round in February 1908, lost the title to Billy Papke the following September, but regained it from Papke in November.

In 1909, he took on heavyweight champ Jack Johnson, who enjoyed a thirty-six pound advantage. Ketchel had the champ on the floor, but Johnson rose to hammer Ketchel in a viciously memorable fashion. All total, in sixty-six bouts, Ketchel won fifty inside the distance and three on points, drew five, lost four, and fought four no-decisions.

While eating breakfast one October morning in 1910 at Col. R.P. Dickinson's Two Bar Ranch in Missouri, Ketchel was shot to death by Walter Dipley. It was alleged that the murderer was jealous over the attention his girlfriend had paid to Ketchel. The former middleweight boxing champion was only 24.

Most of the public's knowledge of Montana pugilism stems from a fight between the great Jack Dempsey and Tommy Gibbons. The men faced off in the little known oil-boom town of Shelby for a fifteen-round World Heavyweight Championship fight on the Fourth of July, 1923. The circumstances that brought a sporting event of international importance to a Montana town with a population of barely 500 have inspired endless words and stories. An octagonal 40,000-seat arena was erected in just over twenty days and temporary hotels were constructed to host the large crowd that promoters anticipated. But the reach of Shelby's promoters greatly exceeded their grasp. In the end, only a handful of spectators saw Dempsey, in his fourth defense of the title, beat Gibbons in a 15-round decision. The supporting banks ran out of cash and had to close, and the primary promoters were left $160,000 in debt.

Of course boxing continued in Montana as it did everywhere. By the 1940s, boxing, baseball, and horse racing were the only three money sports that mattered; their dramas sold newspapers and filled the radio airwaves.

In 1950, the year of Marvin Camel's birth, Rocky Marciano was in the midst of a 49–0 boxing career. Born in Brockton, Massachusetts, to an Italian immigrant shoemaker, Rocky quit school when he was fourteen. He worked a slew of jobs, including candy-making, ditch digging, and truck driving. Short, thick, and one of the hardest hitters ever to lace the gloves, Marciano took the world heavyweight title in his 43rd fight and successfully defended it six times in three years. At the time of his ousting of Jersey Joe Walcott, on September 23, 1952, Marciano weighed 188 pounds.

For decades, the heavyweight champion became the symbol of the toughest man in the world. In the late 1960s, Black Panther leader Elridge Cleaver wrote, "The boxing ring is the ultimate focus of masculinity in America, the two-fisted testing ground of manhood, and the heavyweight champion, as a symbol, is the real Mr. America."

In the late 1970s bigger and more powerful boxers entered the ring. In his prime, Muhammad Ali weighed between 210 and 216 pounds. Some heavyweights weighed nearly 300 pounds. Boxing authorities began to worry that lighter boxers—men of Marciano's size—would have no chance against these giants, so an impetus took hold to carve a new weight class from the heavyweight division. The weight span for the "cruiserweight" division would be 176 and 190 pounds.

That is the division where Marvin Camel staked his claim to boxing history.

05

SPORT OF THE UNDERCLASS

BOXING IS A HARD WAY TO MAKE A LIVING, BUT THROUGHOUT THE twentieth century, young men from downtrodden ethnic groups turned to boxing as a possible escape from poverty and persecution. Early in the twentieth century, nineteen Jewish boxers won world championships, a number surpassed, and only slightly, by Irish and Italian fighters. Later, African Americans entered the rings and won.

Native Americans were—and largely, still are—another disenfranchised ethnic group. On reservations, poverty is abundant, success scarce. Native American Marvin Camel was twenty-two and he could sense success. For the first time in his life, people were paying attention to him, admiring him, complimenting him. He allowed himself to dream of triumph and glory.

Six months before making his pro debut, Marvin married Sherry Clairmont. She was two years younger and they had met in high school. Marvin played the part of the good-looking young man, with neatly trimmed black hair, a dark complexion, and a face that a movie star could have lived in. Sherry was less outgoing and vocal, and that was okay because Marvin loved to talk.

They had much in common. Sherry, whose father was a Salish-Pend d'Oreille tribal member, was one of twelve kids. "We both came from big, Native American families," Camel said. "We respected each other. When I was up in Havre in a tournament, Sherry was in the college there. That's when we made a vow to tie the knot." The two married on February 23, 1973.

When she looks back on her relationship with Marvin, Sherry doesn't remember dates or first impressions. She is, however, struck with a feeling. "All in all, I cared about him, loved him, and he was a part of my life, and a part of me."

Sherry was at her newlywed's side when he experienced a false start as he tried to launch his professional boxing career. First one opponent and then a second ducked out of Camel's first pro fight, scheduled for April 14, 1973. Camel had to settle for a three-round exhibition against an amateur. A few days earlier, on April 10, Camel sparred with sixth-ranked heavyweight Ron Lyle in the basement of the Florence Hotel in Missoula. Lyle, a convicted murderer, brawled with the best during the golden age of heavyweights. In one eight-month period in the mid-1970s, Lyle lost to both Muhammad Ali and George Foreman and defeated Ernie Shavers. One of nineteen siblings, Lyle was born in 1941 and grew up in northeast Denver. At nineteen, the high school dropout was convicted of second-degree murder in the shooting death of a twenty-one-year-old gang rival. Lyle argued he was being attacked with a lead pipe and was not the one who fired the fatal shots. He served more than seven years in prison and nearly died on the operating table after being stabbed by an inmate. Lyle learned to box while in the slammer; Denver cable-television magnate Bill Daniels recognized his talent and asked Gov. John Love to pardon Lyle.

"Ron Lyle was a good, strong fighter," Camel recalled. "He was a rough guy, one of those guys who are their own breed. He was his own man. He went out to the bars and socialized, and was a good guy."

Camel's day in the ring eventually came. "Camel Eager for Pro Debut," trumpeted the headline of Butte's *Montana Standard* on September 18, 1973. The write-up was crowned with a photo of a determined and handsome Marvin Camel warming up to a speed bag. Thin and hawk-like in profile, there was no waste about him, either in body or in movement. He bore no scars on his face, his teeth were white and even as if cast from porcelain. His skin was like brown satin.

Camel understood he was about to step up in class, skill, and aggression. Getting hit in the face, having your eyes cut, swallowing your own blood, trying to move away from your opponent in a dulling mental fog—it is not like bogeying a hole in golf or swinging at a baseball. There are no shifts to catch your breathe as in hockey, no time to sit on your backside and blow gum bubbles as in baseball. "It's a new experience for me, which I hope comes off," said Camel to a friend while preparing for the fight.

The mystery of his opponent was often on his mind. Prior to the days of the Internet and YouTube, his scouting reports were a few lines of ink in the newspaper and word-of-mouth summaries. "I don't know anything about him. He might come out there to tear my head off. Of course, that's what he's there for," Camel said. Camel trained hard for months. His body was keyed toward a diet regimen that would endure throughout his career. He lived on quick, easy meals, water, Ex-lax, and more water. "I needed Ex-lax to feel like I was drained," said Camel. "It made me feel like I needed to work harder. It made me hungrier."

Newspapers recounted that the twenty-two-year-old Camel had an outstanding amateur career (132–26), fought in six national tournaments—three Golden Gloves and three AAUs—was the regional AAU 178-pound champion, and won state AAU crowns in 1971 and 1972. To Marvin, that was an eternity ago; the future was bold. "I hope to get a few wins in the pros," said Camel. "It might be a little tough because it's hard going out there and doing your thing. By starting now I have the opportunity to see how it's like before I get too old...Everybody likes to go all the way. But there are many things you have to worry about, like getting a good place to train and getting good coaches."

The six-foot two, 172-pound youngster described his style: "I move around and look for an opening. I pick my openings. I don't want to run in there and get the other guy excited so he'll start throwing leather from all four corners. You've got to feel them out first. If they get excited and can't do anything, you may as well take 'em out. You're just punishing them if you don't. And I don't like to punish people. So if I've got the opening, I'll take them out."

Camel felt that being left-handed was an advantage: "In some cases, a right-handed guy usually doesn't have many left-handed sparring partners. So it's kind of new for him to fight a left-handed boxer." He was asked how his wife felt about his boxing. "Well, at first she didn't want anything to do with it," Camel said. "But my dad was a fighter and I told her I had the instincts for fighting. I don't know if it's hostility. It's what I know how to do. It's not in the brain or violence. I just fight and I may as well keep doing so until I get the urge to stop."

Before the fight, Marvin stood in the steamy locker room going through his normal workout routine, working up a sweat by stretching, exercising, and shadowboxing. Shadowboxing leans heavily on imagination, and Marvin's imagination projected his hand raised in victory. Marvin paced the locker room in calm purpose and then sat cross-legged on a scuffed wooden bench, high socks protruding from brown leather boots. His face was expressionless; the only sign of stress was his hand clenched around a boxing mouthpiece. His brother Kenny stood just behind him; he was joined by several supporters and friends. In a corner, arms folded on the edge of a wooden railing, sat Elmer Boyce.

"Are you ready for this, Marvin?" he shouted.

"Yes, sir."

September 20, 1973, Butte, Montana

ALTHOUGH THE WEATHER HAD BEEN UNSEASONABLY WARM THAT day, and the weekend's sunshine burst lovely, it turned more wintry than autumnal, and when darkness fell the night was cold. Camel entered the ring as a light-heavyweight (the cruiserweight division had not been created yet) though he weighed only 174.5

pounds, some six pounds lighter than Joe Williamson, also making his pro debut. The fight against 'Jolting' Joe of Tacoma, Washington, came as a six-round preliminary to the Leroy Romero–Sugar Ray Seales main event at the Butte Civic Center.

Under the hood of a heavy blue bathrobe, Camel seemed to be trying to look serious. He had an intellectual appreciation of the anxieties of a fighter, but he had a hard time forgetting how strong he was. He had no time to be afraid. For Marvin, it was if he were listening to the referee's instructions for the first time: "No holding, no hitting on the break, no illegal punches, no low blows. Protect yourself at all times." Flickering images from grainy reel-to-reel film survives. Marvin's robe came off, his mouthguard went in, his seconds climbed out. Then came the bell.

Williamson rushed across the ring, arms and fists flailing away. *Bam!* A left hook from Marvin. Williamson went down. Up again. *Bam!* Marvin slugged Williamson with another left hook and he went down. Up once more. *Bam!* Two lefts and a right from Marvin. When Williamson ate the canvas for the third time, the fight was stopped. The referee raised Marvin's arm in victory. Boyce shouted: *"That's how you do it! That's how you do it!"*

AFTER TAKING OUT BOYCE'S CUT AND GENERAL PRE-FIGHT expenses, out of the $1500 Camel was contracted for, his share came to $375. Soon after the fight, Marvin had a falling out with Boyce—over what he couldn't recall—and he retreated to a small piece of property in Evaro, Montana. "I bought a one-ton truck, cut sixty cords of wood all by myself, and bought and sold wood for a short time," Camel said. "We met up again, Boyce and me. I don't remember who contacted who. But it was time to start boxing again."

Some of Camel's family resented Boyce; they believed Marvin was like clay in the hands of a potter. No matter. Marvin was willing to swallow his pride and believe in someone else in order to push forward. Camel's second fight took place five months later in Pocatello, Idaho, against James T. Jackson, who had won his first five professional fights. Camel used a couple of left hooks to down the Seattle fighter in the fourth round. Camel fought with total control, landing perfectly timed right jabs that snapped Jackson's head. Sometimes Jackson's head jerked back as violently as if he had walked into a tree limb on a dark night.

After the bout, Camel was swollen around the cheekbones and exhibited small welts under both eyes. *Was it really worth it? Were the rewards, as lucrative as they might be, worth getting beaten up, not to mention the hits one must endure day after day in the gym? Absolutely.*

From the beginning, Marvin took pride in the masculinity, marksmanship, and skill required of boxing. "Hey, Marvin, you are some fighter," someone would say. "I'm a boxer," Marvin would reply. "I'm not a fighter. You fight at the bar, not in the boxing ring. In the boxing ring, you box."

A little less than a month later, Camel was on his way to Las Vegas for his third pro fight. The travel routine for his first Vegas fights went this way: Boyce would hand Marvin a bus ticket and the fighter would take the full-day ride alone, staring out the window.

At a trim fighting weight of 177½, Camel used Las Vegan George Clark "for a heavy bag" and easily won his third fight. Camel ended the fight at 1:31 of the fourth round with a straight left to Clark's mouth that left the rangy fighter lying on the ropes. Moments earlier, Camel had connected with a right-left combination that knocked out Clark's mouth piece. The loss snapped an eleven-bout winning string for Clark. Although having had only three professional fights, Camel showed the moves and finesse of a much more seasoned fighter. Clark didn't lay a glove on the swift southpaw in the first two rounds as Camel moved away and worked on Clark's midsection with hard left shots. For the win, Camel's take was $150.

Camel's next ten fights were in Las Vegas. This led to Camel's frequent absences from his new wife. The combination of sex and boxing has long been one of the sport's greatest controversies. Traditionalists believe sex saps a fighter's strength, especially before a fight. Former lightweight champion Ike Williams once said, "I did it once, and I got the hell whipped out of me."

In order to be the best, Marvin chose to remove himself from any and all distractions. And Las Vegas in 1975 was full of them. It boasted a gypsy carnival atmosphere, a place where card sharks cheated novices out of hard-earned money while big-name performers such as Elvis Presley brought in the crowds. And Camel wasn't the only Montanan making a name for himself in Sin City. Butte's Evel Knievel was living hard, drinking harder, and defying death as a motorcycle stunt man. By the time Marvin arrived on the scene, Evel Knievel had already achieved worldwide fame as the quintessential daredevil. Camel would occasionally bump into, and have brief friendly conversations with, the mean, moody, and magnificent fellow Montanan.

By this time Marvin Camel had learned that training seriously took time. To plan for the future, he had to work harder. He had to shake off pain even though it took days to recover from the rounds of hard sparring, his back and neck braided with pain.

In his fourth fight, Camel scored a knockout over Chico Valdez of Phoenix. Camel knocked down Valdez for the mandatory eight count in the first round, then came back in the second round with a series of rights and lefts to the head before putting away Valdez with a wicked left hook to the body and then to the side of the head. Valdez was 36–7 coming into the fight and regarded as the light heavyweight champ of Arizona. Camel had been in complete command throughout the brief fight.

The article in the next day's *Las Vegas Review-Journal* described Camel as "one of the most popular fighters to fight on the Slipper card in sometime" and the knockout as one of the "cleanest" in "several months." It may have been one of the most beautiful punches Camel ever threw, a short left coming from the body and rising to strike Vasquez in the right temple. Whenever Marvin connected with such power and precision, a tingling sensation similar to an electric shock traveled directly from his hand to his shoulder. It was a tremendous feeling.

For Camel the win was more satisfying than usual: older sibling Tommy, who was considered a title prospect before losing a leg in Vietnam, had been working with him for the fight. Marvin said that his brother's courage had a great deal to do with his own dedication to the fight game.

Camel next battered heavyweight Jack Johnson for eight rounds to win a unanimous decision. He hit Johnson so often that he lost energy. Johnson proved he could withstand a furious pounding. The fight even brought a pair of firsts for Camel: the first time he did not knock out his opponent, and his first fight to go more than five rounds. "He could sure take a punch," Camel said of Johnson in a brief post-fight analysis.

In the summer of 1975 Camel's goal was to fight as often as possible and to register some impressive victories so Elmer Boyce could get other promoters to take notice. Most of his regimen was spent working out on the heavy bag, shadowboxing, and skipping rope. He scheduled a fight every month. Since turning pro, Camel had registered seven straight victories, six of them by knockouts. Camel yearned for a coach. "Everybody wants a piece of the action," he told a local newspaper, "but I'm the only guy showing up at the gym."

On September 24, 1975, Camel, in his ninth fight, won the "Strip Fight of the Week" main event by knocking out Terry Lee at two minutes, thirty-six seconds of the eighth round. The "Strip Fight" always took place on a Wednesday night before crowds ranging from a few hundred to a thousand. "Not many tourists, but a lot of dealers and bartenders and small-time degenerate gamblers," recalled one longtime boxing writer for the *Las Vegas Review-Journal*. "They'd stand back by the bar and bet every fight, or every round, sometimes taking alternate corners."

Camel and Lee engaged in an ugly, mutually dirty affair. The headline on the *Las Vegas Sun-Journal* article read: "Camel Lacks Finesse, But Wins Main Event." The third paragraph of Jim Hunter's story described the night: "Camel, to put it bluntly, looked sloppy. He knows it and Pete Jovanovich, [his new co-]manager, will admit it. Camel, always a favorite at the Silver Slipper, fell out of favor somewhat because of some questionable tactics. Not out-and-out dirty, many fighters have been much worse, just that it wasn't the type of stuff one has come to expect from Camel."

A left uppercut to the head dropped Lee early in the eighth round. He was up at the six-count and was met by a straight left on the head that had him down until the seven-count. Camel rushed in, delivering combinations until a right finally floored Lee for the third and final time. During the fight, instead of sticking and moving, Camel lunged and dove after Lee. He said later that he was frustrated by Lee's counter-punching style. He defended his new tactics, which included a rabbit punch or two, "a little hold-the-neck-down-and-punch-up," and quite a bit of shoving. "They're some of the tricks you pick up through experience," Camel told a reporter afterwards. "It's been done to me in a couple of other fights I've had here."

Elmer Boyce had brought in Pete Jovanovich, a fight manager from Anaconda, Montana. Jovanovich got his start as a boxing promoter when the city of Butte refused to negotiate with light heavyweight Johnny Persol in a bout against "The Opportunity Kid," Roger Rouse.

In a November 13, 1967, feature story on Rouse in *Sports Il-lustrated,* Jovanovich's role was described: "Jovanovich heard that Butte wouldn't put up the $3,000 to bring Persol in. 'What a crying shame,' Jovanovich remembers thinking. 'Here's a kid with all the potential, and he can't get off the ground. I went out on the street and caught a couple of guys on the way to the post office. 'Hey,' I said, 'we got a chance to get Persol.' Within an hour and a half Jovanovich had raised $53,000 from 10 businessmen who later incorporated themselves as Montana Boxing Enterprises to promote Rouse's fights in Montana."

Even though Rouse was the leading man among Jovanovich's boxers, the latter was interested in Camel. Jovanovich said it was uncertain when Camel's next fight would be. "With the price of everything today, they try to use as many local kids as they can. That's why we were talking about getting a stable (of Missoula fighters), to eliminate bringing these guys in to cut down on the terrible expense of airplane tickets and meals."

Regardless of where his next bout took place, in a short period Marvin Camel had already given fans and the state of Montana a preview of the thrills to come.

06

FRIENDLY FACE IN THE CORNER

Marvin Camel's last fight of 1975 was a ten-round unanimous decision over the five-inch shorter Danny Brewer, on November 19. Labeled by a *Las Vegas Sun* sports writer as "one of the most exciting bouts of the year," Camel showed he could take a punch. All in all, the bout taught him to be cautious of a purported underdog.

Camel began 1976 with a second-round knockout of a Texan named Pedro Vega. Nearly twenty pounds lighter than his opponent, Camel started the fight with a pair of left hand leads that bloodied Vega's nose. In round two, Camel caught Vega in a neutral corner and shot Vega a short right hook to the head. Vega crumpled to his knees and hung between the ropes. Vega crawled back from under the middle rope but was counted out on his knees.

"The right moves put him in the corner," Camel said. "The moves just came. I was working on moving to my right and jabbing. But if you get an opportunity like that, you take advantage."

Camel credited veteran handler Frank Masterana with handing out the necessary advice. "Like Frank said, if you don't force yourself, the punches will come." Vega, described by a reporter as "flabby-looking" and a "known stiff," wasn't the quality of opponent Camel had been facing. Camel's pro record improved to 11–0.

In his next fight one month later, Camel was so dominant he

could afford to be a gentleman. Early in the third round, his light heavyweight opponent, Donny Meloncon, found himself halfway out of the ring after throwing and missing a punch. He was in a defenseless position, and as he pulled his head back through the ropes, he expected to get it knocked off. Instead, Camel backed away, giving Meloncon a chance to recover.

Meloncon grunted, "Thank you." Camel said "you're welcome" by dropping Meloncon three times in the next minute and winning by knockout at 2:24 of the third. Meloncon, from Houston, went into the bout with an 11–4 record. "He [Maloncon] must be confident," said fight promoter Bill Miller before the fight. "He took the fight without even blinking an eye, and it's been hard to find fights for Camel."

Camel was active in 1976, fighting nine times. His normal day began at five in the morning with road work, followed by a full day as an employee of Elmer Boyce at Montana Music Rentals. He moved, repaired, and serviced pinball machines, juke boxes, and various other machines in businesses through the area. "Many fighters after running will relax awhile. I don't," said Camel.

At this point in his career, Camel wanted to feed on more than just ham-and-eggers, boxing slang for run-of-the-mill pugilists of little consequence who earn only enough to pay for meals. He was happy to be in Montana for his next bout because it allowed him to fight in front of the home crowd and to spend time with family, friends, and his new wife Sherry. The absences caused by out-of-state fights had been difficult for him, making him realize just how much he needed her company.

Sherry understood how much boxing meant to Marvin. She supported his dreams of greatness and talked him down from his anxieties of failure. She understood that Marvin's career demanded that he be away from home a great deal. She needed to acclimate to his singular occupation—and preoccupation. If she held dreams of settling in one place to relax, slow down, and gaze into a blazing fireplace, he didn't.

Sherry showed few signs of resentment in those early days. But they were still young and immature—neither had experienced anything approaching a serious romance with anyone else. Yes, training combined with his regular job meant a lot of time spent away from home and family. Yes, demands required of Camel to become a top-notch contender were arduous. But the couple committed to not drifting apart. One solution was for Sherry to become part of her husband's entourage, and when another helper was needed to assist trainer Frank Masterama, she became part of the team.

Boyce told newspapers that Sherry volunteered and said the three-year-old marriage had been strained by the hours Camel had to spend in training. He said, "Mrs. Camel volunteered to help out in a shortage of trainers." Sherry said she was asked by Boyce and Marvin—who cooked up the idea.

"She learned the basics of the job from Marvin," Boyce told the Associated Press in 1976. "And Frank is teaching her the more technical skills like wrapping his hands and so on."

Sherry's exchange of her kitchen apron for a ring apron scarcely seemed unnatural to anyone. Not only did Sherry assist with the workouts, but beginning with Camel's fight on May 8, 1976, she worked in his corner as a second, giving him water and rinsing his mouthpiece.

"I was on a trail most people don't do," Sherry said. "It's a male-dominated sport and there are not many women in the corners. Then, when you put it into perspective, our trail—two people together who were man and wife —to be in those roles as boxer and corner person, it was very different."

Boyce said that as far as he knew, it was the first time a professional boxer had his wife in his corner as a ring second. "It has given them a chance to have more time together," said Boyce. "Especially with Marvin being as dedicated as he is."

Sherry seemed to enjoy the work, even taking on the same duties for her brother-in-law Ken, who made his professional ring debut on the undercard of Marvin's next fight.

"I came to enjoy a lot about boxing," said Sherry. "In boxing, there is no tag team or nobody on the bench to put in. It's a different kind of thing without a benchful of twelve guys."

On May 8, 1976, at the Field House at the University of Montana, Camel punched his way to a unanimous ten-round decision. Early in a career, boxing records normally represent managerial maneuvering more than a fighter's merit. But at 30–16—2, his opponent, Angel Oquendo, had fought some of the top contenders, including Victor Galindez.

Camel, at 173 pounds, had Oquendo, 178 pounds, in trouble twice during the bout. In the sixth, Sherry watched from her husband's corner as he closed Oquendo's left eye and drew blood from the New Yorker's mouth. Then Camel used a couple of combinations to send Oquendo reeling against the ropes, only to have the bell end the round. In the ninth, the Puerto Rican-born Bronx resident leaned on Camel to stall for precious seconds, retrieving his senses. The durable Oquendo, who reportedly never had been dropped in 43 fights, fought the last few rounds on stamina.

After the bout Camel said he had put on the best all-around performance of his career. Camel won every round on all scorecards. Two judges scored the bout 100–86 for Camel. Judge Billy McFarland had it 100–90. It was Camel's fourteenth straight win.

Camel's previous eleven fights were in a Las Vegas casino, and the fight with Oquendo was only his second pro appearance before local fans. Among the crowd of 3,400 were several familiar boxing faces, including former heavyweight contender Jerry Quarry, who handled the color commentary for television, and World Boxing Council light-heavyweight champion John Conteh of England.

In the last fight of a four-bout card, Kenny Camel won his professional debut with a unanimous decision over William Williams of Cincinnati. The younger Camel, giving away nine pounds at 160 for the middleweight contest, had Williams reeling in the fourth and final round, and received a narrow edge on all scorecards.

Throughout the night, the Camels played togetherness to the hilt. Marvin said he was proud to win a fight with his wife on the ring apron as part of Team Camel. Sherry, in turn, said she felt blessed to have worked with Marvin and her nineteen-year-old brother-in-law. Boyce saw a future in both siblings. He was not the least bit hesitant to involve Kenny in pro fights, even though the youth had only two amateur bouts to his credit.

"There's no sense in fooling around fighting as an amateur when you're ready to make some money," said Boyce. He was quick to take credit for steering the brief careers of both Camels. He sensed that his men were not going to be relegated to the lower rungs on the boxing ladder for long.

Marvin was ready to distance himself from the ordinary as well. He knew he had to keep fighting. He found that he was never more alive than when he was in pain, pushing harder for higher achievement. In that struggle, there was magic.

Camel's next bout was part of the undercard of Bob Foster's fight with Al Bolden. Foster, a light-heavyweight, was one of the top fighters of the late 1960s and early 1970s. Though virtually unbeatable and the world champion from 1968 to 1974, he did not always receive respect because of the weight class he labored in. On this night, Foster stopped Bolden, who entered the fight with a record of 16-8-1, in three rounds.

Camel would appear as an undercard to Foster in his next three fights. Over the course of a single month, Camel fought—and beat—Chicago native Johnny Townsend twice in a pair of ten-rounders. "Townsend had the body and the shape of Mike Tyson," Camel said. "He hit like Tyson. He had my eyeballs rolling a few times. I needed to use the stick and move approach, so he couldn't get set up." (Townsend may have hit like Tyson, but he lacked Tyson's menacing success, retiring in 1981 with a 9–18 record.)

Foster, then thirty-seven, fought one of his 14 successful title defenses in Missoula, on April 4, 1970, stopping Roger Rouse in four rounds. He said he viewed the match as a stepping stone toward a bout with Joe Frazier, who later demolished him. Out of Foster's career 55–6–1 mark, five of his six losses were to heavyweights.

"I talked a bit with Bob Foster in Missoula," Camel recalled. "Since we weren't going to be boxing, we could have breakfast or beers together. He was more or less exiting when I was coming up. His trainer, Billy Edwards, later worked my corner. Most of the time, ninety percent of the time, he'd sit at the café and keep to himself. He was not a loudmouth, and he was a good guy to be around. Definitely not boisterous. Anyone in boxing recognized the name Bob Foster."

In 1990 Foster was inducted into the International Boxing Hall of Fame.

07

BLOOD SPORT LOSS

In a violent sport filled with tales of desperate men rising from humble and troubled beginnings to become celebrated world champs, few can rival the history of Matthew Saad Muhammad, aka Matthew Franklin. His story is one of the most compelling in boxing.

Matthew's mother died when he was five years old. He and his older brother Rodney, age 8, moved in with relatives. But the burden of having extra children became unbearable to them. After just a few weeks, his aunt realized she couldn't afford to raise both children, and she told Rodney to take out his younger brother and not come back with him.

Rodney led Matthew to the Benjamin Franklin Parkway and said, "Let's have a race." Rodney bolted. Matthew tried to keep up but couldn't. His brother simply ran away.

Hours later the abandoned child was found by a Philadelphia policewoman. Matthew was wandering aimlessly along the busy parkway, lost and scared. Police took him to the Catholic Social Services and the nuns gave him the name "Matthew," after St. Matthew, and "Franklin," after the parkway where he was found.

Franklin turned pro in Philadelphia in 1974. He was 19. It wouldn't take long before everyone in boxing knew his surrogate moniker. He took an aggressive path to the top and quickly became the idol of those who relished the triumph of brute strength over science and skill.

Camel knocked down Franklin in the fourth round of their match on July 17, 1976, in Stockton, California, but Franklin brawled back, knocking down Camel once, and won a split decision.

Camel slowly walked back to the dressing room, a loser for the first time as a professional. Despair hung heavily in his heart. He got dressed and quickly left the stadium. His friends and entourage told him that he fought a courageous fight, but he didn't want to hear a word.

"To be truthful, that fight was one of my worst," Camel said later. "Not only was it my worst as far as how I looked, but it was the worst I felt. I just wasn't there. And I really couldn't tell you what was wrong."

Some would say Camel had a valid excuse if he cared to exploit it. Two weeks before the bout, Camel was in a car accident that left him with more than twenty stitches in his forehead and minus about a pint of blood. That accident was on a Friday and Camel returned to his training—mostly roadwork—the following Monday.

"But somewhere along the line I lost something," Camel said. "I don't think I'll really know where. But I'm getting it back. I feel I'm getting my power back." Power was what he didn't have in Stockton.

Camel got another crack at Franklin in a rematch on October 23 in Missoula. Franklin, at 16–1, and Camel, at 17–1, couldn't have been more evenly matched.

"I think, hopefully, that I can stop him within eight rounds," Matthew said to the press after arriving in town one day before the event. "Sometimes, a fighter can change some of the things that he does, but not everything. I've been watching his moves carefully."

Franklin said he took the return bout "to show a guy I can beat him. If I lost, I would want a rematch. He feels he can beat me and he deserves a chance. Of course, the money's good, too. I wouldn't have taken the fight if it wasn't or if I had something better coming."

Actually, Franklin had a bout scheduled in November against Domenico Adinolfi of Italy, Europe's second-ranked light-heavy. This was a step into the upper echelons of the division less than three years after Franklin had turned professional. With that kind of bout only weeks away, it was strange that Franklin would take a rematch with a dangerous fighter like Camel—particularly in the hostile confines of Camel's hometown.

"I know he's from Missoula," Franklin said, "and I hope the people don't rob me, that I can go back to my state and tell them it's a fair game here. I came to fight. And I hope they give it to the person who is the most aggressive and throws the hardest punches—that they give it to the person who wins."

This time Franklin proved much more difficult for Camel, much quicker, much more aggressive. He had Camel off-balance on several occasions and relented—perhaps wary of Camel's dangerous left uppercut. Franklin released his punches faster than Camel, who managed to evade a number of them but absorbed ample punishment as well.

Camel couldn't control the tempo of the fight because Franklin cut down the ring. He forced Camel into exchanges when Marvin would have rather bobbed and weaved and jabbed and moved. That is not to say that Franklin dominated. He pressed, but, in doing so, fell victim to some hard shots to the head, often taking one punch to land two.

Camel overwhelmed Franklin in the second round but got into some trouble when Franklin connected with a stiff combination. Franklin had Camel backpedaling in the third. Franklin could not, however, follow up on his leads. Franklin came on strong in the middle rounds, but Camel reversed the momentum in the eighth and appeared to steal the tenth with solid defense.

Camel won with a split decision. Judge Joe Antonetti had scored the match a draw. Judge Billy McFarland scored the fight 98–96 for Camel, and referee (and boxer) Bob Foster scored it 100–91 Camel, giving the hometown fighter all ten rounds. However, the decision was protested by Frank Gelb, Franklin's manager, and a "no-decision" was declared until a special board met.

In an awkward scene, Gelb tried to inspect the score sheets and discovered that no one from the Montana Board of Athletics was left in the arena. Board members Sonny O'Day and Bob Blome had left before the bout ended in order to catch a bus for their homes in eastern Montana.

While the post-fight hassle spoiled an entertaining fight, Franklin did have reason to balk. According to one newspaperman, the protest "might save Franklin a loss—a loss most of the spectators apparently thought he didn't deserve." Another writer reported that, "Certainly, the Philadelphia fighter took the fight to Camel all the way. His counter-punching and combinations to the body took their toll on Camel, who tired visibly at the end."

One month later, the headline of an Associated Press report trumpeted that "Marvin Camel is the winner." The story said the "Montana Board of Athletics ruled that a split decision by light heavyweight Marvin Camel of Missoula would stand as a victory over Matt Franklin of Philadelphia."

The news media was very critical over the way the decision was handled. One writer said, "All the post-fight brouhaha did was cast a cloud over boxing in Missoula and Montana—a cloud that cheapens the sport, the town and the state."

More controversy would come Camel's way. In fact, controversy would become the norm.

As for Matthew Franklin, the next year in just his twenty-first pro fight, he knocked out veteran Marvin Johnson to win the NABF light heavyweight crown. He defended that title with wins over Billy Douglas, Richie Kates, and a fired-up Alvaro "Yaqui" Lopez. In 1979, he battled Marvin Johnson again for the WBC light heavyweight title. Bleeding from cuts above both eyes, Matthew scored an eighth-round knockout. The round was named "Round of the Year" by *Ring Magazine*. Shortly after, Franklin converted to Islam and changed his name to Matthew Saad Muhammad.

In Saad's fourth world light-heavyweight title defense, in 1980, he again fought "Yaqui" Lopez in what was later named the "Fight of the Year" by "The Ring." The first half of the fight was dominated by Lopez and in round eight (also named the "Round of the Year") Lopez pinned Saad in a corner and landed twenty consecutive blows. That served as a punch-filled, glorious wakeup call. In one of boxing's greatest turn-arounds, Saad dominated the remainder of the fight, flooring Lopez four times in the fourteenth round before the fight was stopped.

Saad made eight successful world title defenses, seven of which came by knockout. In 1981 Saad lost to Dwight Muhammad Qawi via a tenth-round knockout. In the rematch eight months later, Saad was stopped in the sixth round. He retired in 1992, with a 39–16–3 record, winning only one of his last nine fights.

To the world of boxing, Saad Muhammad was "Mr. Excitement," "The Comeback King," or, as one writer put it, "Boxing's Boomerang." He displayed tremendous recuperative powers, and though frequently hurt, was rarely stopped. He was inducted into the International Boxing Hall of Fame.

08

NOT FANCY UP HERE

FOR SOME BOXERS, SUCH AS THE FAMOUS HEAVYWEIGHT CHAMPION Mike Tyson, boxing was a natural extension of their inner rage. Growing up, Tyson's neighborhood was a harsh slum. Violence and crime were common, even tolerated. When he was five years old, Tyson witnessed a murder. Frightened, he did not leave his tiny apartment for three months.

Tyson was reported to have been arrested thirty-eight times for petty crimes by the time he became a teenager; he was locked up seven times after becoming the youngest heavyweight champion in history, at the age of twenty, in 1986. He has been arrested for felony drug possession and assault and battery, as well as the famous arrest, in 1991, for the rape of Miss Black Rhode Island, a charge for which he was convicted and served three years in prison.

For Johnny Tapia, who committed suicide in mid-2012, violence was the core element of his life, from start to finish. Despite being declared clinically dead five times as a result of drug overdoses, he still managed to win titles in three weight divisions. But Tapia's story couldn't be told without mentioning his hard-luck upbringing in Albuquerque's Wells Park neighborhood. His father was reportedly murdered before he was born, and his mother was murdered when he was a small child. He was raised by his grandparents and struggled with mental illness, addiction, and criminal arrests throughout his life.

For such boxers, using their violence within the ring was little different than using their violence on the streets.

Marvin Camel wasn't like most boxers. He rarely let anger sweep away his mind. He didn't stay up late or roam the bars, and he disliked night life and all of its seedy elements. He knew that in the street there was always someone bigger, stronger, meaner, luckier, someone with little to lose, someone with a knife or a gun. Camel valued life too much to risk being badly injured for nothing.

At home in Missoula, Marvin Camel's life was a cramped, home-made gym behind big, dirty windows. When he was in Las Vegas, his existence was a standard gym smelling of cheap cigars, hot liniment, dirty socks, and sweaty jock straps. In Missoula, he largely trained alone. In Las Vegas, there were dozens of fighters of all sizes, shapes, and talents, and all the punching bags, skipping ropes, exercising, shadowboxing, and sparring in the ring.

No matter the location, Camel worked hard. And when he did, Boyce scribbled notes—punches too unruly, needs solid balance, not enough leverage, legs too far wide, stride a bit too long, better defense, don't stand up too straight, needs to get more body into punches, use combinations better, relies too much on jab, stronger right hook. The list was endless.

"Elmer Boyce was a great boxing brain," Ken Camel said. "He was the one who taught me how to hit the speed bag the right way. That's right, a 78-year-old man in business clothes taught me the slow motion of the speed bag. Ka-boom. Slow. Ka-boom. Slow at the beginning. Ka-boom. Ka-boom. Start slow, soon you'll be spinning it so fast you can't see it."

Boyce rode Marvin hard, and Marvin responded. On June 28, 1977, Camel fought Chicago-born light heavyweight Danny Brewer in Seattle. Two years earlier, Camel had earned a ten-round unanimous decision over Brewer in Las Vegas.

In Seattle, Camel had Brewer in trouble through much of the first four rounds, knocking him down twice. "The first time he went down," Camel said, "he was a little off balance and it didn't take much to put him down, but the second time, I hit him with a good left and he didn't have anywhere else to go but down."

Near the end of the fifth round, a head butt opened a gash over Camel's left eye, and the bout was stopped, either by the referee or by the ring physician. Camel felt he could have gone on, but Brewer was awarded a TKO. To Camel, the head butt didn't seem like an accident.

Camel hoped to have a rubber match with Brewer, but his foe canceled, citing religious observance. Brewer only fought once more, wrapping up his career with a 13-11-1 record.

In the summer of 1977, *Ring Magazine*, often referred to as "The Ring" or "The Bible of Boxing," had Camel rated fifteenth at light-heavyweight. Marvin didn't put much stock in it. Camel believed boxing ratings had more to do with who you know than how good you were. He acknowledged, however, that in the long climb to the top, having your name among the leading contenders helps pave the way to fights against the people who count.

Camel told friends that the guys who spout off at the mouth like Muhammad Ali are the guys who seem to make all the money. "I'm not much for that stuff. I guess I'd say I think a guy ought to go out and do it and get it done."

The only way to be the best, in his view, was to show more desire than your opponent. At twenty-six, he understood his time was short. "I'll know within the next two years whether or not I'll make it," he said. He didn't talk much about a shot for the title but the thought certainly entered his mind. "Sure a guy thinks about it. As long as a guy is in boxing he has to have his heart on the top spot." Camel said he planned to pull out all the stops while he was in the profession and then quit when the right time came, unhurt, with a future outside boxing.

His schedule was hectic. In order to reach his goal—and provide for his wife and their new baby Louis Alfonse—prolific training and fighting had to be done. The money from boxing was handy, but not sustainable. "It pays a few bills and what-not," Camel said, whose son was born July 17, 1977. "I won't let it influence me in any way of living because you just don't know when it is going to stop coming in."

At times, boxing felt like just another job. "I really enjoyed it as a kid," Camel said, "but not so much now." So why fight? "I guess I'm not really doing it for myself anymore," he would say, "but for the people of the reservation, Indians, whites, whoever...the people of Montana."

On the Flathead Reservation, Camel's fights were starting to feel like celebrations, not just for the Indians of today, but for what they once were. Camel's followers had begun to climb on board for what they believed would be a long ride.

In August 1977 Camel scheduled light-heavyweight Ron Wilson of San Diego to fight at the Pony Palace, an indoor rodeo arena five miles south of Polson with seating capacity for 2,000 people—and 85 box stalls for horses. Appearing in a card on the reservation meant a lot to Camel. "It's something I have to do for the people."

Camel was confident he could take Wilson at home because he faced the California fighter two years earlier in Las Vegas and won a ten-round decision. "He's a tough guy, a very durable man," Camel said.

Wilson was definitely no slouch. The bout was the one hundredth in his professional career. He had won 64 times, including his last five outings. Some of his opponents included Mike Quarry, recent world light-heavyweight champion Jessie Burnett, Johnny Wise, and Johnny Baldwin.

Camel entered the fight with a 21–2–1 record and fresh memories of his recent cut-stoppage loss to Danny Brewer a month prior. "It's healed and I'm ready," Camel told the Ronan *Pioneer* a few days before the fight. "We aren't fancy up here in Montana. We don't use fight films to train with, but we'll be ready when Saturday gets here."

The five-bout card began at 7:30 pm and approximately 3,600 fans paid admission fees of $15 for ringside; $12 for raised ringside; $7.50 for general reserve; and $5 for general admission. On the undercard, Kenny Camel tangled with Albert Rodriquez in an eight-round middleweight fight. Kenny knocked out his foe in a single round.

Marvin's ring walk was lined with well-wishers and greeters. He stepped through the ropes and paced the ring, counting the steps, sucking in deep breaths. Carefully he ignored the faces of friends in the crowd and found his corner. He was all business. He was the hometown kid. *The local Indian is going to whup some ass.*

Camel loosened out his arms, shadowboxed. The crowd let loose unmistakable cheers, no discernible boos. He heard wolf whistles and cat calls as if from under water.

Using a swift right hand jab, Camel dismantled Wilson's defense early in the bout to run up points. The shorter Wilson could not counter Camel's speed and was unable to establish any rhythm. Both men moved cautiously in the early going, but Camel's looping rights began to connect and his left began to shut Wilson's eye in the third round.

In the fourth round Camel unloaded a series of combinations that sent Wilson retreating. Camel reverted to a stick-and-slide offense in the next round, while Wilson missed counter attempts. In the seventh and eighth rounds, Wilson caught Camel with a few jolting shots. With only ten seconds elapsed in round eight, Wilson stunned Camel with a right hand flush on the jaw, which sent Camel sprawling to the canvas. Camel got back up for the standing eight count. He closed out the round by thumping Wilson's head with a right and a pair of left hooks.

In the ninth and tenth rounds the fight turned into a brawl, with neither man backing off one inch. Camel's right eye was cut badly in the tenth. Wilson absorbed tremendous punishment to the body. When the announcement was made that Camel, who was comfortably ahead on all three judges' scorecards, had won the fight, the partisan crowd thundered its approval.

"Marvin has really improved," a puffy-eyed Wilson said after the bout. "His right hand is quite a bit better and he's an awful lot smarter. I've fought the best in the world, both right and lefthanders, and Marvin will go a long ways. Guys will fight lefties if [the lefthanders] aren't that good. But Marvin's good, and he's a lefthander, and a lot of guys don't like that."

Successful managers like Elmer Boyce knew that a good prospect like Camel had to be handled carefully. The trick was never to overmatch a talented young fighter, but at the same time not to limit his opponents to mere pushovers—known in the craft as "tomato cans." Boyce was looking for a "worthy opponent," a boxing term that connoted fighters who were decent, but not distinguished, and were capable of testing a boxer's resolve. Camel's 25th opponent, Karl Zurheide, fit that bill admirably.

Camel trained in Johnny Tocco's Ringside Gym in seedy downtown Las Vegas and spent his nights sleeping in an uncomfortable makeshift bed, layered in blankets and a few pillows, inside of his beat-up van, which he parked behind the gym. Johnny Tocco's gym was the ideal training site. With frayed, yellowing fight posters layering the walls and the mustiness of hot air, it was like a safe haven for world champions who could prepare in seamy tranquility. Mythic icons and two-bit pugs exercised in close quarters. Marvin sparred and showered in the gym, then retired to his van to sleep.

One night he received an unexpected visitor. "I heard someone trying to open the door," Camel said. "So, I popped right up and out of the bed. I surprised the guy. He looked like he had just walked into a beehive nest. I think he was going to try to steal my Credence tapes."

Camel knocked Zurheide down and out in seven rounds on Pearl Harbor Day, 1977.

Around this time, Camel had another near fatal brush with death—another traffic accident that could have ended far more severely. One Friday afternoon, Marvin and Kenny were driving a pickup truck full of pinball machines to Elmer Boyce's Montana Music Rentals' second store in Polson. Marvin's recollection is a bit murky: someone crossed the center line, someone else reacted, and then, bang, in knee-jerk response to avoid a head-on crash, Marvin swerved and the pickup crashed in a ditch.

"Ken and I came out unscathed," Marvin said. "The truck was totaled and the machines disintegrated. We were out of the hospital the same day."

In the latter part of 1978, Marvin Camel was asked by a friend why he fought. He replied, "It's the only thing I really get along with. I feel that I was born and bred to fight. Sure, it takes hard work and dedication but I'm my own man." Camel said that as long as he could equate boxing with work, it wasn't a chore but an occupation like anything else. "I fight very well. Why not continue with it? I've had no major setbacks yet so I'm going as far as I can."

Camel faced what could have turned into a "major setback" on November 11, 1978, when he faced Tom Bethea, who was once ranked among the world's leading middleweights and light-heavyweights. Before the fight with Camel, "The Bomb" had dropped six straight to top-flight opposition, including losses to Mike Quarry and Michael Spinks.

"Tom Bethea was a very good New York fighter," said Don Majeski, a New York-based boxing promoter who became involved with Camel through Elmer Boyce. "Bethea had fought all over, even in Madison Square Garden. A win over a guy like Bethea was what Marvin really needed at the time."

Bethea had met six world champions and challenged some of the world's top fighters in their home countries and cities. Fighting Camel in Missoula did not bother him. "I beat home-town guys before," said Bethea. He also said he was not concerned about fighting a lefthander. "That don't bother me," he said. "I'm just goin' out there to beat him."

Majeski told the press that Bethea was thirty-two years old and had a 25–8 record. Before the fight Bethea said that he was "34" and had "40-some fights" behind him. *Ring Magazine* listed Bethea's record as 21–16–3 through 1976. His date of birth was not listed.

At Adams Field House, a basketball arena capable of holding approximately 5,500 spectators, only 1,500 fans watched the match, which was billed as the Northwest Light Heavyweight Championship.

It was over quickly. Camel had Bethea clinging to the ropes midway through the first round. When the bell rang, Bethea was on the canvas.

In his corner, Bethea looked slow and lethargic. At the start of the second round Camel moved in for the kill. He hunted Bethea, scoring at will, picking apart his defense, and repeatedly pinning him into the ropes. A barrage of rights and lefts ended it. Dazed and wobbled, Bethea turned his back, staggered to the edge of the ring, and slumped over the ropes. Referee Billy O'Neil had no other option but to stop the fight at two minutes and thirty seconds into the second round. It turned out to be Bethea's last fight of his career.

Camel's trainer for this fight, Billy Edwards—the second of former light heavy champ Bob Foster—had told him to go all out for the KO immediately. "This guy's got so much reach," Edwards said of Camel. "Bethea didn't have a chance."

The win was sweet, but Camel expressed bitterness toward Montana audiences, saying, "What they don't understand is that tickets to bouts pay the bills. We've had trouble promoting our fights in Montana and we've brought in some really class guys."

The crowd was better on April 24, 1979. In fact, not since the days when Roger Rouse attracted buses of fans from Butte had Montana seen such an armada of vehicles in the parking lot of a boxing match. Some 3,000 people paid five dollars each to see Marvin Camel fight David Smith, again at the Adams Field House. "It's the finest crowd we've ever had," proudly huffed Elmer Boyce.

Most of the crowd originated from Camel's home ground of the Jocko and Mission valleys. "I just came to see Marvin fight," said Victor Lumpry of Arlee. "I just came to see Marvin win," said seventy-five-year-old Jocko valley rancher Abel Combs.

Feeding off the excitement of his fans, Camel won handily. "King" David Smith of Los Angeles, a 175-pounder, hunkered down behind his gloves most of the fight. Camel pressed Smith constantly, keeping his foe's back pressed against the ropes. At the start of the tenth round, Smith refused to continue.

The fight was more of a social event for proud Montanans than a fiercely contested nail-biter. "It was a splendid success as a barn-dance," wrote the *Missoulian*. The paper went on to describe the card as "a social get-together that drew into communion people from all over western Montana, from all strata of society, from every political and religious persuasion."

Indeed, Marvin's hunger for success, with its elusive promise of legacy and wealth, crossed all the lines of race and class. His sporting world blended native and white, rich with poor, in ways encountered in no other segment of society.

On March 9, 1978, Camel won a blood-splattered decision over southern heavyweight champion Bobby Lloyd at Wichita's Century II Convention Hall. Lloyd thinned down to light heavy-weight for the fight. A sparse crowd of 1,000 looked on. Camel floored the Bahama native once with a left but most of the night he jabbed and waded in. By the end of the fight the referee was as bloody as Lloyd, who had a cut over his left eye.

After a pair of victories in Montana (over Pete McIntyre in Butte and Chuck Warfield in St. Ignatius), Camel scheduled an August 22, 1978, fight against Ibar Arrington in Coeur d'Alene, Idaho. Part of a five-bout card in front of approximately 2,000 people, the main event provoked excitement.

A powerful heavyweight from Seattle, Arrington was a top-twenty contender with knockout power and tenacity. He faced several top national and international contenders, including a memorable meeting the year before with soon-to-be World Boxing Council champion Larry Holmes at Caesar's Palace in Las Vegas, a contest Arrington came within a whisker of winning.

In the ring Arrington displayed a potent left jab and a powerful right, but his best asset might have been an ability to absorb a licking. He had, in boxing parlance, a great chin, meaning he could take even the most vicious blows and remain upright. Not once in his pro career was he ever knocked out.

Promoter Al Rose tried to stir up pre-fight animosity between the fighters. "Ibar punches so hard, I think Marvin's people are a little afraid he might get hurt," he said. "This Ibar, he can hurt you just in the clenches—he can break your ribs with punches. Marvin's never been knocked out, but it's no disgrace if one of the toughest heavyweights on the coast beats a light heavyweight. I'm surprised Camel is fighting this guy. He's giving away 20 pounds, and this guy is really tough." According to Rose, Arrington had won his last five bouts by knockout.

Camel and Arrington teed off from the opening bell. Camel made a mockery out of Arrington's slow-footed, wild-swinging style and went on to win by unanimous decision.

Afterwards, Arrington did not deny that he was clearly beaten. But in the frustration of a post-fight interview, he came up with dozens of excuses for losing. "He was getting away with the backhand—that's what swells up the eyes," griped Arrington. "I can't take anything away from his ability, except for the dirty stuff—the backhands, a few low blows. We've got rules, let's abide by them. Warnings aren't going to help, you've got to take action."

Referee Dale Trumbo did warn Camel about low blows and Camel didn't deny Arrington's accusations. "With a guy like that, what can you do?" Camel said. "There's bound to be mistakes. You can't watch every move you make. If there were any backhands, I'm sorry about that. I don't think it affected the outcome of the fight."

Arrington also said the conditions for the fight were ideal for Camel but to his own disadvantage. "There was a difference in the ring size when we got here," claimed Arrington. "They had a 16-foot ring scale, but they changed it to 20 by 20 feet. I've always used 8-ounce gloves, but they changed them to 10-ounce. They claim that the 10-ounce gloves are mandatory in Idaho, that it's in the rule book, but when I asked to see the rule book, they said they didn't have one. Things like that make you feel depressed before you even start the fight. It makes a big difference mentally as well as physically."

Camel said he doubted the ring size or gloves' weight would have made much of a difference, and matchmaker Al Rose admitted he was disappointed in Arrington's inept performance against Camel. "I didn't realize Marvin Camel was that good," said Rose. "He just beat one of the top heavyweights on the west coast. Marvin went in there and out-slugged him, out-danced him, and out-fought him. I thought Marvin would be on the floor two or three times."

Looking forward, Camel talked of promoting a fight in Ronan, his hometown. "They deserve it," Camel said. But fight cards in Montana, even with Camel in the main event, had been notorious money losers. "When I started boxing," Camel said, "we figured if I was gonna make any money, I was gonna make it in Montana. But the only time we made any money is when Bob Foster came to town…since then all we've been doin' is losin'money."

Around this time Camel embarked on a personal public relations campaign to interest more Montanans in professional boxing. "Lotta people, they say, I wonder who Marvin Camel is. Are you Marvin Camel? Lotta people still don't know me except by name. I just go out and meet people, talk to 'em one-one-one and let 'em know who Marvin Camel is—that I'm not too good to talk to them, that I'm just like anybody else. Then everything gets alright. A lot more people are comin' out to see me fight now."

At 26, Camel said that his long-term plans may include a possible role in politics. "I've been thinking about migratin' back to the reservation when I'm done boxing and see if I can do any good up there," Camel said. Working with youngsters had a special appeal for Camel. "A lot of kids on the reservation are athletically minded. If I can do anything that might help them forget the booze, I'll do it. Oh, I know they won't forget about it altogether, they're going to indulge a little bit. Everybody does."

Less than a month after defeating Arrington, Camel won a twelve-round decision over Dale Grant, half-brother of Sugar Ray Seales, in Butte. (The two had fought to a draw February 15, 1977, in Seattle.)

Between fights, Marvin fixed pinball machines and hauled them across the incomparably lovely, yet equally lonely, spaces of Montana. Then one summer day in 1979, Camel received word that he would be fighting in an elimination tournament for the World Boxing Council's new cruiserweight title, and he was listed as the number one contender.

Marvin felt vindicated that all those days of shadowboxing and more shadowboxing, of heavy bag exercises and physical extremism, had paid off. *I bucked the herd. I didn't conform. I took a certain mindset. I've arrived.*

Boxing's alphabet soup of organizations and rankings has always been confusing. In 1963, a conglomeration of governing boxing bodies, including the BBBofC, the EBU, and several American state organizations merged because they were turned off by the arrogance of the newly formed World Boxing Association. These groups felt the need to band together, and they formed the World Boxing Council (WBC). The WBC was the first organization to create the cruiserweight division.

"It means quite a bit to me to be rated number one in the cruiser division," Camel said. "I think I have a real good chance to fight for the world title, and even win it in the cruiserweight."

In order to fight for the WBC's world championship belt, Camel first needed to acquire a suitable subtitle—the North American cruiserweight championship. The first step was a fight against Bill Sharkey, the WBC's number two cruiserweight.

"Bill Sharkey was a tough, durable New York fighter," said Don Majeski. "We felt as if a win over Sharkey would get us much more exposure back east. A very tough guy was Sharkey—a stablemate of Vito Antuofermo."

Sharkey had made a belated debut in pro boxing in 1975 when his uncle convinced him to use his experience at street fighting to make some money. "Ever since I was a youth I was involved in a lot of street brawls and got into trouble with fighting," Sharkey said. "But there were no dividends and no rewards. I was getting nowhere. But I never lost a street fight and I had plenty of them. My uncle convinced me I could make it pay off."

Sharkey's path to boxing was all too familiar. One day, when he was 19, Sharkey came home and saw police cars all over the block in front of his house and wondered why they were there. His father and mother had been murdered. Two years later, in 1970, Sharkey and another man drove to a home in Queens and shot and killed a man. Charged with murder, a jury convicted him of manslaughter. He was sentenced to 10 years but was released in 1974. He later told people they had locked up the wrong man.

The 30-year-old Sharkey had compiled an 18–3–1 record against heavyweight opponents while weighing only a bit over 190 pounds. When the cruiserweight division was created, Sharkey said it "was the greatest thing I ever heard. I'm a natural 187-pounder. That's what I weigh today. I used to have to eat four meals a day to keep my weight up."

On June 5, 1979, the two combatants saw each other for the first time at a mock weigh-in at the Southgate Mall in Missoula. Both men weighed 188 pounds. Resplendent in buckskins and flowing Indian headdress, Camel was asked if he was concerned by Sharkey's high percentage of 13 knockouts in 22 fights. "No," he replied. "I don't really think so."

"As I see him today," Camel said, "he doesn't look any different from an average fighter. After seeing him, it made me feel a little better. The way he looked in the paper, he looked awful muscular and powerful. It makes the adrenalin flow a little easier to see him."

Sharkey said it was a disadvantage for him to have never watched Camel fight. "From all I've heard," said Sharkey, "he's a classic fighter who moves and punches well. And that's what I've trained for." Sharkey said fighting a lefthander didn't bother him: "I've fought heavyweight southpaws before. They still only have two hands."

In the bout at Adams Field House, it was boxer vs. fighter, and the contrast was accentuated as the bout progressed. From the second round forward, Camel conclusively dominated the action, frustrating Sharkey with a sharp right jab. He kept Sharkey at distance and staggered him repeatedly with looping left hooks and uppercuts. Following the fifth round, Sharkey started to complain, blaming the altitude and atmosphere, griping, "I can't breathe this mountain air."

Camel staggered and dazed Sharkey several more times, but there were no knockdowns and Camel was unable to finish him off. The two judges scored it 120–108 for Camel, while referee Gene Fullmer had Camel up 120-105. "Marvin really outboxed Sharkey that night," said Beau Williford, Sharkey's trainer. "Sharkey didn't cut off the ring. Marvin wouldn't allow it."

The day and night before the fight, Camel had been in Butte fixing pinball machines. Minutes after beating Sharkey, Camel told Boyce and Majeski, "I forgot something."

"What did you forget, Marvin?" asked Boyce.

"I forgot to do my roadwork."

With that, Marvin laced up his sneakers and ran three miles around the university's field track. It was another example of his work ethic.

That same night, Marvin's brother Ken scored a split decision over "Rugged" C.J. Brown of Eugene, Oregon, in a ten-round light heavyweight bout. It would be Kenny's final professional boxing match.

Following the Sharkey bout, Elmer Boyce said that the people of Missoula "will never see Marvin Camel" fight again. He said he lost $21,000 on his latest card. Only 1,426 people paid to attend and some of them expressed criticism of the overall value of the card. "I thought I was trying to do something for Montana," said Boyce. "I gave them my best, and they don't want it. I could close my tent in the middle of the night and leave—and that's what I'm going to do."

Boyce also said Camel wanted to leave Missoula. "He's unhappy, too, real unhappy," Boyce said. "Nobody supported him." He said boxing had brought people to Missoula who spent money in bars and restaurants, but the owners would not reciprocate and support boxing. He claimed most of the people attending the Camel-Sharkey fight were from only one or two places in Montana and Idaho. He was hurt, angry, and disappointed that the public did not rally around Camel's cruiserweight subtitle bout.

"I quit once before, then got softhearted," said Boyce. "But they've proved they didn't want boxing in Montana."

There had been criticism of the quality of opponents Camel fought in the Missoula area. "They [Montana fans] keep getting ticked at Elmer Boyce for bringing in these stiffs," Camel said. "But I think they're starting to wake up to the fact right now. I really feel there is no competition for Marvin Camel."

Marvin participated in one more tune-up fight before the next round of cruiserweight eliminations—a two-round beating of Macka Foley. That fight took place in Las Vegas, and one day before it transpired, Camel shook the hand of the boxer from whom he took his middle name: Joe Louis. Paranoid and feeble, Louis was a greeter at Caesar's Palace; two years later, he was dead at age sixty-six. "A lot of people thought it sad, him making a few dollars shaking hands," Camel said, "but he died a happy man. Everyone who walked through those doors had the privilege to meet a great champ."

Now Camel's path was straightforward: beat one more man to win the North American title and then fight for the world title.

On August 30, 1979, Camel fought David "Maceton" Cabrera of Mexico, in the border town of McAllen, Texas. A folk hero among the Mexican and Mexican-American fans, Cabrera was a motorcycle policeman in Mexico City until he crushed his knee in a traffic collision. No longer able to satisfy police duty and devoid of any disability compensation, Cabrera needed to find other employment. Nicknamed "Big Head" in Spanish, Cabrera picked boxing, and he started fighting professionally in 1977. He would later become the Mexican light heavyweight champion multiple times.

"It was the most humid place in the world," Don Majeski said. "It was also in the heart of another guy's hometown."

In Majeski's words, Camel "demolished" Cabrera. "The Indian" knocked down Cabrera in the second round with a wicked left-right combination. By the beginning of the third round, Camel had opened up cuts around both of Cabrera's eyes. Camel decked Cabrera twice in the third round—once at 1:05 and again at 1:30. At that point, Cabrera's corner tossed in the towel, and Camel had won the regional North American cruiserweight belt by technical knockout.

In an interview with KYLT Radio, a Missoula sports talk station, immediately after the fight, Elmer Boyce said the win virtually assured his fighter of a world title match. He was right. Within hours, the WBC announced that Camel would face Mate Parlov of Yugoslavia for the championship. Parlov, the reigning European light heavyweight champion, owned a professional record of 27–2–1. He won the middleweight gold medal in the 1972 Olympics and earned the world light heavyweight title in 1978, which he subsequently lost to Marvin Johnson.

Monte Carlo; Las Vegas; Washington D.C.; Trieste, Italy; Morocco, and even Montana were potential sites for the championship fight. However, it was destined to take place in Split, Yugoslavia, a resort city on the Adriatic coast and Parlov's home ground.

Camel would earn approximately $40,000 and some ancillary rights—by far his biggest payday. Did Marvin feel any bitterness over the amount of money for the fight, considering that years earlier Muhammad Ali received five million dollars for a bout? "Nope, I don't miss all that money," he told the *Ronan Pioneer*. "What would I do with it? To me, $40,000 is a heckava amount. The one good thing about this fight is that no one can avoid Marvin Camel anymore." Indicating that the temptation of a huge payday was indeed compelling, Camel said that success in the ring breeds remuneration. "Next fight, I'm almost guaranteed $125,000 by the promoters and the next one after that $175,000."

Following the Cabrera fight, Camel had verbally reprimanded fight fans in western Montana—an indication of the disappointment he began to feel with his home state. "I don't feel like Montana is backing me as much as I am backing Montana," Camel said. "I know there are some people who say 'I don't give a damn if he makes it.' Why should they? Sometimes it makes me wonder if all those years were worth it."

Even though Camel now had the valuable competition he craved, even though he had made it to the top ranks of world boxing, an innate yearning for recognition at home kept him troubled. No matter what happened in Split, a fracture had formed between Marvin Camel and Montana.

09

DISGUSTED

Now was Marvin Camel's time and he knew it. Lean and hungry, he traveled to Yugoslavia in the winter of 1979 with a single purpose of mind and spirit: to become champion of the world.

The new Gripe Sports Hall filled to capacity with 8,000 fans. Ringside seats cost about $30. Since both fighters fought southpaw, the potential for fireworks was great.

Bursting with zeal, the American trotted into the ring dressed in feathered, floor-length Indian headgear. Many in attendance didn't know what to make of the man with the eagle feathers and hand-stitched vest. They could sense that Camel's eagle feathers were sacred pieces of spirit—a reflection of his vision, an expression of bravery, humility, and special perspective.

In Camel's mind the feathers served as a constant prayer floating on the wind. Feathers were no mere casual adornment, but the link between the earthly and the ethereal.

Split was a city of just over 200,000 inhabitants. It had begun as a settlement around a palace built by Roman emperor Diocletian in the early fourth century A.D.

Camel arrived in Split two weeks before the December 8 event. He jogged in the early morning hours, increasing the length to ten miles, traversing the Adriatic scenery with increasing ease. At the conclusion of one morning's run, he turned to Boyce and promised, "I feel like I can run twice as far. Parlov better be training as hard."

He ate as much steak as he could hold, always sure to accompany it with plenty of green stuff—salads, vegetables, whatever—to give him the roughage that helped him digest proteins easier. His stay was comfortable, and he was at times transfixed by the elegant scenery—splendid, ancient architecture a far cry from the plain structures of his home state.

"We stayed in probably the best hotel there," said Camel. "I had a suite—a two-bed-roomer—all to myself. It was real nice. It had two bathrooms and a kitchen…People were friendly to us everywhere we went…In a way, when it was time to leave, we hated to leave Yugoslavia. There was a sense that we were leaving friends."

Even though she was eight months pregnant, Sherry was there, too. (She gave birth to Marvin "Little Fox" on December 30.) "That flight was eight or nine hours long—the longest in the world, it seemed," said Sherry. "But I was no innocent bystander. I wanted to be a part of it. It was not a bad thing."

At the weigh-in, Parlov was about three-quarters of a pound under the cruiserweight limit of 190 pounds. Camel weighed 184¼. Camel verbally outpointed Parlov. "The match will end before the 15 rounds are over," stated Camel. "What I heard and saw about Parlov does not bode well for him."

"I'm not disturbed over the optimism of my opponent," Parlov told newsmen, calmly dismissing the American's self-praise as a "mannerism of all American fighters."

Before the first round was over, Camel realized it was going to be a long fight. Parlov, shorter and heavier than the American but lacking Camel's long reach, clearly dominated the first three rounds. Parlov slipped one punch after another. He was known as a mover who could dodge and deflect, but Camel learned that facing him was like looking in a mirror. Camel spent more energy hitting air than hitting flesh, and it began to wear on his confidence. *Why am I not landing punches? What is wrong with me?*

Camel came back in the middle and final rounds to take charge. The fact that Camel kept a close right guard apparently upset the Yugoslav in his plans to unleash his powerful left. Camel and Parlov exchanged dozens of hard right jabs and crosses, waiting to use their lefts. But such opportunities were scarce and most were ineffectual. Camel seemed to have a greater capacity for absorbing punches.

In round seven, legendary boxing trainer Gil Clancy told television viewers that he was impressed by the precision and effectiveness of Camel's persistent jab: "Parlov can't see that jab coming. This jab is the same type Kenny Norton gave Muhammad Ali all that trouble with. Camel is just going to jab him to death." One television announcer predicted that Camel's birthday, just weeks away, would be a very happy one for the Ronan product.

At times, the spectators seemed restless, perhaps frustrated by the lack of sustained action and unable to relate to the pressures and demands that Camel and Parlov faced every moment in the ring. If one ever feels their life is accelerating too fast, they should step into the ring. There, time becomes incomprehensible; every second is different. Punches are thrown and blocked in split seconds. Distance is constantly measured and adjusted—increased, decreased, increased, decreased. Every ten seconds is an epoch of cruel intentions.

Although it did get sloppy in the late rounds, with French referee Raymond Baldaire reprimanding Camel for hitting below the belt and for butting, the overall fight had been a very good technical performance by two skilled boxers.

Announcers on CBS's "Sports Spectacular," which broadcast portions of the fight live, had Camel clearly winning. "We have Camel way out in front with the final round coming up," said one announcer.

The rounds go on and on, Camel thought. This was his first fifteen-round fight—and it showed. Heading into the final round, his eyes were blackened, face bruised, hair in disarray. In general he looked like he had taken a beating.

Fifteen rounds had been grueling for both men: you could see it in their eyes. With legs burning and lungs on the verge of exploding, they relayed signals of respect to the other without saying a word. In the last minute, the harder Parlov hit Camel, the tougher Camel charged back.

There was no knockout. The match was decided by points awarded to each boxer by the two British judges and the referee.

Referee Baldaire scored Camel 147 points and Parlov 142. Ringside judge Sid Nathan awarded both contenders 143 points, and ringside judge James Brimme gave both boxers 144. The bout was ruled a draw, the worst sort of outcome: pointless, irritating, numbing.

The CBS announcers could not believe the judgment. "It's been ruled a draw!" said one. "No!" replied the other. "I think that's only one official's card." "No, it has been ruled a draw," repeated the first announcer. "I'd sure like to see those cards individually."

"We went berserk in that ring," Don Majeski said. "It was such a terrible decision. It was laughable because it was so unfair."

Even the partisan crowd seemed stunned by the judges' voting. When the decision was announced, "It was like little green men invaded the earth," Camel said. "For an instant everything was so quiet you could hear a pin drop…then chaos. Nobody was happy with it." Security guards immediately rushed ringside to protect Camel, unsure what the crowd response would be.

"Marvin won the fight hands down," Sherry said. "The people threw roses into the ring for Marvin because they didn't like the decision. They treated us real nice—even though security surrounded us for our own safety."

"Everybody was whistling. That's booing in Yugoslavia," Elmer Boyce told a reporter.

Indeed, the decision appeared to violate a universal sense of fairness. Many Yugoslavian fans stayed until Marvin was done with his final interview. Then they gave him a firm, fair applause. Some lined up along the aisles and patted Marvin on the back as he walked by. Someone handed him a rose. "They were all sayin' 'You besta box,'" said Boyce.

Even the Belgrade daily *Politika Ekspres* said that Camel was shortchanged by the decision: "According to the view of all those present (at the match), the outcome was unfair. Everybody regards that Camel (in fact) has won this match and that he should have been proclaimed the winner." The paper added that "according to some interpretations," there can be no draws in world title matches, and that "this rule was not observed at Split last night." The paper said that the Yugoslav did not manage the fight equally until the end and that Camel had initiative in all but the first two and last two rounds. "The impression is that what Parlov showed in the last round and at the start of the match was not enough to overcome the far better prepared opponent," *Politika* said.

Camel said that the local populace believed he had won the fight. "In places we ate (after the fight), even old people with big glasses on were saying 'We see you on TV. You win boxing match.' The people in the press showed us around the town." "The people of Yugoslavia embraced Marvin as the champion," Majeski said.

Parlov, who had pointed the finger for his earlier struggles in pro boxing at weight problems, said that his new weight had reduced his overall resilience. (Parlov had lost his light-heavyweight crown to American Marvin Johnson one year earlier. He also blamed weight problems for that defeat.)

"[Camel] was an unpleasant opponent," Parlov admitted. "It was hard to fight a boxer with such a close counter-guard. Only at the end could I go in for all or bust, but I was rather tired by then."

Camel charged that Parlov, born in Split, had a hometown advantage that helped make the match a draw. "Mate Parlov is a national hero in Yugoslavia," said Camel. "But the people realized that the national hero is at the end of his rope. It's too bad Yugoslavia was put in the position of looking like it caused the decision. It's too bad I was the fall guy for it. Somebody had to be the fall guy. I just hope—it's not settled yet—I hope I get the belt or a rematch with Mate Parlov. The only thing that'll be lost was me to receive the belt over national TV so all the people could see."

In reality, hometown fighters generally have the advantage of the crowd's reaction. The crowd cheers when their man even comes close to landing a punch and derisively taunts the opposition's aggression as ineffectual. Sometimes that reaction influences the judges, who will keep a fight tight on the scorecards if there is no spectacular knockdown or visible damage.

It's a robbery," fumed Camel. "If he's honest, he will accept a rematch in the United States. But I doubt he will because he has no chance there. I gave him an opportunity here."

Parlov said he thought he earned "at least a draw." But he didn't refute Camel's accusation. "If the match was held in the United States, I would've lost," he said.

Perhaps it was a way to attain mental clarity, perhaps it was mere physical addiction, or perhaps simply an understandable coping mechanism: upon leaving the Gripe Sports Hall, Marvin Camel ran to his hotel.

Rest was hard to come by. Instead, he sat mute, shaking his head. For hours he listened to his own thoughts in the black silence. *Fifteen rounds. Fifteen rounds for nothing.*

The next morning, Camel gingerly sat up in bed, pivoted, placed his feet on the floor, and stood. Physically, he couldn't move without pain, but mentally, he felt somewhat better. Deep in his blood, he knew how to turn a losing battle into a winning war.

Marvin Louis Camel, seven years old. His middle name was bestowed in honor of boxing legend Joe Louis.

Some of the Camel family in Montana. From left to right: Ken, Paula, Bobby, cousin Roberta Fairbanks, Renee (foreground), Florine, Terry, and Marvin.

Camel, his wife Sherry, and their son Marvin Junior.

On April 24, 1979, Camel fought "King" David Smith at the Adams Field House in Missoula, Montana. At the start of the tenth round, Smith refused to continue.

On May 5, 1981, Camel earned a 12-round decision over Rahim Muhammad for the USA Nevada State cruiserweight title. Both men took a beating. By the end of the fight, Camel's left eye was nearly closed and Muhammad's face was cut and bruised.

Camel joins a ceremonial dance with Phillip Paul on the Flathead Indian Reservation in 1979. Marvin is wearing the North American Boxing Federation's cruiserweight title, which he won days earlier in Missoula.

Camel listens to Mitch Small Salmon explain the significance of a ceremonial lance that was presented to Camel in 1980 by the Confederated Salish and Kootenai Tribes. The eagle feather was added to the lance in honor of Camel winning the world title.

Camel and his manager Elmer Boyce talk with a Yugoslavian radio host prior to Camel's fight with Mate Parlov. The bout would be the world's first cruiserweight title fight, a division created for boxers 176 to 190 pounds.

Camel takes a deep breath before battling Parlov. The bout took place on December 8, 1979, in Parlov's hometown of Split, Yugoslavia, and ended in a hotly disputed draw.

In the rematch against Parlov months later in Las Vegas, Camel won a unanimous decision to become the World Boxing Council's first cruiserweight world champion. He poses with the championship belt and trophy.

Camel often wore his eagle-feather headdress into the ring.

Camel's hand-stitched buckskin vest was made by his first wife, Sherry, who frequently served in his corner. Later, in marital discord, Sherry was rumored to have buried Camel's vest, headdress, and world championship belt in the woods.

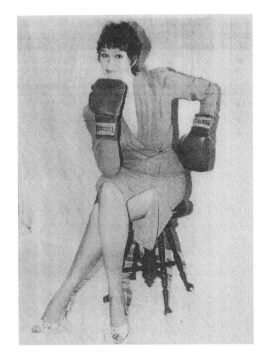

On December 13, 1983, Camel traveled to Nova Scotia, Canada, to win the International Boxing Federation's first cruiserweight title fight; his opponent was Roddy MacDonald, a 23-year-old fighting out of Toronto. Forty-seven seconds after MacDonald decked Camel in the fifth round, Camel stopped MacDonald with a hard shot to the body. Mistakenly suspecting it was a low blow, a number of fans charged the ring and had to be restrained by policemen.

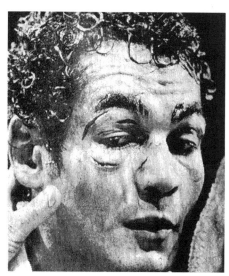

Camel was known as a "bleeder" because his face was often cut during fights. The worst instance was his first WBC title defense against Carlos "Sugar" De Leon, which Camel lost. Camel's crimson mask was so startlingly repugnant that this image appeared the next day on national television news.

In 2006 Camel and Parlov were reunited in Croatia at the World Boxing Council's 44th annual convention. They got along marvelously. Upon hearing of Parlov's death two years later, Camel broke down in tears. "I considered him a friend," Camel said. Courtesy World Boxing Council

Camel stands next to legendary middleweight "Marvelous" Marvin Hagler at the WBC convention in Croatia. Courtesy World Boxing Council

Camel chums it up with one of his boxing idols and contemporaries, Muhammad Ali.

10

SERENE

Every talent must unfold itself in fighting.
—*Friedrich Nietzsche*

Saturday, March 29, 1980, Caesar's Palace, Las Vegas.

DON KING, THE ECCENTRIC BOXING PROMOTER KNOWN FOR HIS wild hair and for arranging titanic bouts, looked at his new protégé and was pleased. Marvin Camel was muscular and healthy. Appearing loose and chipper at the press conference, Marvin had some boxing business to reckon with—a rematch against Mate Parlov for the WBC cruiserweight title. And this time, Camel was in the United States with the sport's greatest publicist and mercenary at his side.

On a professional level, Camel understood and even respected King's role as the ringmaster of professional boxing. Part of what King did was assess the talent and shoot down the pretenders. In Camel, he saw potential—and money.

Camel ignored King's past, which could not have been shadier. In 1954, King killed a man who tried to rob one of his gambling houses. The shooting was ruled a justifiable homicide, sparing King a prison sentence. Thirteen years later he was found guilty of second-degree murder for killing a gambling associate who owed him $600. The charge was later reduced to manslaughter, and King served three years and eleven months in prison. He was released in September 1971 and began his rise to the top of boxing. Dogged by accusations of rampant corruption (according to legendary trainer Teddy Atlas, the WBC stood for "We Be Collecting") Don King was, for better or worse, a manifestation of the American dream.

Marvin Camel stood at the podium, engulfed in silence. There was commerce attached to the mission, and it seemed as if all other people were capitalizing. While others collected, he was cautious and careful not to dishonor anyone. His manners came at his own expense. *Should I tell these people how tired I am that I don't get the money or the attention I'd like? I can show them the crazy Indian they expect.*

"Why do you wear the headdress?" asked a reporter. After buried in thought for a moment or two, Camel smiled and said, "You know where Montana is at?"

Camel knew he was playing second fiddle—or fifth, really—to heavyweight champion Larry Holmes who was fighting LeRoy Jones in the main bout. That very morning Holmes's workout ran late and he used Marvin's scheduled ring time. Unflappable, Camel sparred on the grass outside the arena.

Camel certainly had reason to feel stressed, and similar to other fights, the days before the rematch were fraught with problems sleeping and eating. In truth, Camel felt ignored. Of the five world championship fights on the card that night, his rematch was the only one that was not being nationally televised.

"I haven't had the taste of the good life," Camel told the *Las Vegas Review-Journal.* "It hasn't bothered me. I'm not really a socializer. If I do get some money, I'll probably invest in some ground."

Camel was slated to earn $30,000—a smaller purse than the $40,000 he received when he fought Parlov less than four months prior. Parlov, on the other hand, received the same amount as he had for the first match: $50,000. Considering that King had already turned many of his fighters into millionaires, the sums seemed small.

In 1974, when Don King Productions arranged for champion George Foreman to defend his heavyweight title against Muhammad Ali, King guaranteed each fighter an unprecedented $5 million. It was "The Rumble in the Jungle," and it jumpstarted King's financial empire. Heavyweight champs Muhammad Ali, Larry Holmes, Evander Holyfield, and Mike Tyson all worked under King at some point in their careers. King helped make them rich while boosting his own net worth. His wealth came with accusations: many fighters, most notably Tyson, claimed King defrauded them of millions. Jack Newfield, who authored King's biography, *Only in America: The Life and Crimes of Don King*, wrote: "Forget death and taxes. The only sure thing is that, win or lose, Don King is counting the money." King has faced serious indictments of tax evasion and insurance fraud. He has never been found guilty. He has denied any allegations of fixing fights and manipulating rankings to ensure that more of his fighters received title shots.

"My opinion of Don King was the same opinion that I had of my first manager," Camel said. "They are looking for the best talent to put on their cards. Don King gives kids a chance they would never have otherwise. Whether he treated them bad, good, or indifferent, he gave them an opportunity they couldn't get anywhere else. Without Don King, a lot of boxers would have never got to where they got. Where would Marvin Camel be if Don King had never been around? Boxers need connections like Don King."

King visited Camel in his locker room before the fight. He watched as Camel shadowboxed for an extended period, working up a good sweat so he could enter the ring hot and ready to fight. To keep the heat in his muscles, he put on a white flannel robe and his blue silk robe over it.

The scene in a dressing room before a fight is an elaborate slice of theatrics. Fighters work off their nervousness, each in their own distinct manner. Some like Camel threw punches in the air or into their trainers' hand pads. Others listened to music to soothe themselves and danced their butterflies away. And still a few others were in the bathroom relieving their bowels or spitting or blowing their noses to clear their respiratory tract. Some fighters pray to the gods of pugilism, masculinity, and chance that they will exit the ring on their own two feet and not on a stretcher wrapped in a neck brace.

Marvin felt as if every detail was magnified by the importance of this match. So much depended on him. The hopes of his people, his state, and his own ambition seemed more than just symbolic.

Days earlier, Camel supporters from across Montana descended on Las Vegas. "I had about 170 people come down," Camel said. "I wanted my entourage. Don said he'd give me two tickets to his party at Caesar's. I said, 'What about the other 168 people?' He said, 'That's all I can do.' I said 'Well, we are going to have our own party.'"

There was all the usual pomp and circumstance associated with a title bout at Caesar's Palace. The atmosphere was electric. Photographers, cameramen, newspaper reporters, and fans competed for space along all four sides of the ring. Past champions were introduced and waved at the crowd. Hollywood stars, noted boxers, and prominent politicians could always be counted on to attend an important fight. Bill Cosby. Tom Jones. Joe Louis. Ken Norton. The unbeaten Larry Holmes, who had pocketed $1.3 million earlier that night for stopping the previously unbeaten and second-ranked LeRoy Jones to retain his World Boxing Council heavyweight title.

Now it was time for the WBC cruiserweight world championship: Camel versus Parlov. At nine P.M., trainer Elmer Boyce stepped into the dressing room and said, "Marvin, all these folks know is that you are going to beat Parlov. You did it once. Do it again." Boyce taped Camel's hands, a familiar, soothing ritual for both of them. Boyce stretched the tape diagonally across the fighter's palms and then straight across the knuckles, curling Marvin's fingers into a half fist. Boyce said, "Keep cool. Relax. It's all yours to win. Now go take what those bastards should have given you. Take it again."

Camel watched Boyce work, occasionally flexing his fingers to test the bandages and to feel the tape against his skin. He told Boyce, "I'm ready to go fifteen. I'm trained for fifteen. I'll wear him down late. He's through."

Camel had another asset for this match. His cornerman was 68-year-old Eddie Futch, a boxing legend, his heritage traced to the Joe Louis era of the 1930s. In boxing's atmosphere of grinning smooth talkers and brashness, Futch was a quiet and confident man who had gained his knowledge of the sport from the inside, having started his career as a lightweight in Detroit. He was definite in his attitude toward his fighters. He worked on mind as well as body, and if a fighter wanted Futch as his trainer, the fighter had to listen. Futch finally retired at 86, having helped his fighters dethrone so-called unbeatable champions like Muhammad Ali and Roy Jones Jr. In his lifetime, he trained six heavyweight champions.

Camel and Parlov, each weighing about 185 pounds, emerged from the darkness of the arena tunnels into the white pillar of light that illuminated the ring. The referee gave the traditional centering delivery of instructions. The boxers touched gloves and went to their corners.

The bell rang and Camel picked up where he left off in Yugoslavia, flicking a stiff right jab and scoring tough body shots. He scored at will in spite of Parlov's protective shell. Parlov retreated and lost the first pair of rounds.

After a sluggish and indecisive third round, Parlov stepped up the aggression in the next three rounds, countering effectively. Parlov opened a gash near Camel's ear in the fourth, and Futch had difficulty closing the wound because the laceration ripped away a small chunk of skin.

In the sixth, Parlov cut Camel's left cheek near the sideburn.

But despite the chants and flag-waving by his Yugoslavian coun-
trymen, Parlov could not sustain his advantage.

After an even seventh, Camel took control. He re-established
his right jab in the eighth round and dictated the remainder of the
fight with it, his most dependable asset. As the fight progressed,
Camel discovered that he could deliver this punch from a crouch,
and that Parlov could not counter effectively when Camel was in
this stance.

Camel continued to move forward in the tenth round, but he
seemed to alternate aggressiveness and caution, backing off after
scoring with punches. There would be a seemingly random flurry
of punches and then a series of discrete, carefully plotted moves: a
feint, a clinch, some quick blows to the ribs, a crazy swing above
the head. It was as if the fighter in Camel wanted Parlov elimi-
nated, but the boxer in him just wanted to tally points.

In the eleventh Parlov split Camel's left cheek again and target-
ed his swelling right eye. Camel won the twelfth by a narrow margin and then lit into Parlov with his heaviest punching and scoring
in the thirteenth and fourteenth rounds. A profusion of lefts and
rights puffed and bloodied Parlov's face and gave him a nasty gash
over the right eye. Camel scored a smattering of left hooks to the
head and a wicked left to the midsection before referee Ferd Her-
nandez directed the Yugoslav into a neutral corner to have ring
doctor Donald Romeo examine the damage. The fight continued.

Camel scored the best punch of the fight in the fourteenth, a
right hook that landed squarely on Parlov's face, staggering him
into the ropes. With his backpedaling opponent off-balance and
dazed, Camel went in for the kill, pursuing his prey with wild arm
and body punches. Parlov somehow retrenched and survived the
round.

In his corner before the last round, Camel stood rigid, muscles flexed, staring through his opponent—ready to fight. Parlov
slumped on his stool, looking tired. His eyes wandered. Camel
answered the bell for the fifteenth round shuffling his feet as if it

were the first round. A sizable delegation of Montana fans chanted, "Marvin! Marvin! Marvin!"

The round began with harmless action. In a split second, however, it was thundering. One minute passed. Marvin launched himself through the air and Parlov sidestepped. Their boxing was now a duel of right hooks to the left rib and left hooks to the right rib. Two minutes passed. Then Parlov clipped Camel with a glancing right jab that tore open an inch-long cut on Camel's right eyelid. It bled profusely, forcing the referee to consult the ring physician. As their hero's face streamed blood, Camel's supporters gasped, fearing the doctor would stop the fight with less than a minute to go and Camel clearly ahead.

Although the cut looked serious, Camel's veteran trainer, Billy Edwards, wasn't overly concerned. "I knew [the round] didn't have long to go. I didn't think they'd stop it." Sherry Camel, who was also working her husband's corner, said she wasn't bothered by the nasty gash, but she did worry about the referee's next action. "I was just crossing my fingers, hoping he wouldn't stop the fight," she said.

Romeo gave Camel a cursory inspection and raised no objections. Parlov tried in vain to stay aggressive. Lacking knockout power and the explosive arsenal of a knockout artist, Parlov couldn't take advantage of Camel's bad cut. Camel, his vision clouded by streaming blood, dodged and clinched his way through the last agonizing moments. In this desperate culmination of 45 minutes of two men beating on each another, Camel held on to glory while Parlov flailed futilely.

This time there was no controversy. Mexican judge Jose Guerra scored the bout 148–141 for Camel; Judge Angelo Toletti of Italy had Camel winning 149–141; and Judge Harold Buck of Las Vegas marked his card 144–141 for Camel—a unanimous decision. Marvin Camel—the half-black, half-Native American pinball mechanic from a Montana Indian reservation—was the first cruiserweight champion of the world.

After the fight, with a small trickle of blood oozing from the cut over his right eye, Camel credited a strategy he discovered in his previous fight with Parlov: "When I fought Parlov in Yugoslavia, I went into a crouch in the seventh round and found he couldn't hit down." Camel waited until the eleventh round to go into the crouch but when he did, he was able to pepper Parlov at will. "All I had to do was stay low and come back in with a counter jab," he said. Asked if he felt he was in command of the fight, Camel answered, "I never feel I'm in complete control even if the people on the sidelines think so. No matter how fast I'm going, I want to go faster."

Camel was asked abut his cuts. "Yeah, in the last round she was bleeding pretty badly," he said. "The only thing a guy could do was to put on a little more pressure. By doing that, you make the ref think everything's all right. At the last, I started backpedaling." Asked if he would stay idle for a while because of the cuts, Camel answered, "Us Indians heal pretty fast. My cuts don't stay open very long." After the bout, Camel's team spent at least thirty minutes trying to close his wounds. Futch said Camel would need at least 19 or 20 stitches to close the four cuts.

Perhaps a fighter is most naked in the first moments following a glorious victory. Too drained to create a camouflage of false words, too fulfilled to hide behind an illusion of modesty, he speaks his truths. "My life is complete now," Camel said. "I've been working 18 years for this green belt. I'd like to enjoy this, any champion would like to enjoy it. I'm the first champion ever out of the state of Montana. More importantly, I'm the first champion ever in my tribe."

In a land obsessed with disadvantage, Camel was the ultimate meritocrat: a man who succeeded whatever the accidents of his birth. When he reflected on winning the WBC Cruiserweight title, Camel credited three people: Sherry, Kenny Camel, and Elmer Boyce. "Sherry was definitely a part of it," Marvin said. "She always was there with the bucket, the water, and the towel, keeping track of things. She was always helpful. Kenny was there day and night, getting me ready. Boyce, too."

That night, everyone, including Don King, thought the Montana native was destined for greatness. King said the cruiserweight division would become a "super class" for fighters too big for light heavyweight and too small to compete with the massive heavyweights. "I thought it was a super match," King said. "Marvin handled himself well. And I thought he worked a little harder to make this a decisive win after the draw the last time. I think this is going to be a good weight." The victory raised Camel's record to 35–2–3.

Elmer Boyce spent the night on the town, eating and partying like a world champion. At his hotel room somewhere around midnight, Marvin received a knock on the door. He opened it to find a rugged looking prostitute in a bright, floppy red wig and shabby clothes—perhaps the cheapest variety of call girl one could envision. "Elmer Boyce sent me," the woman said.

"Geez," responded Marvin. "I'm tired as hell. But, well, c'mon in."

Paradoxically, even though Camel had fought in Las Vegas frequently, he more or less felt out of place there. For a man who was, essentially, a loner and an honest workman, the glittery and glitzy stuff never appealed. His world was a gym full of old fight posters and misshaped heavy bags held together by duct tape. "There isn't much to do here besides working out," said Camel. "I mostly eat my meals in my room…If I want to see the lights I can just look out the window. Course you know, they don't have any left-handed slot machines down here anyway."

Sitting on top of the world put life into sharp perspective, and that perspective was always framed in the context of birth, upbringing, and the need to both run away and return. His roots were still strongly embedded in Montana. "Yeah, but experience's the thing," Camel once said. "You can't sit up in Missoula, Montana, all your life and talk about how the other half lives without seeing for yourself."

Now Camel had seen exactly how the other half lived: his blood, toil, conditioning, training, running, and dedication were things that helped push him into the other half. Camel's life was his conscious decision, a sharp rebuke of the barriers of culture and a strong endorsement of the power and self-pride of the warrior.

Camel felt more alive and more authentic than at any time in his life. It was as if he entered a room where no one else was permitted to go, where there was no confusion and nothing to be afraid of, where he felt happy and at peace, despite taking part in merciless brutality. In a strange way, that made sense to Camel: he found boxing's warlike nature serene, almost beautiful, a pure, almost too-wonderful-for-words sensation that he could not attain anywhere else. He would miss this moment terribly for the rest of his life.

One week later, the tribes welcomed home the champion. Marvin and Sherry drove a borrowed car past colorful, hand-painted signs that began at the southern boundary of the reservation and continued for miles. On Evaro Hill the first one proclaimed "WELCOME HOME MARVIN CAMEL!" Signs decorated fences, bridges, and businesses the rest of the way to Pablo. A series of signs along a fence declared: "FIRST INDIAN—FIRST MONTANAN—FIRST CRUISERWEIGHT CHAMPION— MARVIN CAMEL." Others were simpler, more direct: "Camel power," "Super Chief," and "No. 1 Marvin." Signs in several businesses read: "Home of world champion Marvin Camel."

Camel eventually arrived at the St. Ignatius Community Center to be greeted by fifty to sixty friends, relatives, and members of the Confederated Salish and Kootenai Tribes. He held informal court at the Community Center for a couple of hours, signing posters of himself in Indian dress, entertaining the crowd with stories about the fight, and amiably chatting with young and old alike.

Camel spoke with eighty-year-old tribal member Mitch Small Salmon of St. Ignatius, who had designed the ceremonial lance that the tribes had presented to Camel after his first fight with Par-

lov. Now Small Salmon added an especially large eagle feather to
the lance. He explained: "This is the finishing feather. It means he
has reached the top of his struggle—each time he wins he has another feather. You know, a warrior when they have these, they got
a feather for each enemy they kill. I told Marvin he's different—he
doesn't kill his enemies, he just knocks them down."

Camel made modest plans for his earnings. It seemed as if everyone and their tribal councilor knew that Camel made $30,000
for the fight—an attractive sum by ordinary Montana standards
even though local papers touched on the fact that it was substan-
tially less than the money earned by the other boxers that night.

"I may move the trailer house to Ronan," Camel said. "I got
ideas. But I don't think I will change. It's not going to change my
lifestyle versus being sociable or unsociable. If I've got an extra
dollar, I'll get a piece of land...I like money just as well as the next
guy, but the fact that I got this rematch is worth more than waiting around for a big purse." Camel spoke of paying off the money
he owed on 80 acres of land near Ronan, and even becoming a
rancher someday. "I may set up a training camp on the ranch," he
told one reporter. "Because of the price of gas it's kind of hard to
run into Missoula every day to work out." Elmer Boyce had sold
the Missoula-based electronic game business where Camel had
worked for several years, so aside from boxing, Camel was without
a job.

Marvin scoffed at having other interests. "Hobbies?" Camel
said. "It doesn't seem like I have enough time. After I work out I'm
bushed. Maybe I'll have enough time to go fishing or something...
it's just not the time. But getting this fight out of the way relieves a
lot of pressure. I could not stop working till I got it."

Standing tall in the fistic heaven, Camel hoped to reap the
benefits and lead a better life. Perhaps he could now box professionally full-time. But the big question on his mind was whether
anyone had an interest in a Montana Indian who was champion
of a weight division no one paid much attention to. The day af-

ter the fight the sports section of *Las Vegas Sun* said Camel was a native of Butte, Montana—illustrating the relative obscurity of Camel compared to other champions. A writer for *Ring Magazine* admitted the publication refused to recognize the cruiserweight division, saying it wasn't justified. *This controversy may go on for years,* Camel thought. *I need to fight harder to protect the crown and lift the division to world prominence. It's like fighting Parlov every day of my career.*

11

VISION

CAMEL BEGAN WORKING OUT ALMOST IMMEDIATELY AFTER returning home. He could hardly wait to get back into the ring. *I'm proof that an Indian from Montana can learn the ropes and see the world. My temperament is different than ninety-nine percent of the people out there. I've been to places people only dream about going. Football is played with eleven members on the field at one time; boxing is just one man. Me.*

To Marvin Camel, boxing was democratic, dynamic, glamorous, virile, and violent. It held all the addiction of a marvelous danger, and he moved toward the ring like a moth to the light. He was much like any other boxer except that he always had something of a philosopher's streak. He paid close attention to what went on around him and pondered the meaning of cowardice, strength, courage, and survival. He fulfilled Picasso's concept of an artist: "You must do what is not there, what has never been done."

The cruiserweight division ranked a number of solid opponents who were eager to challenge Camel. On June 1, 1980, the Associated Press reported that Marvin Camel prepared to meet Victor Galindez in a nationally televised title fight in California on June 14.

Galindez was born in Buenos Aires, Argentina, and had amassed a 52–9–4 amateur record. He represented Argentina at the 1968 Olympic Games and turned pro in 1969. Galindez captured both the Argentine and South American light heavyweight titles in 1972. In 1974, he challenged for the vacant WBA light heavyweight championship and stopped Len Hutchins in thirteen rounds.

A busy champion, Galindez traveled the world defending his title ten times against formidable names. He lost the crown to Mike Rossman in 1978, only to regain it in a rematch the following year. He then lost the title to Marvin Johnson.

Camel would be paid $200,000 for the fight, by far the biggest purse of his career. He flew to Los Angles where the fight was slated for the Disneyland Exhibit Hall in Anaheim and live national television on CBS.

Unfortunately, the match never took place.

News reports said the fight was called off "after Camel sustained an eye injury while using a welding torch on a pinball machine." One report said "a piece of metal flew up and hit him in the eye." Another report claimed it was a spark in the eye. No account was true.

"Here's the thing," Camel said. "I got thumbed in the eye by a sparring partner. I guess I dipped when I should have dove. If the athletic board knew it was boxing related, I probably couldn't fight. So Boyce fabricated the pinball thing. We figured that if the injury seemed like it came from a pinball machine, instead of in the ring, we would still be able to fight."

Camel actually had a detached retina in his right eye. It was discovered by Los Angeles ophthalmologist Matthew Bernstein during a required prefight examination one week before the scheduled bout.

Bernstein recalled that Elmer Boyce became incensed when Bernstein told him he would report Camel's detached retina. "Camel's manager went up the wall when I told him what I intended to do," said Bernstein. "He told me such a report would mean Camel couldn't get fights anywhere, that it would end his career. His payday for the fight in L.A. was $200,000, so he was already putting a guilt trip on me for costing him that." According to Bernstein, Boyce treated the issue solely as a matter of finance.

Bernstein compromisingly submitted a report saying that Camel had "corneal abrasions" and that "they wouldn't heal in time for the fight." In return, Boyce promised Bernstein that Camel would have his retina repaired and they would never again make an effort to box in California.

"I felt sorry for the poor guy," Bernstein told "The Ring" years later, after discovering that Marvin was still fighting as late as 1989. "I remember he came into my office wearing his championship belt. And he was terribly disappointed he wouldn't get that $200,000 payday."

Seeking a second opinion, Camel asked Dr. Glen Almquist, medical director of WAY Athletic Enterprises, to examine the eye. The Corona del Mar physician asked Marvin to read the eye chart. He recited each letter correctly except he stumbled when he tried to identify the ones in the bottom rows. Next the doctor dilated Camel's pupil and inspected his retina. After he finished, he paused. Marvin could tell by the doctor's expression that he was about to tell Camel what no boxer wanted to hear.

"There is definitely a partial detachment," Almquist said. "And you don't have much time. If you don't take care of this in the next week or so, you could go blind in that eye."

"When can I box again?" asked Marvin.

"Well, you shouldn't. You should not fight for at very least a month. And you should consider never fighting again."

"Never box again? I've got a title. I'm on top."

Camel sat down with Boyce and mulled over their options.

"You know it's up to you," Boyce said. "Do you want to continue or quit?"

"Nothing can keep me away," Camel responded. "As long as I can see, I want to go for it, keep on fighting."

A detached retina is a thorny issue in boxing—and a common occupational hazard. No one wants another Sugar Ray Seales, the 1972 Olympic gold medalist who today maneuvers his way around Seattle with a red and white cane, blinded by eye injuries that went undetected for years because he memorized the eye charts. Still many ophthalmologists insist that a boxer who's undergone successful retina surgery is at no greater risk for another retina injury than anyone else. In spite of everything, they say, Sugar Ray Leonard, Pinklon Thomas, Bob Foster and Earnie Shavers had retinas repaired and all continued to box without any further obvious injury. In recent years, ophthalmologists have encouraged states to adopt thumbless boxing gloves because most boxing-related retina injuries are caused by the thumbs on gloves.

"Marvin has a deep corneal laceration in his right eye," Dr. Almquist told the media. "The injury was treated in Missoula and a foreign body was removed but he reinjured the eye in sparring Thursday. There was the secondary possibility of infection due to the injury. And because of the new threat of infection he will be wearing an eye bandage for five to ten days and taking antibiotics." Once again, another physician did not publicly disclose that Marvin had a detached retina. Perhaps that was because of a similar "guilt trip" to the one Boyce and Camel placed on Dr. Bernstein.

Nevertheless, Camel had his retina repaired in Los Angeles. He knew that such a surgery had consequences. He understood that California would not allow a boxer with that medical history to ever fight there again. So Camel skirted around this scenario in a move more brilliantly choreographed than any he used in the boxing ring: He underwent the surgery under an assumed name.

The surgeon, according to Marvin, gave his approval for him to box again. "That surgeon told me that my retina was stronger than it was on the day I was born," said Camel.

Jesse Burnett replaced Camel against Galindez and earned a unanimous twelve round decision. It was Galindez's final fight; in an ironic twist, he was forced to retire because of issues with a detached retina. Galindez then pursued his other dream of becoming a stock-car driver. In October he was standing in the pit area at a race in De Mayo, Argentina, when he was struck and killed by a careening car. He was 31. In 2002 Galindez was inducted into the International Boxing Hall of Fame.

Camel was deeply demoralized. Before he boarded a plane to Missoula, he told the media that he wasn't angry—just extremely disappointed: "Nobody is as dedicated as me when it comes to fighting. I've dedicated myself for a long, long time to winning the title. Sometimes I do my roadwork in forty-below-zero weather. I haven't made $100,000 in my boxing career. Now this has to happen. I'm going home."

12

DONE IN BY DE LEON

Monday, November 18, 1980.

The Superdome, New Orleans, Louisiana.

ONE WEEK REMAINS UNTIL MARVIN CAMEL MAKES THE FIRST defense of his world cruiserweight championship. On this mild, mid-70 degree day, Camel is attired for the pre-fight press conference in an Indian chief's headdress and warrior's clothing. His opponent, Carlos De Leon, is asked to pose with Camel and boxing promoter Don King with a symbolic knife "to scalp the Indian," as King puts it. De Leon refuses. "Where's the peace pipe?" asks Marvin.

De Leon steps away from Camel. The Indian's eyes miss nothing. "I hope you are in shape," Marvin says. "Because your opponent over here is in great shape."

BOXING IS A CRUEL PROFESSION THAT DEMANDS THAT THE MAN who masters it stay astride it as if he were constantly riding a bucking horse. Camel found himself holding on tighter than ever. He was now the proving ground for fighters, old and young.

Camel's first defense of the WBC 190-pound class championship came against Carlos "Sugar" De Leon of Puerto Rico. The fight brought Camel a $90,000 paycheck, the biggest of his career. De Leon was hell bent on making him earn every last nickel.

Prior to scheduling the match, Elmer Boyce had cautioned Camel to avoid De Leon. He felt Camel's style wouldn't match up well against De Leon's brawling, knockout-seeking aggression. "Boyce knew that the smaller guys always gave Marvin trouble," Ken Camel remembered.

At ringside before the fight, the announcers—Larry Holmes, Les Keiter, and Don King—described Camel. "A very articulate young man, too" King said. "He speaks very well. He handles himself quit admirably."

"I can tell you something about Marvin Camel—he's a proud champion," Holmes added. "He wears his belt in the lobby. He wants to be recognized. He wants people to know who he is. This man is coming out here to fight tonight, because he wants everyone to know that Marvin Camel can fight and that he is the champion."

As Marvin Camel entered the ring, there was more talk about the novelty of his race, origin, and state of birth than about his ring credentials. "Marvin Camel is a southpaw, he's a real Indian," said King, who imparts his own clever spin and emphasis on syllables and sounds. "It's Indian Marvin Camel. He won the title and he's from Missoula, Montana, and defending the crown. He has a good left hand."

Even though Camel's match was a championship fight, it was, in truth, a footnote to the night's biggest story: Roberto Duran's "no más" quit against Sugar Ray Leonard, which happened immediately before Camel's bout.

Roberto Duran was seen as the "man" fighting the "boy," Sugar Ray Leonard. Thus, many pundits picked Duran over Leonard in their return match for the World Boxing Council junior middleweight championship.

Duran, the titleholder, was twenty-nine; Leonard, the challenger, twenty-four, but eons separated the two in terms of experience and actual combat. Duran's official professional record listed 73 fights over a period of fourteen years, 55 won by knockouts and a lone loss eight years prior to Esteban DeJesus in what Roberto called "a freak because I was tired." The records don't list the hundreds of fights that "Stone Hands" won and lost in the street brawls of his native Panama. He had dodged knives, bullets, baseball bats, and iron chains. He butted, kneed, clawed, and slugged his way through an adolescent jungle to emerge as a boxer.

One of Duran's wins was a dominating defeat of Sugar Ray Leonard for the WBC welterweight title in their first meeting. Ray was undefeated in 27 professional fights. Duran, a living legend among boxing fans, came into that contest with an impressive record of 71–1. Duran hurt Leonard early in the second round with a right hand-left hook combination from the outside. After that, Leonard elected to fight inside with Duran, which was Roberto's game. The final scorecards were 145–144, 146–144, and 148–147 in favor of Duran.

When Duran walked into the Louisiana Superdome in New Orleans, he fully expected to keep his belt. He was so confident that he told anyone who would listen that Leonard was "afraid" of him and called Leonard a "clown." But Leonard, the son of a night clerk at a grocery store and named after the blind singer Ray Charles, had come up with a different game plan for the rematch. Ray would keep Duran turning, hit him with shots coming in, pivot off the ropes, spin out, slip the jab, and move over. He refused to box toe to toe. Instead, Leonard utilized his quickness, flashing from one side of Duran to the other, using a variety of looks. He taunted Duran, sticking out his tongue, frustrating, mocking, and angering the champ.

Duran was not his typical self on this night. His timing was off.

He appeared flustered, confused. But, above all, Leonard's taunting caused Duran to unravel. In the seventh round, Leonard stuck his face toward Duran and mocked him with a shoulder-shrugging dance. The crowd of 40,000 cheered vigorously. Two minutes and forty four seconds into the eighth round, a weary Duran put his hands by his side, turned his back, and then waved a glove at the referee. Some say he uttered two words: "No más." No more. He had surrendered.

In a sport often called the theatre of the unexpected, this outcome was completely bizarre. Chaos ensued. One of Leonard's corner men charged Duran, taking a swing at him. Bodies swirled around the ring, a mass of confusion. Embarrassed, Duran pretended that the round was over. Then he claimed he had injured his shoulder. Later, he explained to the press in his scratchy voice, "'I don't want to fight any more.'" He later said that he developed stomach cramps in the fifth round, that they grew progressively worse, and that he couldn't take it any longer by the eighth round.

The match was officially ruled a knockout, with Leonard narrowly ahead on all three judges' cards. Hours later, Duran flew to Miami, hiding for a week, shielding himself from the world, in disgrace. Rumors flew. One explanation was that with Leonard clowning around, sticking out his chin, taunting Duran, making him look like a fool, quitting was Duran's way of saying, "The hell with you."

For a span of five decades, from 1967 all the way to 2001, Duran won 104 of 120 fights with 69 knockouts. He won four world titles, two against younger men at junctures in his career when he was considered washed up. Except for one inexplicable night in New Orleans, Duran had never given less than everything he had in the ring, even when he was pathetically out of shape later in his career. Yet he will be remembered mainly for perhaps uttering two infamous words: "No más."

⬦

THE DURAN-LEONARD FIGHT AFFECTED CAMEL. IN ADDITION TO the bedlam that broke out after Duran quit, there was another delay because a ring floorboard needed repair. "I heard all this about Duran quitting and I was excited," said Camel. "The adrenaline started really flowing. I was throwing the jab and jumping around. But then they said I'd have to wait five minutes because the ring collapsed. Boy, I just went right down again. I had to wait there 15 minutes."

In the locker room, Marvin confided to Sherry that this fight was more important to him than any of his previous bouts.

"This is going to be the ultimate," said Marvin.

"Ultimate?"

"Being on closed circuit television is the ultimate for me. What I didn't get with Parlov for the title, I've got now."

"The Indian" entered the ring with a look of confidence. For some, it was their first close look at a "real Indian." Most had seen caricatures from a century of Western movies—befeathered and war-painted warriors, often cunning and cruel, sometimes drunk and ignorant, and mostly silent, except when whooping war noises. Marvin Camel was no caricature of the past. Handsome, soft-spoken, gentlemanly, he was antithetical to the prevalence of "the Indian" as a stereotype.

Sauntering to the ring, De Leon looked like a serious challenger. He had the cocky look on his face as if he felt he was going to swat away Camel like a fly. He had worn that smirk for the whole week before the fight. It had struck Camel as an attempt at a major psych-out, somewhat ineffective. But De Leon seemed incredibly sharp and focused on putting on one hell of a show.

Camel was fighting eights months after his previous match. His rustiness showed. The twenty-one-year old Puerto Rican came to brawl, catching Marvin in the first round with some heavy shots, harassing the champion in the early going. Larry Holmes questioned the fatigue factor: "Marvin doesn't look as fresh as De Leon right now. It might be a sign of tiredness." In between the first and second rounds, Don King reminded listeners that Marvin was a "real Indian."

De Leon opened the second with body shots, chasing Camel. Marvin's best shot of the second was a low blow that was missed by the referee in the tail end of the round. Bruises appeared on Camel's face after the second. Camel's nose began to bleed midway through the third. De Leon reacted like a great white shark in a hemophiliac ward. He pressed his advantage in the fourth, attacking Camel's cut lip.

Getting hit is nothing, thought Camel. *I can take a punch. I'm proud of that. I can take real punishment. I used to live with an angry dad. Punishment is satisfying. Shit, it means that Marvin Camel is working hard.*

De Leon ratcheted up the aggressiveness in round five, while Camel responded with combinations and a fierce left uppercut. De Leon began to show wear and tear and the effects of Camel's slick counterpunching, especially on his eyes and bloody mouth. "He was eating leather that round," commented Les Keiter.

Camel's right eye began bleeding profusely, courtesy of De Leon's crisp power and a sixth round clash of heads. Bad blood and enmity flowed; after the sixth, the fighters ignored the bell and kept swinging. It was a professional-turned-personal grudge: Camel had said he disliked the way De Leon conducted himself outside the ring, and De Leon didn't appreciate Camel denouncing his character.

Camel's biggest concern was that the fight would be stopped by the referee because of his bleeding. That caused him to further change his tactics and fight more cautiously. Sherry and Edwards pled with the ringside physician not to stop it. "The ol' doc came out there in the ring with his coattails flapping to check my eye," Camel said. "Sherry and Billy were in my corner yelling at him. They talked him out of it. Man, this is a once in a lifetime opportunity."

De Leon continued to attack the wounded warrior in the seventh. Midway through the round, Camel was cut over the eyelid, brow, and nose. Conversely, De Leon's right eye abrasion swelled. Despite the punishment, Camel said he never felt he was in danger of being knocked out. "I felt like De Leon and I were boom-boom-boom, bumping heads all the time," said Camel. "But I never felt that I was staggered or hit hard…as much as I got cut."

Camel bloodied De Leon's mouth in the eighth. De Leon discovered that even though Camel may have hit like a mosquito, by the midway point of the fight, the champion's sustained punching had caused cumulative lumping all over his head. Indeed, Camel understood positioning—how to hit in a manner that supplied the entirety of his weight at the end of his fist. De Leon's arms seemed to lose their power, resting on the ropes as Camel snapped blazing lefts. Camel leaned against his challenger in the tenth, wearing him down.

De Leon reversed the momentum in rounds eleven and twelve with explosive energy. De Leon had acquired the reputation as a knockout artist; with each punch, the adulation wasn't far behind. Boxing fans have forever been infatuated with fighters who could annihilate the opposition with a single blow. Many fans live vicariously through their heroes in the ring, and nothing is as dramatic as one human being sending another to the ground, the bloodier the better.

De Leon's knockout reputation had influenced Camel's trainer Billy Edwards to alter Camel's regular style. "I put my life in Edwards' hands," Camel said. "I felt by him having three world champs prior to me he'd know what I should do. The way he wanted me to fight was to do a lot of running, a lot of backpedaling. But that's not my way. I got to go in and chase guys…do a lot of punching."

Although bleeding profusely from cuts over and under his eyes, Camel refused to quit. His face looked like it had been shaved by a blind man with a sharp razor. At fight's end he was nauseous, dehydrated, and his left hand was throbbing, as if someone had injected needles into his knuckles.

Despite the cuts, Camel scored often and well with long lefts and stiff rights. It was closer than Marvin's face indicated. Judge Roberto Ramirez of Puerto Rico scored it 145–142 for De Leon, Ray Solis of Mexico had it even at 145, and Lucien Joubert of New Orleans called it 145–141 for De Leon.

"That was a blood bath," said boxing analyst and radio host Frank Stea. "Both guys beat each other up unmercifully for 15 rounds...some people thought Camel could have won."

Afterwards, Camel said he hurt himself by training too hard, trying to make up for lost time after the eye injury forced him to stop training for more than a month. "I'm not making any excuses. Don't get me wrong" Camel said. "But I only sparred for five weeks before the fight because of doctors' orders."

He also said that he felt pressure to prove his merits to the press and the world. "I felt like I had to prove to those guys that I'm the best conditioned fighter in the world," Camel said later. "But I couldn't recoup between rounds. Even though I was resting, I felt like I was fighting all the time. Next time I'm going to take more of a break the last week-and-a-half."

Unlike Duran, who left his crown in ignominy, Camel exited like a champ. According to Hank Kaplan's *World Wide Boxing Digest*, "It earned him the love and respect of boxing fans and aficionados all over the world." Camel took the beating of his life. Because of his valiant efforts in that 15-round war, the WBC nominated him for the most exemplary champion in the world for 1980.

Others did not think the carnage was exemplary. Camel's face was a crimson mask, a gashed and slashed mess of wounds. "It was so bad they even put his face on *Good Morning, America*," Ken Camel recalled.

"I wasn't a fan of watching my brother getting beat up and seeing his fights," their sister, Patricia Camel, said. "You've seen those pictures of his face, right?"

Many people who saw the fight on television, or who shrieked at the sight of newspaper photos of Camel's hacked face, believed it was time he retired.

De Leon kept the title four months, then lost it in two rounds to S.T. Gordon on June 27, 1982. He regained the title on July 17, 1983, in a return match with Gordon, and kept it until April 9, 1988, when he lost to Evander Holyfield. "Carlos De Leon is a Puerto Rican boxing legend," Stea said. "He's a three-time world champion at cruiserweight, who never was involved in a boring fight through his prime. That first fight with Camel set the standard for the all-action style that De Leon would provide for boxing fans throughout his career."

Ken Camel took his brother's defeat hard. He loathed the fact that the Puerto Rican pounded his brother to a bloody pulp and stripped him of his world championship. "I felt that Carlos was my enemy," said Ken Camel. "I hated that Marvin lost. I wanted De Leon to face Ken Camel. It drove me crazy. My family conferred on the matter and agreed that De Leon was Marvin's fight. Right then, I decided that I ain't coming back to this bullshit."

Although he wanted to avenge his brother's loss, Ken also had been troubled by trying to develop his own identity. Many of his professional fights were preliminary bouts on the same card with his brother's big-time matches. "I boxed on Marvin's coat tails," he said. "I wanted to break away so bad. I wanted people to recognize me as Ken Camel, not as Marvin's brother."

Right after the De Leon fight, Ken got a call from Boyce that ESPN's *Wednesday Night Fights* wanted him to fight. "I was finished," Ken said. "I wanted to go back to school." At age 23, with a solid record of 17–3–3, he retired.

As much as boxing is physical punishment, it is also mental punishment. A fighter's goal is to take his opponent's heart as mercilessly as an Aztec priest, to leave him with his will so shattered he will take the pieces to bed with him every night for the rest of his life.

Following the loss, Camel could not come to terms with the

disappointment. Those close to him said that for the next few days Camel looked stricken as if in mourning, silent, reverent. "He was emotional," his wife Sherry said. "He'd lost it all." Sherry said the pain of seeing Marvin's disappointment after his defeat was even worse than witnessing the fight itself.

In boxing, one fight can radically change a boxer's career, legacy, and financial standing. That strain showed in Marvin's eyes. After all, for years and years he had diligently performed roadwork, punched bags, and shadowboxed. He avoided coffee, late nights, and anything else that would mute his fighting edge. His drive helped him win the world championship, but what the hell happened? Camel wondered if he would ever get his mind right for another shot at the title. He agonized over whether he would ever be pronounced medically fit to do battle again. Camel worked hard to isolate himself, to gather his thoughts, and to regroup emotionally. He stood at an unpleasant point in which dreams collided with reality. *What now?*

I must go on. As the addiction of boxing dictated, Camel was soon back to sweating, toiling, and laboring. It was back to staring at the bare ceiling when doing sit-ups, to hitting the pavement before sunrise for a run, to hearing the squeak of a freshly mopped gym floor as he shadow boxed. He hoped more sacrifices would lead to future payoffs. He hoped more sacrifices would create more blessings.

13

"YOU GOTTA PROGRESS."

MARVIN CAMEL FOUND LITTLE SOLACE DURING THE DARK DAYS after the fight, his mind a complicated and excessively self-conscious mess. He felt alternately proud and embarrassed, humiliated and humble. He mentally repeated everything that had happened in New Orleans, criticizing himself as he pondered all the people across Montana he felt he had let down. Some days every little thing seemed to annoy him—the squeaky stationary bike, the rusty weight set, a hissing radiator by the window. As a champ, everything had felt better.

In April 1981, Marvin Camel and Elmer Boyce finally called it quits. Camel was dissatisfied that Boyce recommended retirement, and Boyce, who saw no benefit in a rematch with De Leon, understood that all good things had to end. "He's not working for my benefit anymore," Camel said. "I feel I gotta go for the title again. I feel something has got to change."

It had been five months since Camel lost to De Leon and he wanted some real action. (In March Camel had a scheduled fight in Hawaii with Samoan heavyweight Fozzie Schmitz, but it was canceled after Schmitz reportedly hurt his hand in workouts the week before the match). For weeks, Camel and Boyce went back and forth in the press. All the while, Boyce reiterated his claims of support. "I've got all kinds of fights for him," said Boyce. "He kind of forgets that he was cut up pretty bad in that last fight. And it takes some time to heal." Camel eventually made it clear to Boyce that he wanted to negotiate his own career on his own terms—meaning a rematch with De Leon. Boyce brought in his lawyer, who reminded Camel that Boyce still, in sum, owned the fighter's ass, though, naturally, Boyce could be bought out. Camel and Boyce reached an agreement: Boyce would take a lump sum of $1,000 up front and retain whatever revenue he could muster for selling Marvin's contract.

While contractual discussions lingered, Boyce did get a fight for Camel, a sixth-round technical knockout of Ron Draper in Billings, Montana. Journeyman Draper, who ended his pro career six fights later with a record of 7 wins and 28 losses, was the perfect opponent for the resurgent Camel. Draper was an awkward plodder who suffered from bad instruction and worse technique. "He had no business being there," Camel said. "He accepted, but he accepted every fight. He was in it for the money." The April 24 contest earned Camel a purse of $3,000.

A fighter must defy all the rules of logic, all common sense, and fight. But in order to fight, a boxer needs a matchmaker. Camel quickly aligned himself with Fred Harbeck, a Missoula businessman who bought Camel's contract for $1,500 and immediately went to work promoting a rematch between Camel and De Leon. A native of Sioux City, South Dakota, Harbeck was president of Harbeck Footwear, a company his father founded in 1940. After a stint in the service, young Fred moved to Missoula in 1968 and opened a strip club named Fred's.

With a new manager and hardened desire for a rematch, Marvin wasn't just thinking about himself. He was thinking about his immediate family. He now had three sons, and while Camel did not put his family first in terms of emotional commitment—boxing took center stage—he was not one to neglect them financially. "When I was fighting, I may have had $17 left in my pocket every two weeks," Camel said. "Those are my three kids, and I'm responsible for their care. It was okay to starve a little bit."

With an eye on the future, Camel began a new career, of sorts.

He negotiated the construction of a multi-purpose recreational center in Ronan. The $130,000 facility's main purpose, Marvin predicted, would be to establish a "new, non-polluting industry on the Reservation," or a "factory" to turn out world champions. The 3,500-square-foot center would house a snack bar, a penny arcade, and an office for Marvin. Farther down the dream trail, Marvin hoped the center would evolve into a complete health complex, with a swimming pool and a spa.

Camel fought Rahim Muhammad in Las Vegas on May 5. For such large boxers, the pace was hectic. Camel floored Muhammad with a left hook in round four. In round eight, Muhammad was cut above the left eye. Muhammad gave back hard rights that stunned Camel.

"Camel is a busy fighter for a big man, he keeps moving," said one announcer. The other added: "Marvin knows every trick, when to hold on, when to spin out of that corner. He's busy. He's slick."

As the fight wore on, Camel's defensive position was disciplined, with those long arms bent at the elbow to form a gloved fortress protecting his torso and head. The mustachioed Camel had experienced trainer and cornerman Jimmy Montoya on his side, who shouted instructions throughout the twelve rounder.

By the end of the twelfth round, both fighters had absorbed a beating. Camel's left eye was nearly closed and Muhammad's face was cut and bruised. Camel earned the unanimous decision. Muhammad lost twelve of his next thirteen fights before retiring with an 8–19 record.

The fight's best photos were taken by Linda Platt, an attractive, talented Las Vegas photojournalist with whom Camel had a series of short liaisons. Indeed, his relationship with Sherry had dissolved into a little more than a formality. "In my life," Camel said, "I've taken a few wrong steps. But, overall, I hope I've taken more right steps than wrong ones."

On August 11 Camel returned to Las Vegas to fight Willie

"The Cannon" Shannon for the Nevada state cruiserweight title. If Camel ever had a "Rocky" movie moment in his career, it happened in this fight.

In the first two rounds Shannon picked apart and bloodied Camel. Marvin had a cut over the left eye from what he said was an elbow, and a cut on the left forehead from what he said was a head butt. Camel admitted he had been hurt in the first round.

Early in the third round Camel ripped a picture-perfect left hook to the jaw that deposited Shannon on the canvas. Some of the fans at the Showboat Casino called it a lucky shot. Others called it ring experience. Shannon was fending off right jabs and did not see the shot coming. He sat on the canvas, glassy-eyed. He could not make the count, and the referee jumped in to stop the fight and save him. Shannon was out for at least five minutes.

"Marvin had power when he needed it," Don Majeski said. "He wasn't just a southpaw or just what some would call a boxer. He could deliver real power when he needed it, like the night of the Shannon fight." "He caught me once or twice," Camel said, "but experience and conditioning pulled me out."

Shannon may have had other things on his mind. In the spring of 1981, Shannon reportedly started stalking teenaged neighbor Jamey Walker, daughter of nightclub owner James Walker and past Las Vegas NAACP President Eleanor Walker. On May 10—three months before the Camel fight—Jamey's body was found 47 feet below a bridge in the Lake Mead National Recreation Area, a half-hour's drive from where she had been abducted near her home. An autopsy showed she died from a massive skull fracture sustained in the fall.

When questioned by Metro Police, Shannon denied involvement, saying he was busy training for the upcoming bout. Despite the initial absence of hard evidence—DNA testing was still years away—authorities never dismissed Shannon as a possible suspect, and he knew it.

Shannon fought only one more time as a professional. By 1985 he was in prison for kidnapping and battery. He got out in 1998 and returned home to Florida, where he kept secluded. In December 2010, 60-year-old Shannon was arrested for Walker's murder. He was convicted on DNA evidence obtained at the crime scene and sentenced to life in prison.

Following the Shannon victory, Camel was the WBC's number-one contender in the cruiserweight division and first in line for another bout with De Leon. "They want to fight me," Camel said. "But they're taking their time about it."

The major obstacle in negotiating a rematch was the Puerto Rican's manager. "Bill Daly is the guy causing all the problems," Camel said. "He's 86 years old and he swore he'd die with a world champion. It looks like he will if he doesn't have a fight pretty soon."

While he was waiting for a possible title shot, Camel had to take a fight against Bash Ali for $2,500. "I'm not spoiled getting big money," Camel said, "but I wish someone would spoil me." Having to fight Ali because the WBC wouldn't enforce a mandatory rematch made Camel mad. "I take these $2,500 fights to stay in good graces with them—to stay the No. 1 contender. And then they send me a telegram saying I have to fight this elimination fight. I shouldn't have to do that."

Formerly a wrestler in Nigeria, Ali was in the United States as a political science major at the University of California. Physically gifted, he had taken up boxing to seek a big payday. Ali had four wives in Nigeria and one in the United States. In his first pro fight, he only made $400. "I nearly cried because I had promised my mother I was going to send her money to buy a car and do other things," he said. "The guy who fought in the main event netted close to $300,000. So, I decided to take up the sport full-time and also to work hard and be very good at it. And if I won a lot of fights, it was a way to become president of Nigeria."

The fight was billed as a WBC title final eliminator, with the winner getting the USBA cruiserweight title. Compared to Camel's, Ali's pro experience and 11-3 record was limited. But those limitations often seemed irrelevant.

Ali opened the fight headhunting, going for an early knockout. His aggressiveness won him the first round, but Camel came back with an effective jab and lefts to the body to even the score in the second.

In boxing, the cornerman is no mere spectator. He is there to provide solid guidance, to calmly and quickly deliver instructions that will help his fighter win. In this fight, Camel did not have a cornerman. "He is his own man," said one announcer. "He is making his own decisions." Early on, Camel could have used a little guidance.

Despite the reputation of not being a particularly hard puncher, Ali landed the heavier shots in the third and fourth. Camel stayed active with a right jab that repeatedly found its mark. As the fight wore on, Ali's inexperience showed, especially in the fifth and sixth. Camel was able to absorb his opponent's best punches and pile up his own points. "Camel approaches the fight without a knockout in mind," an announcer said. "The decision is where he wins his money."

At the start of the seventh round, the crowd began to chant, "Ali, Ali, Ali." Camel facetiously joined in the cheering. For a moment, it appeared as if Ali's youthful ferocity would triumph. He hammered Camel with a hard combination to the head, followed with another blow to the temple. Resiliently, Camel weathered the storm—he even resorted to what appeared to be an intentional head-butt—and finished the round without being too hurt.

Throughout the eighth, ninth, and tenth rounds, Camel scored often, although he was warned about low blows in the ninth. Ali's best round came in the eleventh when he rocked Camel with heavy blows. The crowd came to its feet as Ali chased Camel around the ring, sensing, tasting, and some even hoping for a knockout. Once again, Camel survived.

The twelfth and final round saw Ali land the harder blows.

Bleeding from a severe cut between his left eye and nose, Camel was efficient and slick enough to win the round and earn the decision. Referee Jack Campbell scored it 115–113, judge Rudy Ortega 115–114, and judge Jack Danny 115–111. Camel did enough to win. Not too shabby a performance from a man who, according to one of the fight's announcers, was such a "mellow fellow" that he even "fell asleep at the weigh-in."

"Bash Ali tried to go from a political science major to a boxing major," Camel said. "It didn't work out." (Ali didn't become president of Nigeria, but today represents asylum seekers as an immigrants' rights activist in Canada.)

Camel headed back to Montana to spend time with Sherry and the boys. Surrounded by mountains where grizzly bears roamed, Camel isolated himself from the bright lights and sizzle of Las Vegas. He forfeited anything that might dull the wicked sharpness of his fighting machinery.

14

CALL ME BLEEDER

FOR ALL THE ATTENTION THE REMATCH BETWEEN CAMEL AND DE Leon received, many boxing pundits felt it made no sense. De Leon had won most rounds of the first fight, and at the end of the 15 rounds, Camel's face looked like an abstract painting by Picasso.

It's curious, but understandable, how great athletes never allow themselves to consider the possibility of defeat. Indeed, great athletes expect more greatness. Ted Williams expected to get a hit whenever he stepped to the plate. Tiger Woods was confident he could win every golf tournament. Rocky Marciano was always certain he would win. As if governed by some fundamental natural law, the athlete who dwells upon losing will do just that.

Marvin Camel couldn't allow defeat to enter his thoughts as a real possibility. Even in losses as an amateur, Marvin believed he had really won. He was as convinced as any man of his own infallibility. It was one of his most important assets. *I avenged both my other losses. I came back to beat Danny Brewer and Matthew Saad Muhammad. I'm a boxer. I can bear all the mental and physical torture you can throw at me.*

In the brutal world of boxing, the psychological hurdles that have to be cleared for a boxer to avenge a loss are immense. Mental scars from a bad beating are sometimes far more permanent than physical ones. But not for Camel. He didn't dwell on the loss; he dreamed of vengeance. *There is no peace in defeat.*

Camel knew it was going to be a rough, tough fight. He hoped to take the Puerto Rican the whole fifteen rounds because he believed he could punish De Leon in the later rounds.

De Leon presented himself as a unique combination of cockiness and arrogance, and going into the fight, Camel had been publicly critical of the 22-year-old champion and his training habits.

Ringside commentators referenced the viciousness and disdain between the two fighters and said that De Leon appeared visibly angered by Camel's comments that the Puerto Rican was an unworthy titlist. In the weeks leading up to the event, Camel said De Leon "didn't wear the belt well" and that he had been "ducking him for eighteen months." Apparently Camel was feeling his own sense of manifest destiny.

Camel's spirit was willing, but his flesh was weak. A third-round punch opened a gash on his right eyebrow. Camel said later that he had been cut badly in that very spot a week earlier and that he knew full well that one good punch was going to split him apart again.

Camel's cornermen stemmed the bleeding but the cut was opened a second time in the fourth. His eye puffed up almost to the point of closure. In the fifth round a bloody nose was added to the cut.

Marvin worried about his own propensity to bleed. *Will the bleeding cause the ref to stop this goddamn fight? Will the blood and cuts just be excuses for my not being able to beat this guy? Is there a point when even a bleeder like me has exhausted too much blood supply? Why can't this sonofabitch be the one drenched in his own crimson mask?*

Despite the cuts, the first six rounds had been scored evenly. In the seventh, just as he had predicted, Marvin began to pick up steam. But the bleeding was too much. Between the seventh and eighth rounds, a New Jersey doctor said the eye wound was too serious and advised the referee to stop the contest, which he did. De Leon kept the title.

Despite the stoppage, Camel retained the good legs and quick reflexes of a much younger fighter. He was strong and rugged and apparently had lots of stamina. He could take a punch. He had the skill to use little twists and moves to keep De Leon off-balance. De Leon found that Camel was easy to hit, but not easy to hit effectively.

Nonetheless, Camel did not win, and here came the blame. Camel employed Las Vegas trainer Johnny Tocco for the bout. It was a move he regretted. "For 15 years, I've trained with the rigor and enthusiasm of a racehorse or a wild dog," Camel said. "I put my life in Johnny Tocco's hands and he tells me all the time to 'Slow down, Slow down.' Well, I can't train like that and then go out and fight."

Marvin Camel believed he was a highly intelligent and collected boxer. He believed he was better than most and that he could still outbox and outhit many of his contemporaries. One of the reasons virtually all the sportswriters liked Camel was because of his naturalness and honesty. But was he being honest with himself? Deep down, did he sense that it was time to walk away? Was it time to leave with his physical and mental sensibilities intact? Gone was the splendor of the golden throne. Gone was the beauty of the silver garden. Gone was the title.

Emotional and headstrong, Camel was addicted to pugilism. The recognition, the money, the security, the sense of self-purpose—everything that mattered to Camel depended upon winning again. He had saved every last penny and looked to turn his earnings into something even more profitable. In an effort to appease Sherry and strengthen the bonds of family, he had moved them out of their small trailer house into a commercial building that he would turn into a restaurant and arcade. He would rent the property from the tribe. It was only a matter of time before he entered between the ropes once more.

"Marvin Camel is a unique fighter who will take it to you from start to finish," commented one analyst before the title bout between Camel and Leonardo Rodgers for the USBA Cruiserweight belt. "I take every fight as a big fight," Camel said in the prefight interview. "I'm hoping for another WBC shot much quicker and I've lost four fights which have been crucial to my career. I'm going out there to bang heads." Camel, still embittered by the losses to De Leon, took one last swipe at the Puerto Rican, who by now had lost the title. "De Leon took fifteen months to fight, to defend the title…he put the cruiserweight championship back into the closet, where it's hidden."

Camel felt the cruiserweight champion should constantly promote the crown. The path back to that prestige had to go through the Civic Auditorium in Omaha, Nebraska, and Leonardo Rodgers, a Dominican with a reputation for dirty tactics, fighting out of Brooklyn, New York. "Omaha and Lincoln (Nebraska) have almost as many people as the whole state of Montana," said Camel's promoter Fred Harbeck. "Hopefully, some exposure here can help us get Marvin a title fight."

"Look at that head dress on him," commented one announcer as Camel was waiting in the ring for the formal introduction. "He looks almost too pretty to fight tonight." Pretty? Sure. But the look in his eyes was unmistakable: it was do or die. Indicative of the seriousness that Camel placed on the bout, he hired veteran cut man Bill Pursand, who had more than forty years' experience tending boxers' wounds.

Ranked outside of the WBC's top cruisers, Camel felt slighted. "He has a heart as big as this ring," said one announcer. "When times are tough, champions pull it off with heart. Marvin is loaded with heart."

Strong, bullying, with a losing record and 179 pounds of muscle, Rodgers was one tough guy. Marked by slow pacing and reluctance, the first round was uneventful. In the second and third, Rodgers pushed, shoved, and crowded Camel. But soon, Camel had turned the tables on the well-built brawler. "Indian" Marvin outsmarted Rodgers, who was slow afoot, awkward, and off-balance much of the time, and too wild with most of his punches. Gaining greater confidence with each round, Camel became so dominant that Rodgers refused to come out of his corner for the fifth round.

Boxing's alphabet soup of associations is uniquely complicated. The United States Boxing Association formed in December 1977 and during Marvin's time it served as a stepping stone for boxers on their way to the World Boxing Association (WBA), one of the two international sanctioning bodies. The other was the WBC—the belt which Marvin formerly held. After beating Rodgers, Camel owned the USBA cruiserweight belt, but the USBA hardly mattered to most boxing fans.

One month later, Camel ended his brief partnership with lounge owner and shoe store mogul Fred Harbeck. Harbeck said that, because of financial difficulties, he sold Camel's contract back to him one year after purchasing it. "This was probably one of the most difficult things I've ever had to do," Harbeck said. "But I promoted a fight for Marvin…and it just didn't work out financially. I'll always be his No. 1 fan."

"Now I'll work as an independent until somebody comes along that wants to offer me some money for my contract," Camel said.

August 10, 1982, western Montana

THE BIG YAMAHA WITH THE NEW YORK LICENSE PLATES RUMBLED off Highway 93 and turned into the dusty parking lot in Ronan. The young motorcyclist unloaded himself stiffly and stretched as he winced into the sun to read the sign overhead: "The Champ's Place." With a wide smile, he strolled inside.

"Hey, are you Marvin Camel?" queried the nervous Easterner.

"Yes, I am," Camel politely responded, extending a hand. "What's your name?"

Thus began a discussion of boxing trivia that continued through the afternoon in-between customers downing Indian tacos and milk-shakes. Camel affably busied himself, clearing paper plates and cups from vacated tables and making change for several youngsters feeding coins into the game machines while the biker perused nearby trophy cases filled with newspaper clippings, championship belts, and photos. Finally the boxer settled into a chair and they talked. Never a hard man to keep in a good humor, Camel's face, as almost always when he was outside the ring, wore a pleasant asymmetrical grin. It was the grin of a shy fellow happy to be recognized.

Once the biker decided it was time to leave, Camel walked him out; the boxer even listened to a bit of motorcycle-related chitchat before bidding him farewell. "Everybody has something interesting about them," Camel said to the man. "Everyone wants to be wanted. I'm learning to be a good listener."

CAMEL BELIEVED THE RESTAURANT, GAME ROOMS, AND WEIGHT room reflected his effort to fulfill an obligation toward young people. He was usually at the weight room or acting as chief cook and bottle washer. He enjoyed telling about his fight experiences and answering questions about his career. For a quarter, newcomers could put on a glove and punch a boxing machine outside the door. Anyone who could match or better Camel's effort had a chance to win the 'Team Camel' jacket inside.

Though outspoken and independent, Camel still found himself deeply influenced by the opinions of others. "I know what I have to do and why, but boxing is a business and you have to care about what people feel about you."

Sometimes it seemed as if Camel had a difficult time figuring out what he was all about as a fighter. He was pleased with his many knockouts but concerned that the other two dozen bouts had gone the distance. He was never known as a head hunter; most of his knockouts were a result of body shots.

"Boom, boom, to the old solar plexus," Camel would simulate to visitors, throwing a few punches.

At this point in his career, Camel had participated in 46 professional outings. That was a lot of punishment. Camel told friends he had "at least three good fights left" and that he hated wrapping up a long, exhausting career "fighting for peanuts."

Camel knew that championship fights weren't plucked from trees and he was hoping that new manager Robert Hudson could get him back to the top. There was talk of Camel fighting Leon Spinks, but that faltered.

Camel continued to run hard; for ten years he had run at least seven miles almost every day. Camel ran as much as twenty miles on some days. He began at 4:30 P.M. on the heavily traveled cemetery road east of town because, "People are moving at that time and they'll see me and know I'm still in there."

Marvin Camel's boxing career was anything but a straight line; it ran up and down. The next down point came in Copenhagen, Denmark, on February 11, 1983, in a non-title bout against Kenyan John Odhiambho.

Once again, Camel was on his own. "You fly in one day, you fly out two days later," Camel said. "The promoters could not afford anything longer. No time to acclimatize or get the people to come out. Not enough time to show the people that this lone stranger from Montana wasn't just a figment of their imagination."

Looking long in the tooth, Camel was dismantled in two rounds. The hungry up-and-comer Odhiambho battered Camel until the referee stopped the mauling. Four fights later, Odhiambho fell short in his attempt to win the WBC cruiserweight title, losing by technical knockout in the fifteenth round to Ossie Ocasio. That was the lone loss on Odhiambho's record; he retired in 1986 with twenty four wins, one loss.

On May 21, 1983, Camel retained the USBA cruiserweight title in what he considered his "best fight ever" against Rocky Sekorski at the MetraPark in Billings, Montana. Sekorski was a sportswriter's dream. Unlike the laconic Camel, who measured his words with a thimble, Sekorski could not keep his mouth shut. He talked about the champ: "I'm sure I can take him out early." He and his trainer elaborated about how they were going to win the fight.

With the nip of Sekorski's words stinging in his breast, Marvin ran in the early mornings and punched speed bags, heavy bags, and sparring partners in the afternoons. He trained and listened. Shortly before the match he ventured an observation: "That Sekorski will make for a great show for the people of Montana."

Marvin and Rocky had words at the weigh-in. Sekorski said, "I'm going to come out smoking! I'm going to bring the fight to him. Camel's a south paw so I'll be moving to my left. I plan on banging on him early. I'll take him out in the sixth round."

Marvin's rebuttle: "The way he explains it, he'll come out and stay on my case! For a guy of his caliber and his experience, he'll be making a drastic mistake. It will be a good fight, but I hope it doesn't go over six. I have to get back and take care of my business in Ronan."

The trash talking between the fighters, while not uncommon to boxing, was rare for a Marvin Camel fight. In fact, Camel seemed especially perturbed with Sekorski's antics. "I listened to his press conference, and I listened to all the things he said he was going to do in the ring. I listened to him talk about all those things he could do. I was no debater or talker. I went to get the job done and went home."

Camel said that Sekorski was more tongue than toughness. "Rocky was a Caucasian guy and that made him a bigger draw, and helped his fight draw money. He wasn't a great fighter. He was put in there because people wanted him to win, which seldom happened."

White fighters have been big draws in American boxing since its inception. In the early 1900s "White Hopes" were part of an effort by promoters to resuscitate the heavyweight division. Camel began boxing at a period when regardless of race, creed, or color, the better man had the opportunity to emerge victorious. But, even in his era, those inclined toward savior-searching looked for another Jack Dempsey—a white heavyweight with a lethal punch, a killer smile, and a common touch. White fight fans still clamored for a dominating presence in the ring, no matter the weight class, and undoubtedly, a little racial conflict never hurt the gate.

"The only thing Rocky Sekorski and Rocky Marciano had in common was the first name," Camel said. "Marciano lived to knock people out, but Sekorski couldn't."

Lumbering and unskilled, Sekorski had braved a number of top-ranked contenders and former world champions. Heading into the Camel fight, Sekorski had won his first thirteen professional matches.

Just before fight time, a budding reporter and a photographer from the Flathead Reservation's Indian newspaper visited Marvin in his dressing room. Marvin asked them who had "paid their way over;" they let him know they had paid their own expenses. For the first time in Camel's long boxing career, the *Char-Koosta* was able to present a first-hand account of one of the reservation champ's fights.

"I'm glad someone affiliated with the *Char-Koosta* and the Tribes was able to attend," said Camel. "I'm glad you could be here." Pictures of Marvin and Kenny Camel appeared in the local paper.

Marvin made a grandiose entry into the ring with his beaded vest, eagle feather war bonnet, and eagle feather staff, which was given to him in honor of winning the world title in March of 1980. The friendly crowd applauded as he danced around the ring.

Rocky Sekorski was six feet tall and proportioned like an action figure. He had arms thicker than most people's legs, a snowplow of a jaw, curly hair, and a chest that looked overstuffed with pride. As he swaggered through the crowd, it was easy to imagine him walking around a prison courtyard.

At one minute fifty-six seconds into the second round, Camel dropped Sekorski to his knees. Rocky got up, but he took innumerable blows to his head and body through the next several rounds. Near the end of the fifth round Sekorski could do little but keep his guard up and protect himself from Marvin's repeated blows. *Rocky can take a good punch*, thought Marvin.

By the end of the eighth round, Rocky looked defeated, and, the referee, sensing his demise, intervened. Sekorski shook hands with Marvin and left the ring with badly swollen eyes and face.

The victory put Camel at 42–5–2. He felt physically and mentally superior. He autographed pictures and score cards before returning to his dressing room.

Following the Camel bout, Sekorski continued to fight boxers of high caliber; his career best was a sixth-round TKO of former world champion Leon Spinks in 1986. "Neon Leon" may have been descending at the time, but the win did propel Rocky into fights with bigger names. On December 18, 1987, flabby forty-something George Foreman was only four fights into his improbable return when he stopped Sekorski in three rounds—the fastest Sekorski had ever been dispatched. Rocky never went down, but he ate hefty punishment. Overall, Sekorski compiled a professional record of 23–11, with thirteen kayos, during a twelve-year pro career.

Robert Hudson, fight promoter and match maker of the United States Boxing Association, arranged to have Marvin Camel's cruiserweight belt delivered to Bell Airport in Missoula—the airport named after the very same man his absent father once worked for. Along with the USBA belt, Marvin received verification of being recognized as number-two cruiserweight in the United States in the World Boxing Association (WBA).

On July 1, 1983, the Missoula Chamber of Commerce presented Marvin with the key to the city of Missoula. Marvin appreciated the gesture: "The first thing I'm gonna do is take this here key to the great city of Missoula and drive directly to the South side bank and see if it fits." Missoula mayor Bill Cregg also proclaimed the day as "Marvin Camel Day."

"I've been fighting out of Missoula for 12 years and I'm proud to be a friend," Marvin said. "Bill Cregg is one of my good friends."

Camel's younger brother Kenny said he was grateful for the recognition that Marvin received. "I've been very glad to be back in Marvin's corner to do as much as possible to help," Ken said. "We're not your everyday fighters. We have to work hard for every fight we get, paying our own way nearly all the way down the road to the championship fight. Some days we only had time to go from one eight-hour job to the plane and to the fight, then to the plane again heading for home to our eight-hour jobs. But it's worth it and I'm glad that Marvin is getting his recognition for it now. He is interested and concerned about his career in boxing. Thinking about all the hard work that goes with it almost scares a person out of it."

Camel placed the key to Missoula with the many trophies and gifts at his Ronan business, right next to the key to the city of Ronan. As happy as Camel was about all the events of the day, he still had business on his mind.

"I've got the USBA title now and I challenge all those fighters out there who've been dodging me. I've got the title and I'm here to fight so come and get it."

15

HOME LIFE

ONCE CAMEL RETURNED TO RONAN AFTER THE SEKORSKI victory, it became apparent that his domestic life was no longer solvent. Aware of her husband's occasional infidelities, Sherry had been demanding he spend more time at home, but retirement wasn't on his mind. Retirements didn't mean much in boxing. *When I retire, they are going to have to scrape me from the ring. I decide when I'm done. Marvin Camel decides. I just came off my best fight ever. There's more inside, more reserves of strength.*

Marvin was a boxer whose greatest strength was his tunnel vision: train, fight, win, train, fight, win. And for a boxer, narcissism is the way of life. He runs on it. He feeds on it. Anything less tempts weakness. But that narrow vision was a weakness when it came to dealing with those who should have been closest to him.

Camel explained to Sherry that before he had fallen in love with her, he had been in love with boxing. Boxing was his first love, and he didn't want to give up the one thing he could do best in life. If it came down to it, he'd choose boxing over his wife and children, however painful that decision might be.

His home life wilted. He was a casual visitor in his own domestic circle. He seemed to love his children in a distant, abstract way, never allowing a birthday party or family get-together to interrupt the regiment of boxing. *Many boxers have some latitude in their domestic arrangements*, he thought.

It was clear to Sherry that Marvin was not a man who would

153

put his family first in terms of emotional commitment. After all, how could someone who needed months of preparation to focus on less than an hour of action adjust to the time requirements of another? Marvin's life was a study in scrupulous self-management, and Sherry had wearied of it. "I was gone too long," Camel said. "I was gone too many times."

Marvin and Sherry had long realized that a prizefighter was not ideally suited to be a husband. Now they discovered they were different sorts of people. In the quiet of a chilly night, Marvin asked, "Do you want a divorce?"

She turned towards him, her face anguished, a face that didn't want to explain.

"Yes."

He put up a hand in acknowledgment.

"Has it been that bad?"

"Yes."

Sherry's answers, according to Marvin, were swift and firm. Still, he was surprised. Marvin petitioned the court for a divorce.

In 1983, Larry Holmes, Ray "Boom-Boom" Mancini, and Marvin Hagler were a few of the marquee names in boxing. All were world-class fighters who lived far away from Montana. Most of them probably never even heard of Ronan. However, they had a peer from there who deserved to be noted.

Marvin knew one reason he lacked recognition was that he boxed in a relatively new weight division. *How many times can I explain the weight limit of 176 to 190 pounds? How many times do I have to tell them that the division was designed to keep a small heavyweight from being outweighed by a boxer of 220 pounds? Will cruiserweights ever gain the interest of the boxing world? How can I answer that? Can't I just go out there and fight the best way that I know?* Living on an unknown Indian reservation in fly-over Montana did not help his popularity, either.

Camel contemplated retirement. Champions before Camel had said they were through with boxing, through with getting up for roadwork in the faintest early morning light, through with pounding speed bags, heavy bags, and sparring partners, through with having their brains scrambled and their faces cut, through with urinating blood and enduring blinding headaches after tough fights. And most of them meant it—at the time.

There was always a catch, a void between intention and action. After they retired, where could they get a job that paid tens of thousands of dollars for a single night's work? Where could they work in front of screaming, adoring fans? How could they adjust to ordinary life outside the ring? Camel was well aware of too many former boxers scrambling just to make ends meet. *Is this what I've got to look ahead to?* Camel was not immune to the psychic rewards of being the champion, but more importantly, he needed money to pay his expenses and to survive.

"For a while I went back to the Flathead Indian Reservation and thought about quitting," Camel said. "I contemplated finding an 8–to–5 job. I even applied for several jobs, but no work. My life is boxing. I had the glimmer of light, the bead of fire installed in this brain when I was 11, and I've carried the torch until now."

Camel's business venture in Ronan—the arcade and restaurant—had become an overwhelming drain on time and resources; it shut down after only a few months. His marriage ended. In the divorce decree, Marvin ceded 35 acres of his family's ancestral lands. Child support added up. At 33, he could still fight a few more years, but time was running out. He needed to do something big.

In the summer of 1983, Marvin Camel made a decision that would change the rest of his life—and change the way his own family and others on the Flathead Reservation viewed him. With little money and a chip on his shoulder, Camel hopped on his Honda 750 motorcycle and headed to Los Angeles. He packed a pair of boxing trunks, photo identification, and a notebook with names and contacts. He left behind three children, several brothers and sisters, friends and critics, and the only home he had ever known.

Camel went to Los Angeles because he was tired of fighting in Montana for little pay—tired of his home life, tired of losing money, and tired of not having adequate sparring partners. Filled with bitterness and recrimination, he was tired of the psychologically inferior structure of his birthplace lands. He felt as if people were out to demean him and demolish his sense of accomplishment. On the reservation, he felt like a faded pencil drawing—you could see him, but you couldn't quite make him out. He couldn't even quite make out himself.

"There were some things Marvin was saying in the newspapers about the reservation that hurt and angered a lot of people," said his sister Renee Camel. "His quotes about the reservation were very angry."

When he reached his destination three days later, Camel observed streets littered with a bewildering array of signs and billboards; everything imaginable was for sale. Through the sight-binding smog, he observed countless faces. Tucked in between donut franchises and gas stations, Marvin found a small motel surrounded by people with whom he would never care to be associated.

On July 17, at a boxing tournament in Los Angeles, Camel met a woman who would become his second wife. Norma Josey was a "second" in another sense, too. She was the "second" in the corner of a boxing ring, serving as an assistant to legendary cut-man Chuck Bodak, who had worked with Rocky Marciano, Muhammad Ali, and Oscar De La Hoya.

Indeed, Norma's life was boxing. Born in 1944 to Irish-English parents in upstate New York, Norma, along with her brothers, had been taken by their father from their hometown of Niagara Falls into Buffalo to watch boxing. "I have three older brothers and my dad used to take them to the fights," she said. "I begged him to take me, too, and he finally did. That's how I got interested in the fights. I used to spar with my brothers, too."

From the beginning, Norma found an authenticity in boxing that she felt was lacking in all other forms of competition. "I saw something fair and upfront in boxing," Norma said. "Football can be sneaky and nasty, with you hiding behind others. Boxing was honest. 'Hey, I'm going to try to beat the shit out of you, and vice versa'."

By the time she met Camel, Norma, 38 and twice divorced, knew a thing or two about boxing. She was living in Redondo Beach doing public relations and promotional work for the World Boxing Hall of Fame. She had recently finished a class in public speaking at El Camino College. By night, she was ringside at the Olympic Auditorium.

"I'd been going to matches since I was in my early twenties," she said. "My girlfriends went clubbing but I went down to the Olympic Auditorium on Grand Avenue—the best place in the world. You could be sitting next to a grease monkey on one side and a Hollywood producer on the other."

Following a meeting with Bodak and boxing promoters Dick and Ray Marconi, who were organizing a stable of fighters, Norma was invited to get her "second's license." She was one of the first women licensed as a second in California. "Chuck thought I might be nice window dressing in the corner for his fights," she said. "So I went to the commission and got a license. I was more than just decoration. I was not an airhead about boxing."

Having a female second had its advantages for unknown fighters. Photographers and camera operators were always directing their attention to the corner with the lady in it. "Made our boys more notable," Norma said.

Ironically, Norma did not know that Marvin was a boxer when she first met him. She was working as a second and he was a spectator in the bleachers three rows behind her, wearing a pair of "large, mirrored sunglasses—horrible looking things," Norma recalled. Still, she thought: *He's an unusual looking celebrity of some kind. Very unusual looking.*

The last thing Norma set out to do that day was choose a man. But she thought it a pity that this uniquely striking man was alone.

After the fight, she sought him out. She didn't recognize his face, but when he said his name, it registered in her boxing brain. They talked—and later that night shared the kind of intimacy that sometimes sneaks into the lives of two dispersed strangers.

Many women had been struck by Camel's good looks, his obvious intelligence, and his pleasant manner. "He had a beautiful smile," Norma said. "I've seen a lot of beautiful smiles in Los Angeles, but Marvin's was the most beautiful. Beautiful teeth. He never even mentioned he was a boxer."

To Norma, Marvin was a fixed point of rugged cool in a city of spectacle and flux. He was well mannered—even charming—and could be comfortable in any social setting. He stayed away from unsavory boxing people, avoided cocktail parties and drugs, and didn't seem the least impressed by socialites or entertainment figures.

Of course, Marvin and Norma had something in common that was stronger than class or character: their love of boxing. While each of them had lived through good times and bad, they now seemed destined for a final call of fate and chance together.

16

CHAMPION AGAIN

PEOPLE WANT TO BE AROUND YOU WHEN YOU ARE THE MAN, thought Marvin Camel. *They want to be associated with the lime-light, but when the limelight is gone, they're gone, too.*

Even though Camel had the USBA subtitle, he felt pain and discontent when he thought about losing the WBC world title. "After you lose a world title, your life is so quiet you can hear a pin drop," Camel said. "For three years, all I heard from the people of Montana was, 'Why don't you quit?' or 'Why don't you retire?' I lost the title and I was abandoned by my people."

Marvin Camel's life felt lonely. Boxing had always been a solitary pursuit, but the overnight liaisons with speedbags and heavy bags now felt even lonelier. Shadowboxing made him feel empty. Marvin drifted back and forth between Montana, where he stayed alone, and Los Angeles, where he stayed with Norma. When on the Flathead Reservation, Marvin engaged in a tough conditioning routine that involved chopping wood, running, and repeating heavy-bag drills. Day after day. He thrived in the outdoors and the seclusion at his home. He exercised solo. He thought and over-thought his next career move. Then just when it seemed as if he were on the precipice of mental calamity, a phone call changed his entire outlook.

Despite two defeats at the hands of De Leon, Camel was sailing high in the rankings. When the International Boxing Federation (IBF) released its list of fighters in contention for its cruiserweight title fight, Marvin Camel was on top. (The IBF was formed in 1983; the World Boxing Organization in 1988. For better or worse, this confusing fragmentation made it possible to have four world champions—WBC, WBA, IBF, and WBO—in each of the seventeen weight classes.)

Marvin was invited to fight for the IBF title against the second-ranked cruiserweight Roddy MacDonald in Halifax, Nova Scotia—MacDonald's backyard. When Camel left Missoula for Halifax in early December 1983, nobody seemed to care. There were no bon voyages or well wishes. Local newspapers paid scant attention. Family and friends shrugged their shoulders. Marvin felt slighted.

"When I left the airport in Missoula, I felt alone," Camel remembered. "I looked down and felt alone. As the door to the airplane shut, I looked out the window in disgust." Part of his bitterness was that he literally alone: no manager, no trainer, no cornerman. He would train in Nova Scotia for four weeks before the fight—alone.

The flight to Nova Scotia seemed exceptionally long, and Camel had too many thoughts. *You are too old. You need to retire. I've put myself on the butcher block for you, for you Henry, for you Sherry, for you Elmer Boyce, for you Montana. Shit, I'm doing this for Marvin Camel. I have made sacrifices.*

It was a dizzying, turbulent ride and Camel felt relieved after his plane touched down. The night was dark but very clear, and the stars were bright in the northern sky. On his first morning in the chill of the Canadian winter, Camel rose early and ran hard on cement and asphalt.

Perhaps it was the euphoria of the moment, but Marvin Camel felt in the prime of his career. On the outside, he looked wonderfully conditioned, his body an anatomy of function. In the northern cold he pounded his body hard until all traces of flab and gentleness were exorcised and all that remained were the survival instincts of an animal.

Most fighters carry doubts, and Camel may have been carrying a few since his two losses to De Leon. But those doubts, if any, were mental. Physically, Camel knew he had what it took to succeed, except for one problem: his right eye began to "do funny things."

The problems started weeks earlier. Camel had increasing bouts of double-vision. He even visited a doctor in Missoula who said that the surgically reattached retina was slowly beginning to peel back, or detach. Camel knew that if he had his eye inspected by physicians in Canada, he would never receive the medical clearance to fight.

Before he left for Canada, Camel called Robert Hudson to inform his new manager and friend that the surgery he had undergone to repair his detached retina had started to lose its effectiveness.

"The doctor says the detached retina is coming back," Camel said.

"What do you want to do about it? Do you want to fight?" asked Hudson.

"I didn't come all this way for nothing," responded Camel.

"The decision is completely your own. You make the choice."

"I will only have one opportunity to be the first IBF cruiserweight champion of the world. I would love to accomplish this feat."

"How are you going to avoid the prefight exam?"

"I have no idea."

"Can you squeak by?"

"I can sure try."

A fighter who over-trains is as likely to lose as the fighter who doesn't put in the work. Marvin disregarded any suggestions of moderation; it was his duty to lead an existence of nonstop sparring and to leave his partners with bumps and contusions. He had sparred more than a hundred rounds since he'd entered Canada. But would he be allowed to compete? That thought thumped his head every second of the week leading up to his prefight appointment with Canadian physicians. Five days before the fight, he showed up for his scheduled examination, where two old men with Canadian accents and little black hats asked him to smile, speak, and cough. The doctors did not check his eyes. "I squeaked by," Camel said. "Call it luck or the fate of God."

Around midnight, less than twenty-four hours before the fight, Marvin jumped out of bed and went to the bathroom to look in the mirror. For ten minutes, he did some shadowboxing. The exercise was geared more to checking out his mental state: Was he willing to put everything on the line? The answer was a resounding *yes*. Was he willing to put his body and blood on the line? *Yes*. Was he willing to live beyond the edge and do anything, to press the resolve, to never quit? *Yes, yes, yes*. He slipped back under the covers.

December 13, 1983

The pungent smell of sweat and cigars hovers over the 40,000 spectators wedged shoulder-to-shoulder inside the Halifax Metro Centre. The arena thwacks with energy and expectation. Fans swig beer and place bets on tonight's historic match, the International Boxing Federation's first world cruiserweight title fight.

Most, if not all, wager their money on the first fighter to duck under the ropes: Roddy MacDonald, 177 pounds, a 23-year-old Canadian with roots in New Waterford, Nova Scotia, and fighting out of Toronto. He can taste the crowd's overwhelming support.

"There was only one other person there who wasn't Canadian," Camel recalls, referring to Alvin Goodman, IBF director and legal counsel. "I felt a lot like Custer with three thousand Native Americans coming at him to get his scalp."

MacDonald warms up, stretches his arms, and bounces lightly side to side. A second warrior enters the ring: Marvin Camel, nearly 10 years older, weighing 186 pounds. Wearing an eagle-feather headdress that trails to the mat, Camel shuffles his feet in a slow, measured dance around the ring, flourishing a wooden staff decorated with blue beads and leather fringe. The war bonnet stays on during punching practice. It has a feather for every win. In the Salish Indian tradition, he is preparing for a battle. *This is my second contest for the world cruiserweight title. No problem. I've been here before.*

The referee signals it's time to start. Camel carefully removes his war bonnet and hands it to his makeshift cornermen, a pair of local boxing-gym owners. Final reminders are issued to the fighters, then the referee steps back and boxing begins.

Does this guy know about how bad my eye is? Is he going to go for it?

MacDonald is confident, strong. He starts off aggressively and ratchets up the violence for four intense rounds. In round five, MacDonald catches Camel with a crushing right to the bridge of the jaw. Camel is decked for an eight count. *I've got to get up. Get up. I need the strength to get up. The rainbow hanging high over my head, come to me. Restore my limbs. Restore my body. Restore my feet for me.*

Camel said that at split-second intervals throughout the fight his right eye felt "beaten-down." "I felt like I would need to pick it up off the floor," said Camel. "But I wanted to be the champ, and I needed to keep boxing."

Forty-seven seconds after eating canvas, Camel delivers a hard right to MacDonald's gut, dropping him to his knees. Referee Bobby Beaton hesitates. Was it a hard, legitimate right to the solar plexus that should start the count? Or was it a low blow that requires Camel to be reprimanded or even disqualified? As MacDonald groans on all fours, Beaton signals a low blow. He is promptly overruled by IBF director Goodman. Beaton then starts the count, and MacDonald cannot continue.

Tens of thousands of spectators jeer and throw debris into the ring, many shouting obscenities at Camel. Some have to be restrained by police. Camel is declared the winner, and more beer bottles, popcorn, and obscenities rain down on him. MacDonald's father, also his trainer, jumps into the ring and tries to take a swing at Camel. A number of fans charge the ring but are restrained by policemen.

Camel raises his arms above his head, claiming the glory which took three years to reclaim. He no longer has anything to prove. He is the world champion once more.

In an interview after the fight, MacDonald was asked whether the blow was low. "I don't know, you'll have to look yourself. He hit me fairly. There wasn't a low blow to own up to. He hit me fairly." MacDonald's record drops to 25–4; he hits a 4–6–1 skid and then retires.

Afterwards Camel said the blow was fair as did one of his Canadian cornermen, Tom McCluskey of Halifax. Referee Beaton admitted he didn't see the blow but did not explain why he signaled it was low. "From where I was I wasn't sure…so I checked with the supervisor [Goodman] and two judges and they said it was up in here," he said, pointing to the solar plexus. The punch was legal.

Once more, Marvin Camel had achieved greatness. The flight back to Missoula was full of all the memories that led to this point in his life. *His father's intimidation. Lost days of youth. Training, thinking. Personal sacrifices. The toll on his body, his family, and his relationship with his people. The helpless feeling of being a packaged commodity to sell and sell. To sell and use. To sell and discard.* No matter. Camel had established a reputation as a durable and tough fighter who could win the big fight.

The Missoula airport was especially frosty when the new world champion arrived. There wasn't a familiar face in sight——not a single reporter, not a friend, not a fan. He had gone to the fight alone and he returned alone. The people didn't believe he could do it; maybe now they didn't want to believe he had.

When he got home to Ronan, sheltered with warmth, safe from

the winter cold, Camel placed the shiny world championship belt on the mantle and looked it over. He examined the souvenir up and down, memories of former fights and personal demons rushing through his head like a rolling train. Blood. Pain. Glory. Legacy.

Camel sat there in the silence of night. Everything up to this second had been theory. In his arms, he tightly held the result of all those years of practice, patience, and training. One of the hardest fights in his life had always been the fight for recognition and respect. Now his pride was in good standing. Now, it was just Marvin Camel and the belt. His belt.

Was it worth it?

Hell, yeah. No mess or worry could make this smile disappear.

Marvin Camel never felt better.

In the subsequent days and weeks, letters arrived from Canadian fans apologizing for their brutish and unfair behavior. One letter read: "Please accept my apologies for the expressing of displeasure to you and the IBF following your fight with Roddy Mac-Donald. I now accept the fact that there were no low blows and that you are the undisputed champion of the world. Continued Success and Merry Christmas."

17

BACKYARD BLUES

*"After you lose a title,
your life is so quiet you can hear a pin drop."*

—Marvin Camel

Lee Roy Murphy was a mean dude. Outside the ring, he had the reputation of being ungovernable, bad, with a temper just a hair trigger away from violence. Hailing from the west side of Chicago's meanest parts, he was an inner-city tough with a substantial chip on his shoulder. "I grew up in the projects and I fought out of the projects," said Murphy. "Boxing saved my life. I was one of the luckiest ones to make it out of the projects."

In the ring, Murphy—nicknamed "Solid Gold" by his trainer-cutman Jim Strickland—was a knockout artist and a crowd pleaser. He won the 1979 light-heavyweight National Golden Gloves and was a member of the 1980 United States Olympic team. His first six pro fights were fought as a light heavyweight. He then went up to cruiserweight. In conjunction with boxing, Murphy worked as a physical education instructor and playground supervisor for the Chicago Park District, and he worked part-time as a deputy sheriff for the Cook County Sheriff's Department. When he fought Marvin Camel in October 1984, Murphy, age 26, was undefeated in his 20 professional fights.

Murphy came to Montana with a big, nasty attitude. Murphy wore a "Camel Jockey" t-shirt at the weigh-in and predicted he could finish the champion in two rounds but promised the fight would not go past six.

"I don't predict but I can predict his prediction is all wrong," countered Camel, who appeared as cool and placid as a glacial lake in a blue dress shirt and a traditional Native necklace of tricolored beads. "There's always a chance of one punch, a lucky punch. The knockout punch will have to wait for Lee Roy Murphy and his undefeated string is going to stop. I'm a spoiler." Camel would be defending his world title in front of his home crowd—one of his dreams.

YEARS EARLIER, TRIBAL ELDER WALT MCDONALD HAD WARNED Marvin that anyone who would go into a sordid sport like boxing without a heavy dose of skepticism and doubt would be a fit candidate for a mental ward. Boxing is known for its sleazy foundations and brutally unfair decisions.

A referee's decision to stop a fight without a clear knockdown always reeks of controversy. On March 17, 1990, in perhaps the most sudden finish to a fight in the history of boxing, Julio Cesar Chavez—far behind on two scorecards—stopped Meldrick Taylor with seconds remaining.

Taylor, a young, undefeated former gold-medal Olympian, was touted as the second coming of Sugar Ray Leonard, with perhaps the fastest hands in the sport. He turned pro at eighteen, won the IBF light welterweight title a few years later, and was only 23 when he took on Chavez, a Mexican icon with a perfect 68–0 record. Chavez, the WBC light welterweight champion, was known for his ability to dish out pain and punishment. Both fighters staked their 140-pound titles to unify the division.

From the opening bell, Taylor appeared quicker and stronger, dazzling the crowd with a variety of combinations that baffled Chavez. Taylor pushed Chavez around with confidence and control, even showboating in the middle rounds. However, the few shots landed by Chavez did more damage to Taylor than Taylor's shots did to Chavez. Taylor's face swelled badly, his mouth bled, and fatigued showed. Nonetheless, after eleven rounds Taylor was comfortably ahead on the score cards; HBO scored a near shutout. Hoping to stymie any potential complacency, Taylor's corner told him he needed to win the last round; Chavez's corner told their fighter that only a knockout would salvage his performance, "Do it for your family, your country."

At the start of round twelve, Taylor appeared spent and Chavez fresher. In the fight's final minute, Chavez landed a strong right hand that buckled Taylor's legs. Taylor tried to rebound, but Chavez pounced with a barrage of blows. With fifteen seconds remaining, Chavez landed another big right hand that decked Taylor. Mexican fans erupted with chants of "Mexico."

Taylor beat the count, but only by using the ropes for leverage. Referee Richard Steele asked Taylor, "Are you okay?" Taylor didn't answer and looked towards his corner. So with only two seconds to go, Steele stopped the fight, and Chavez won by TKO. On two of the three scorecards, Taylor was well ahead: 108–101 and 107–102. The third scorecard had Chavez 105–104.

CAMEL HAD BEEN TRAINING IN LOS ANGELES SINCE NEW YEAR'S, while Murphy spent the months of August and September in Arizona, working under Sugar Ray Leonard's former trainer Jinks Morton. "I was in Arizona training and working out with Marvin Johnson a lot," said Murphy. "I was boxing every day for eight weeks." Marvin Camel and Marvin Johnson were both southpaws. "Going in, Jim Strickland, my trainer, he would tell me that Camel was easy to cut. I never thought about him being easy to cut during the fight. I just knew it was his hometown and home turf."

The fight was action-packed from the opening bell. Camel threw and landed far more punches throughout, but Murphy's right hand carried much more might. In the third round, Murphy began using his left jab frequently. Camel stalked the bruising Chicagoan and bloodied his nose in the fifth round.

"Cowboys, Indians, and businessmen, they were all chanting for Marvin, and chanting his name," Ken Camel recalled.

Midway through the fifth round, Murphy turned the tide, landing a right that slit open Camel's right eyelid. During the next few rounds, Camel's blood showered the ring until his corner effectively stanched the bleeding. Murphy put Camel on the canvas at 2:35 of the eighth round, though Camel bounced right back up and took a standing count. The white canvas was speckled with blood, most of it from Marvin's eye.

"I dropped him in the eighth or something," said Murphy. "I think he respected me after I dropped him. I was more aggressive in the later rounds. I respected him, it was his hometown. I tried to give him respect."

In rounds eight, nine and ten, Camel picked his spots with more efficiency and landed the better single shots. The later rounds saw both men eager to get it on. Camel started the 13th mad, peppering, talking, and clowning.

In round 14 Camel was bleeding from the old wounds around his right eye that had never fully healed, but he wasn't bleeding as badly as against De Leon. He could still see. He could still stand and box. He only needed to get through one more round to defend his world title. He was ready, and he felt he was winning. Indeed, Camel was ahead on all three judges' cards. Bob LeCoure of Butte, Montana, had the fight scored 127–122; Tom McDonough of Tacoma, Washington, had it 126–121, and James Rondeau of Cameo Lake, Washington, had it 125–121.

But before the final round started, referee Dan Jancic came to

Camel's corner, quickly looked at Camel's cuts, and stopped the fight. All of a sudden, even though winning the match and still ready to fight, Camel had lost.

The crowd of 2,670 people at the Yellowstone Metra booed and showered the ring with beer cups and empty bottles, and chanted obscenities. When the ring announcer announced Murphy the victor, the fans booed louder and threw soda cans and programs into the ring. The police had to escort Murphy and his team out of the stadium. "It was scary," Murphy recalled recently. "But afterwards it was all cool. The people they shook our hands in the restaurant, and they talked to us. There was no problem there. They all said it was a good fight."

"I filled in that night as a judge because someone didn't make it," Bob LeCoure remembered. "Marvin had a wicked bola punch—a devastating body punch, and he hurt Murphy. But Marvin didn't have that big knockout punch. The cut was bad—it's true. But I did not think Jancic should have stopped the fight. I was very, very surprised. But I guess that the referee did what he thought was best."

"Dan Jancic looked like a man without a country," Ken Camel said thirty years later. "He was looking for the cops and to escape. He had a look that said 'how the hell do I get out of here'."

Later Jancic told reporters, "Those two cuts were real bad. They were real deep and [Camel] had trouble on his vision. I stopped the fight on that doctor's recommendation."

But ring doctor H.B. Cabrera told the press a different story. "I didn't stop the fight," Cabrera insisted. He said the cut over Camel's left eye was no worse than the cut that opened over the right eye in the fifth round. According to Cabrera, Camel could have fought the last round.

The confusion over who stopped the fight only compounded the controversy—and concomitant suspicion of Jancic's motives. "Jancic had his mind made up even before he looked at this cut," Camel said. "The doctor looked and said I was okay. I felt I could stick and move and stay out of the way. [Jancic] stopped it because

I had a slight cut. During the De Leon fight, I was cut like a shredder hit my face. Marvin Camel gets cut—that's the way it is. But Jancic walks into the corner and stops it."

"So many people in that arena wanted to get their hands on that no-good guy," Camel said. "They would have torn him limb from limb. He made a mockery of the state of Montana when he rendered the world champion unable to continue. I could have gone that round and retained the title."

For his part, Murphy was clueless. "I thought the fight was close," he said, "but as far as stopping it, that's not my decision." But Murphy did say he felt that Camel was having difficulty seeing in the fourteenth round.

Confusion reigned. Promoter Pete Jovanovich of Montana Boxing Inc. roamed around telling everyone that he was going to immediately protest the outcome. As fans angrily chucked cups, the Camel entourage shook their heads.

"I remember a white guy with a big old beard coming up to Marvin after the fight," Ken Camel said. "He came out of the crowd, lifted Marvin's arm, and said 'Shit, we *know* who won that fight.'"

Ken Camel, who later worked as a boxing inspector in Montana, said that one of the guidelines the referee needs to be mindful of, regarding stoppages, is that a bad cut should not be the determining factor in calling off a match. "Do not let cuts and blood impact the decision," said Ken. "Now that's rule number eight of the ten. They put that rule in there because of Marvin Camel's loss."

The fact that travesties happen in boxing is no consolation to the man on the wrong end of the injustice. In the cold locker room, Marvin sat drenched in sweat. His perspiration, body oil, and tears plopped onto the concrete floor. He stayed there for a few silent minutes. He did not want anyone to see his pain, anger, and grief. He felt old and profoundly lonely. He hated that he ever agreed to fight in Montana, and for the moment he hated his life.

"I followed Marvin into the locker room and he looked like the warrior in that painting, with his head bent down, the last ride, the end of the trail." Ken Camel said. "We were stunned. The doctor walked in with his black bag and so did the television reporter. The television reporter asked the doctor, 'Did you stop the fight?' The doctor said, 'No, I did not'."

In the dressing room some of Marvin's friends and fans were hollering about Marvin being "robbed." A handful of reporters stood there awkwardly. They could feel the heartbreak. Marvin's face was puffed out, his lip cut, his body and arms tired. An exhausted Camel slowly looked up and said, "This is unjust. How could he stop the fight during the break?"

"That's unheard of," Kenny agreed.

"I was cut early in the bout and sustained my composure," Marvin said.

"You were ahead on all three scorecards," Kenny pointed out.

"What was going through his mind? I get cut. Marvin Camel gets cut."

That night was one of the most stressful in Camel's life. Quiet and seeming distraught, the deposed champion was eventually driven to his hotel room, still in his boxing mind, and still silent. His mind replayed the fight over and over: the audience filling the auditorium with boos and catcalls as the decision was announced, the aroused wave of sympathy among many in the crowd, the cheers based on his strong performance. The people were cheering for Marvin Camel, clapping for him, calling out his name in a way he had never heard before. He never realized how much he had hungered for a sound like that, and now here it was—on the night he lost his title.

That night Marvin Camel lost a part of himself he would never get back. To say he had trouble coming to terms with the perceived injustice would be a vast understatement. Just as he would tense his body when physically hit, he now tensed his mind from psychological pain. He tried to clamp it down, tried to wall it off and reject it from his consciousness. The pain kept coming.

Boxing begins in illusion and ends in real blood and tears. Marvin's illusion was that he would not only become champion but stay the champion. *If I train hard, if I run so hard that it feels like an ant colony occupies my calves, if I work my flesh red and sore, I can control my own fate.* Wrong.

Unlike professional football and baseball, there is no central authority that oversees boxing. Instead, boxing is governed by state organizations. The Montana Board of Athletics (MBA) fielded a formal protest initiated by a Billings-based group called "Concerned Montanans for Marvin Camel" and filed by the boxer. Some of Marvin's friends told him to let it go. But he persisted. He pestered, called, made inquiries. *Do the right thing, Montana. Do what's right for Marvin Camel. Don't take away what I've worked so hard for.*

He heard nothing in response.

Camel begged the MBA to overturn the referee's stoppage and rule that the fight ended in a no-decision, which would allow Camel to retain his title. Camel repeated his claim that the referee could not see into his corner and did not discuss the cuts with the doctor. Camel emphasized that if Jancic truly were concerned about Camel's safety, he would have interceded in the fifth round when Murphy cut Camel's right eye. He added that the cuts in the Murphy fight required "ten to fifteen" stitches, well below the "sixty-four" he required after the first De Leon fight.

"If we lose this title," Camel said, "if we are unjustly stripped of this title through an error in judgment, then Montana becomes just another [state]…and Marvin Camel becomes just another citizen, which is fine, but Montana wants a legitimate champion, not to have it taken away like a thief in the night."

Camel even told the board that he was about to show a videotape of the fight in Missoula at no charge so boxing fans there could make up their own minds. If they agreed that he was robbed, they could send letters protesting the outcome and supporting Camel. "If you know boxing as well as I do, you can only come out hating the referee for rendering the decision that he did render," he said.

"If this decision stands, this injustice, it marks the start of my retirement," Camel said. "I have no more goals to strive for."

On October 12, 1984, the Montana Board of Athletics announced that it "does not have the power to hold a hearing nor render a decision" on Camel's protest. The three-member board said the fight was a "World Championship Contest (held) under the auspices of the United States Boxing Association–International Boxing Federation." (The USBA had added the IBF designation earlier that year.) The board recommended that Camel appeal Jancic's intervention to "the appropriate committee of the USBA-IBF for disposition…" The board noted that the USBA-IBF sanctioned the fight, and that "the officials were all agreed upon and approved by all parties involved."

Camel was crushed. "The state of Montana spit in my face," he said later. "Looking back, I'm surprised somebody didn't stand up and shoot Jancic between the eyes. What was going through his mind at the time? He was probably paid under the table. What Jancic did that night will never be forgot. Montana thought they had a world champ and that boxing in Montana was going to stay on the map. What Jancic did will be on the minds of all who were there forever.

"I'm sure he went to dinner that night, looking for a payoff from promoter Cedric Kushner, more than just a pat on the back. Other fights of mine that Jancic refereed, he treated me differently. He was supposed to control a fight, not cast judgment of me, not to show an attitude towards me. But one time Jancic told me, 'I'm going to get you one day, Marvin.' He had issues with me. I should have kissed his ass, but that's not my mode of operation."

In between accusations of a fix, a crooked referee, and other possible chicanery, Camel accused the state of Montana of conspiring to take away everything he had worked so hard to attain. "At the time I felt that the state of Montana, by not helping, was against me," he said.

Writers distort boxing. In order to find the plot—causation, sequence, meaning—they make boxing more intricate than it really is. Sometimes, however, the plot is no more elaborate than a fight is a fight, and a loss is a loss—and there is no massive, hidden conspiracy.

Marvin did not file an appeal with the USBA-IBF and no evidence has ever surfaced that Jancic colluded to subvert the Camel fight with Murphy.

Judge Bob LeCoure, who later went on to promote club boxing in Montana, said that Jancic, a former Anaconda police officer who died in 1995, was a "straight shooter." "Dan Jancic and Marvin's promoter Pete Jovanovich were good friends, as I recall," said LeCoure. "In my opinion, it was absolutely not a fixed or illegal fight. I don't believe that Jancic would have intentionally stepped in if he didn't think that it was the right thing to do. I don't believe that Jancic should have stepped in so late in the fight. But he did."

"If anything, you would think that it would be the opposite," said boxing referee Kevin McCarl, of Helena, Montana, who has refereed professional boxing matches for more than 20 years in Montana, Italy, and Thailand. "You would think that the Montana ref would be biased for the Montana fighter. The thing about it is that you never know what the referee sees or can understand what his eyes see. He saw something."

As IBF champion, Lee Roy Murphy devoured three more opponents with a heavy right uppercut before his devouring of too many meals did him in. In 1986, Murphy suffered his first professional defeat when he was knocked senseless by Ricky Parkey. Depleted from having to shed 30 pounds during training, Murphy couldn't make it through the tenth round. He retired in 1998. "When you win a title, it makes your life harder," said Murphy, who currently works for the Chicago Transit Authority. "A lot of guys need to win a title to get any confidence in life. That's a lot of responsibility because you don't know who wants to beat you up the next day. It's a win-lose situation when it comes to boxing."

In times of stress, a man often does things he later regrets. He acts hastily, without examining the consequences of his actions. Sometimes he repents, but it may be too late for forgiveness. Sometimes a man simply disappears to avoid further psychological or emotional conflict.

It may be a combination of all these factors that led Marvin Camel to turn his back on his home state, his family, and all the people that helped make him a two-time world champion. The MBA decision pushed Camel away from Montana, leaving him with a bitter taste he struggled for decades to overcome. As a boxer, he had long ago made his peace with danger and risk. But he could never make peace with the Murphy decision and its aftermath.

"I remember Marvin coming around after the Murphy fight, and he had nothing," said Bob Camel. "I remember our mother having to give him twenty dollars. He circled around the house, looked like he was deciding whether to take it or not. Look ashamed."

Marvin didn't refuse the payment. "I borrowed twenty bucks from my mom," said Marvin. "I had hit bottom—rock bottom. It was all the money there was. It was all the money there was in the world for Marvin Camel. What did I have? I stood there on Highway 93 with the belt I'd won, a three-piece suit, and no place to go. I had no place to go in the world."

In 2013 Camel said, "The state of Montana did nothing to keep Marvin Camel. They had a world champion who represented Montana all over the world—proudly. They couldn't keep him. They chose not to correct the injustice."

CAMEL LOST TO MURPHY IN 15 ROUNDS. ONLY THREE YEARS LATER, fights were limited to 12 rounds to protect the fighters.

Championship fights had been the standard fifteen rounds until the death of South Korean Duk Koo Kim. On November 13, 1982, Ray "Boom Boom" Mancini made his second defense of his WBA World Lightweight Championship title in a grueling, nationally televised encounter against Kim.

At one point in the 14th round Mancini hurled more than forty unanswered punches. Mancini finally decked Kim in that round, and though Kim beat the 10 count, the referee stopped the fight. While Mancini was celebrating the stoppage, Kim collapsed in the corner. He was rushed on a stretcher to Las Vegas' Desert Springs Hospital, where he had 2½ hours of surgery on his brain to remove a blood clot and relieve pressure in his skull.

Mancini attended a Mass the day after the fight where a priest asked attendees to pray for the dying Kim. Kim had no brain function and lingered in a coma for four days on life support. Under Nevada law, the consent of Kim's family was not needed to stop the life support.

Four months after her son's death, Kim's mother killed herself by drinking a bottle of pesticide. Referee Richard Greene also took his own life. The Kim-Mancini tragedy convinced the WBA to discontinue 15-rounders in 1987, and all other boxing organizations followed suit. Championship bouts would be set at 12 rounds.

"Later rounds were damaging guys," said Mancini, 53. "What is 15 rounds like? Those are the rounds when you get scathed, right? To me, that's stupid. No fighters come away unscathed, but guys would see a lot more damage with 15-rounders again. It'll never come back. Why risk more long-term damage? What's the sense of having three million if you don't know your own name, and if you can't count it afterwards?"

"Fifteen rounds is like the brink of death," Camel said. "The only thing I can compare it to in athletics is—it's like running a three or five mile race in track. You are full of energy, but by the time it is over you are spent. You can't push any harder than that. You get in touch with your soul. You probably sweat out your soul, too. But I trained for fifteen rounds. Didn't matter to me. Those 15 rounds meant something back then—it meant a championship."

18

DARKER SIDE OF SPORT

"I love boxing, that's all."

—*Marvin Camel*

CAMEL STAYED IN MONTANA FOR A FEW DAYS FOLLOWING THE LEE Roy Murphy loss, finding little or no solitude during the dark hours binding those long days. Some nights he would lie awake, mentally replaying everything that had happened in his career: One minute Yugoslavia, the next New Orleans. One minute the Halifax triumph, the next minute the stench of the Billings decision.

Camel knew that thousands of Native Americans had placed their faith in him, hoping he would have a long run as champion; maybe even prove to be one of the dominant names in boxing. That dream was shattered now.

He chastised himself as he thought about all the people across Montana he felt he'd let down, but Camel could not forgive Montana for the Leroy Murphy injustice. "It was the first world title fight in Montana with a Montana champion and it was taken from Marvin Camel by the Montana Boxing Commission. They don't have a rule so that a boxer can overturn a decision. They have rules to protect promoters and managers, but none to protect boxers."

Emotionally, Camel was enmeshed in an abusive relationship with an unforgiving sport. If Camel had known boxing's "glimmer of light" and "bead of fire," he was now seeing the darker side of it, the disposable nature of heroism and the rotten ground on which it stood. He was embittered by the controversial decisions that had gone against him, by the managers and promoters who, he felt, had ripped him off, and by the departure of those supporters who jumped off the Marvin Camel bandwagon as soon as it hit a rough patch. Why, after cheering him from those barstools and punching vicariously with him through the amateurs and the smokers and HBO shows, did they abandon him now? How can they possibly understand the feeling of reaching the pinnacle of their wildest dreams, only to be blindsided by bureaucracy and bad luck? What is it about this culture that builds up heroes only to tear them down?

Camel understood that if he were to walk away, there would be powerful repercussions. For one thing, his ex-wife and three children depended on him for financial support. Quitting boxing would not put food on their table or coal in their furnace. Would he become just another fighter stranded on boxing's boulevard of broken dreams?

Although Camel once viewed himself as "a representative for the city of Ronan, the Flathead Reservation, and the state of Montana," he now wanted out. *What the hell am I staying here for?* And with that sentiment, he was gone. Montana was in the past. Southern California was now home.

Despite reaching the utmost glory of his profession, Camel found himself struggling for financial survival in Los Angeles. His financial predicament had been made worse by his manager for the Murphy fight, a shadowy figure named Clarence Collins, known as "CC Rider." Camel had met him in a southern California gym. Immediately after the Murphy fight, CC Rider took Camel's $20,000 purse and disappeared.

"What's worse than the loss is what that dirty son-of-a-gun manager did," Camel said in 2013. "He took my gloves and money, boarded the plane, and I've never seen him since. Honest to God, I went back to Ronan, and he jumped on a plane to California. I went to California to find that dirty, lowdown, son-of-a-bitch. It was Norma who told me not to lower myself to his class.

"If I were to see him today, if I saw him walking down the road and he was hit by a car, I would just let him lay there. Even though it isn't in my character, I went out there to snuff him out. I was upset, angry, when I got on that plane."

Norma fully corroborates her husband's account: "That bastard never cared about what he did to Marvin's life. He walked away with every single cent from that fight. Who knows what arrangement Collins made to have that fight taken from Marvin. Yes, Marvin was so upset."

Camel never caught up with Collins, whose career as a manager was short-lived. He changed addresses like pairs of cheap shoes and eventually got out of the sport, presumably with plenty of cash at the expense of others.

After the Murphy fight, Camel had said he would retire if the loss stood. He soon experienced a change of heart. Camel entrenched himself in the Los Angeles boxing scene. He tried becoming his own manager, which proved to be a misadventure from the start. His first scheduled bout after the Murphy loss, for the Continental Americas cruiserweight title in Jacksonville, Florida, was cancelled. The Florida Boxing Commission would not allow it, citing Camel's scar tissue around his eyes and his history as a bleeder. Another fight he negotiated against a South African heavyweight also fell through. Camel had hoped a victory in that bout would lead to a World Boxing Association cruiserweight championship showdown with Piet Crous in South Africa. "I want to win world titles in all three organizations," Camel told a friend.

The move to Los Angeles allowed Camel to stay closer to the fight game, as well as find better sparring partners, including Olympic heavyweight gold medalist Henry Tillman. (Tillman's path to the gold medal in 1984 included twice beating Mike Tyson in the heavyweight division. When they met later as pros, Tyson won.)

Camel told friends and family that he had no intention of moving back to Ronan and the reservation. "There is really nothing calling me back," Camel said. "Being a two-time champion wasn't worth a hill of beans on the reservation. What they want is a totem pole, not a real person. I miss Montana, but not to the point where it is saying, 'I've got to come back'."

Camel hoped that with better sparring partners, his timing would improve to help him avoid getting cut. He was acutely aware of his propensity to bleed, and he knew that his history of cuts had his career on the ropes. "I can see the writing on the wall," Camel said. "I said when I was 24 or 25 that I only had a couple of years left. But my skills are just as good as when I was 28." Camel hoped to stay involved in the game as long as possible, either as a trainer or an advisor to a stable of fighters. "But definitely not a manager," he said. "I've seen what it does to people." When asked by a friend what other plans he had, Camel joked, "Maybe I will have some plastic surgery and try to get into television or movies."

Marvin began to work in a warehouse for a company manufacturing brake lights for Laser Corporation. Norma was part of the development team that worked on "the original and the only collision testing avoidance light tested and proven effective by National Highway Traffic and Safety Administration," according to one of its advertisements. Marvin and three other men formed the assembly line, filling and churning out kits for the "Hi-Lite Collision Avoidance Light." A new federal regulation required all cars manufactured after August 31, 1985, to have a third brake light—and the Laser Corporation tried to profit as quickly as possible before the equipment was made mandatory. "The kit had a lens, tape, and the light, which, at the time, was a novelty item," said Camel.

Pictures of Marvin Camel in the ring in 1986 show a man visibly aging: his hair thinned, his waist thickened slightly, and his face, always difficult to read, displayed a disturbed weariness, the look of a fighter who had stepped into one too many rings. He was proving the law of diminishing returns, fighting more and more for less and less. He fought a ten-round draw on May 22, 1986, with Jimmy Bills, in Boise, Idaho, in front of his idol Muhammad Ali. The Northwest Cruiserweight Championship sat in the middle of the ring—unclaimed.

Most of the time, Bills beat Camel to the punch. Camel lunged around the ring, showing the effects of a long layoff. "I'm satisfied with the draw," Camel said "This was an even fight—not one to win or lose. It was the right decision—especially for the shape I'm in and my age."

"That was a toe-to-toe fight," said Richard Jackson, 67, a long-time trainer who was working in Jimmy Bills' corner for the bout. "We kept Jimmy clean. But we were covered [in blood]. The more Marvin bled, the harder he fought. Marvin was a cutter. I've never had someone bleed on me like that. I don't think I've ever seen any more blood." Jackson said the fight was a "gut check" for Camel and he thought Camel had a slight edge. "It was one hell of a fight. The kind you just don't see or forget. Those days you had to suck it up and fight. There is no gentleman around like Marvin today."

The truth was that Marvin Camel's zip was gone, and with it his long-burning hope of winning a third world title. In August 1986 Camel traveled to Buenos Aires to fight José María Flores Burlón, a native of Uruguay who was the South American Cruiserweight champion. Burlón outpointed Camel in ten rounds.

To add insult to injury, a few days after the loss in Argentina, Marvin received a letter from Charles F. Casas, president of the World Boxing Hall of Fame, who apologized to Camel on behalf of the organization for "overlooking" to invite the two-time cruiserweight champion to its annual "Banquet of Champions" dinner—then in its seventh year. Casas wrote: "On behalf of our Board of Directors, please accept my sincere apology and rest assured that so long as I have anything to do with it this shall never happen again." Norma, Marvin's loving partner, served as Casas' recording secretary but only afterwards did she realize the inadvertent slight.

In 1987 Camel, 36, fought up-and-coming Virgil Hill, 23, in

Hill's 16th professional fight, at Grand Forks City Arena, North Dakota. The fight was scheduled for ten rounds, but within minutes of the opening round it was obvious it would end much sooner. Slow and awkward, Camel never had a chance. Nicknamed "Quicksilver," Hill picked off and blocked almost every punch Camel threw while peppering the former champion with a variety of blows. Camel's legs, arms, and head were all rubber. In the first round Hill caught Camel with a short left hook to win by a knockout. Hill went on to win the WBA light heavyweight title twice and WBA cruiserweight crown as part of a Hall of Fame-earning 50–7 pro record.

In his locker room after the fight, Camel soaked his left hand in a bucket of ice, though he did not seem to have landed a punch solid enough to have injured it. "I seconded the Virgil Hill fight for Marvin," Norma said. "It broke my heart to see him out there. He had to get down to one hundred eighty pounds to make weight for the fight. He was weak, just skin and bones."

"It was at the tail end of my career," Camel said. "I'm not upset about it. Hill was a young guy who was just coming out of the shadows. I was happy for him. In boxing, you have over-the-hill fighters, guys who just show up for the paycheck, and that was me, I guess. Money was tight. I took the fight and hoped for the best. That's how boxing is, one day you are at the top of your game, the next, you are mopping floors."

Camel's decline continued. In October 1987 he found himself in Paris fighting the Tunisian-born Taoufik Belbouli. It was bad enough that Camel got beaten up, losing by TKO in four rounds, but worse, he took the punishment in front of a small live audience in a foreign country for a scant paycheck. (Belbouli later won the WBA cruiserweight title.)

"I couldn't tell you a brief story about any of my later fights in foreign countries," Camel said. "I couldn't even tell you a paragraph about a lot of them. You go in and you're out the next day. There is no sitting back and talking, no hashing out conversations. It is just business."

Camel's body was breaking down. When one of his punches landed wrong, the bones in his hand felt like they had broken. His left shoulder kept popping out of socket. Understanding his role as a poorly compensated sacrificial lamb, Camel demonstrated a steadfast disinclination to train and a halfhearted will to fight, a stark contrast to his younger discipline and drive. In all, Camel was beaten material, the quintessence of the shot fighter. He wasn't present.

"Boxing is a dirty, disgusting, sick business," said Bob Spagnola, manager of current contender and former light middleweight world champion Austin Trout. "When you get to be old, you become the opponent. You are pimped, prostituted and turned into nothing, and no one cares."

Don Majeski, who co-promoted Marvin Camel around the time of his Parlov fights, said Marvin at this time "was just a piece of meat. He was a notch in the belt and there were people out there using him."

Majeski said Camel could have easily used his likability and personality to do something far less dangerous than box. "He was so well-liked and well-spoken," Majeski said. "He could have used those traits to work in public relations or be a good spokesman for something. Perhaps his reputation was hurt by the fact that he allowed people to exploit him in these [later] fights."

Indeed, Camel still had an alluring personality. One morning Norma waited to pick up her husband at the Los Angeles airport when she spotted him arm and arm with another handsome gentleman, chatting amiably. The other man was looming, engaging, and possessed an offbeat energy. His heavy-lidded eyes and laconic drawl practically screamed film noir. He was movie star Robert Mitchum, who repeatedly said he was a fan of Camel and listened with great enthusiasm to Marvin's tales as they sauntered to the baggage claim.

On April 26, 1988, Camel fought and lost to German-born Ralf Rocchigiani in Cologne, Germany. Later that year Camel suffered a sixth-round TKO loss to James Salerno in Milan, Italy.

Against Salerno, Camel again appeared overmatched, and he knew it. As soon as the bell rang, Camel beat a hurried and disorderly retreat. He moved backward for no other purpose than to avoid injury or confrontation. Occasionally, he flicked out a harmless jab, but mostly he just endeavored to stay out of Salerno's way. Sensing Salerno's steadily increasing confidence and Camel's lethargy, the referee stopped the fight.

After boxing, Salerno worked as a landscaper. The August 4, 1999 *Orlando Sentinel* reported that Salerno, age 38, had died three days earlier. It failed to mention his boxing career and said he was murdered in Jacksonville, Florida. The case remains unsolved.

Camel's boxing record was becoming badly tarnished. Now his reputation as a serious fighter had begun to crumble as well. Holding out hope that he could rebuild his myth, he ended up tearing it down. *Remember the skill, the speed, the smile. What happened?*

On August 8, 1989, the *Los Angeles Times* ran an article titled "Boxer to Fight in Montana Despite Past Eye Problems." The piece detailed Camel's attempt to keep fighting despite having been confirmed medically unfit to box in California.

Someone from the paper learned that Matthew Bernstein, the Los Angeles ophthalmologist who discovered Camel's detached retina in 1980, did not submit an accurate medical report on Camel's condition. Bernstein said that he "acted against his better instincts" and regretted not identifying Camel while watching the Sugar Ray Leonard–Roberto Duran "no más" rematch on television. All of a sudden the camera picked up Camel coming down the aisle, preparing to box. Bernstein said he was "shocked and sickened." "Here was a guy with plastic material in his eye, from eye surgery. I was afraid the plastic material holding his eye together would fly out right in the middle of the fight. I've regretted the way I handled that exam ever since....I've never done anything like that, before or since."

Contacted in Montana, Camel said he had had sixteen fights since undergoing retinal surgery. "I was assured by the doctor I was at no greater risk than anyone else," he told the *Los Angeles Times*. "Anyone who gets in the ring takes a risk, and so does anyone who gets on the freeway. I love boxing, that's all."

California and New York are the only states that require an eye exam of first-time boxers, and the California Athletic Commission has a hard policy on boxers who have had detached retinas. They can't get licenses, and they can't even spar. CAC officials once halted Sugar Ray Leonard at Century City just as he was about to spar during a scheduled workout.

It is one of boxing's hoary themes: Aging guy announces comeback, takes some beatings in remote towns, hooks a headline, and tells everyone thanks, but he's perfectly capable of looking after his own affairs. Marvin Camel believed he could look after his own affairs. Aging? Marvin scoffed at the notion that Father Time was undefeated. The fact that he needed an income was an incentivizing factor, too.

Since no national medical or safety standards exist for professional boxing, Camel applied to fight in different states. He applied for a boxing license in Oregon. It was denied. Chuck Minker, executive director of the Nevada Athletic Commission, told the *Los Angeles Times* that Camel would not secure a Nevada license either. He said he would be more concerned about Camel's "gray matter" than his eyes: "At what point does someone say to this guy, 'OK, that's it. No more'."

The point was unmistakable. Marvin Camel was coming to the end of the line as a professional boxer.

Nonetheless, Camel managed to sign on for an eight-round fight in Billings, Montana. When contacted by the *Los Angeles Times*, the Montana Board of Athletics said it was unaware of Camel's history of eye surgery and referenced an ophthalmology report from 1980 that cleared Camel to box.

In 1989, Camel fought three bouts in Montana less than three months apart: the first a draw, then a unanimous decision win, and then an 8-round decision.

After only 73 seconds into the first fight, Camel and his opponent Trent Surrett of Tennessee became entangled and fell to the floor. Camel sprang back into action, but Surrett was hurt. "I hit him with a stiff left jab coming in," said Camel. "He kind of grabbed me around the neck and pulled me to the ground. I could feel his leg coming around under me but it wasn't so hard he was going to cripple himself." The fight was stopped and called a draw.

Camel's ex-wife, Sherry Clairmont, and their three children attended his September 25, ten-round victory over J.J. Cottrell in Butte. Watching his dad fight in the ring was one of Cass Camel's earliest memories of his father. The hole-punched, twine-bounded scrapbook, yellow newspaper clippings, and old photos all came to life. "I remember the cheering, the crowd rooting for my dad, and being glad I was there," said Cass. "I was angry at him for a time, still."

Next up was Camel's last victory in the boxing ring—which came in the shape of an eight-round victory over Jerome Hill. "Sometime during the fight, Marvin's shoulder went out," said Kevin McCarl, a veteran boxing referee who was in attendance as a spectator that night. "So the referee gives Marvin the eight count and while he is counting, Marvin's wife [Norma] jumps up on the apron and snaps his shoulder back into place. She popped it back into the joint. And then he goes on to fight."

Marvin imposed his will on the hapless Hill, and the win was a source of pride, a slim silver lining in a darkening career, notwithstanding the fact that Hill was never a good boxer. When Hill retired from boxing in 2002, his career record was 1 win, 48 losses. In those 49 fights, Hill was knocked out thirty times. His sole victory came in September 1987, and he didn't win another fight in the remaining fifteen years he entered the ring.

Nonetheless, Camel interpreted the victory as a sign of encouragement; admitting that he was rusty but encouraged that he could still fight like a contender. This was pure delusion. But Camel kept telling himself that with more training, a few tune-ups, he would be back in top form.

Camel was always supremely confident, if not undeniably detached from the realities of age and natural wear and tear. Norma wanted Marvin to exit gracefully. To her, hearing that he was going to keep returning to action was like hearing that polio was making a comeback.

Camel next fought Joe Hipp, a Blackfoot born on the Blackfeet Indian Reservation in Browning, Montana, across the Continental Divide from Camel's Flathead Reservation. If there is another Native American fighter besides Camel who can offer pupils a wealth of boxing knowledge, it would be Hipp. With his traditional eagle feathered head dress passed down to him from his grandfather—a spectacular representation of authentic Blackfeet tribal regalia—Hipp is an equally proud man.

The two fighters clashed in Lacey, Washington, on December 2, 1989. Like Marvin, Joe Hipp wore his headdress into the ring The fight was stopped in the sixth round when the referee ruled Camel unable to continue.

"Joe Hipp had tricked me," said Camel. "We sparred before and I expected the big lumbering lumberjack that I knew. But when we got together, he got in shape and he was better. In the fight, I hit him with a left hook that popped my shoulder out of the socket. Hipp was throwing his weight around, and the ref saw I was in pain. The referee jumped in because I threw my shoulder out of place, not because I was out-powered."

However, the bout was actually halted because of cuts to Camel's eyes. "They weren't that bad of cuts," said Bob LeCoure of the Ring Hotel, Camel's training grounds. "I was really surprised the doctor stopped it."

When the end came, Hipp was leading on all three of the judges' cards. Camel, at 185 pounds, said he was starting to affect the 230-pound Hipp in the later rounds. "He was grunting like a pig every time I got to his solar plexus." "We figured body shots were the only way to get to this big guy," LeCoure said "Marvin really figured he could go with a heavyweight —and he can. But this guy was just too damn big and young and strong." Hipp bumped his record to 10–1.

Joe Hipp started fighting when he was eight and enjoyed a pro career that included winning the World Boxing Federation's version of the heavyweight title in June 1999. In reality, Hipp reached the pinnacle of his career four years earlier when he challenged Bruce Seldon for his World Boxing Council title in Las Vegas, on the undercard of Mike Tyson's comeback bout against Peter McNeeley. Hipp showed characteristic grit in the knockout loss.

In 2002, Hipp, along with another Yakima Valley boxer, Pete Rademacher, were among 23 boxers inducted into the Northwest Boxing Hall of Fame. Proud, soft-spoken, likable, the Montana native said that even though the two men fought in the ring, his recollection of Marvin Camel is indubitably positive.

"I first met Marvin Camel in Butte," recalled Joe Hipp. "We trained at the Grand Hotel, I believe it was, down in the basement. We were both down there working out, and I got along with him very well. He was soft-spoken, nice, humble, and I enjoyed meeting him. I remember watching him work out, he went fifteen, sixteen, eighteen rounds on the heavy bag. He was a unique person who worked hard, I looked up to him as a fighter. If Marvin could make it, so can I.

"After I came back from Butte and had met him, his name came up for the fight. It was one of the weirdest fights I ever was part of. He kept talking to me the whole fight, kept looking over, kept talking. He would talk to me during a clench, and it was hard for me to get my head back in this fight. He was coming down on his career but still had the strength of the warrior mentality."

At this point in his career, the only thing Marvin Camel should have been fighting was the urge to fight. "There are a lot of 'L' marks on my record toward the end," said Camel. "You know, the last fights I took for the money. When I went out to box, there was nothing there. I couldn't get the job done."

Every fighter has heart. Marvin Camel had heart. A really big heart. What that begins to mean, though, once you scrub away the endearing sound of it, was that he could take endless punishment. He could be pummeled round after round, bleed all over the canvas, endure the cruelest of onslaughts, and then somehow, some way, just before the ref was about to jump in and end the slaughter, mount a rally and keep the fight going. That's a cruel thing to call "heart." Camel showed this ability to endure over and over again in scores of bouts that were frequently futile and didn't serve his career—or bank account—much purpose.

Young Joe Louis took on old Marvin Camel in the feature event of a boxing card on June 11, 1990, at the Hyatt Regency in downtown Minneapolis. It was billed as the "Brawl on the Mall." Afterward, some of the five hundred onlookers, which included members of the Minnesota Vikings football team and other sports stars, referred to the fight as the "Riot at the Hyatt." Louis, 33, claimed a ten-round split decision over Camel, 39, a champion past his prime. Camel was fit and muscular for this fight, but he was out-boxed and out-hit.

It was Camel's last fight—and not necessarily because he didn't want to fight on. Closing in on 40, he was viewed as too shopworn to rivet interest, a veritable geriatric risk. "It took too much to get opposition because of the detached retina," said Camel. "Word got out and promoters wouldn't return calls from my new promoter Moe Smith. They thought I was a has-been. They thought I had had enough."

Whether he wanted to admit it or not, Camel was sapped of energy. In reality, he had lost the prerequisite strength much earlier, perhaps even years earlier when he felt he was robbed in the Lee Roy Murphy fight. He had reached his goals. It was no longer as easy or practical to make the commitments of dedication and self-sacrifice. He was beginning to think about not being a substandard stepping stone. He was beginning to think about a good life away from the isolation and punishment of a training camp.

Camel knew he could stick around and pick up a paycheck here and there, but he also understood that his days as a contender had passed. His opponents were too fast, too well conditioned, too confident. It was time to exit with brains and mind intact, to begin again. After 17 years of professional boxing, Camel's final record was 45 wins, 13 losses, and four draws—and two world championships.

Marvin Camel loved boxing. He loved everything about it. He loved the punches and all the lavish footwork. He liked the sweat and the smell of leather. He liked the tit-for-tat exchanges and the spiraling out of control. He liked the diet, the exercise, the routine, the configuration of each day. He liked the individuality, the respect of other fighters, the admiration of fans. He loved the privilege of being considered a fan favorite. He even came to love the shining dizziness and bubbling drunkenness that came after being punched.

He would miss all of it.

19

DISRESPECTED DIVISION

WHEN CAMEL BOXED, THE CRUISERWEIGHT DIVISION WAS NEW, fringy, and subcultural, and too unknown. Today the cruiserweight division remains boxing's proverbial red-headed stepchild—an indistinguishable bracket of unpleasant associations. It garners little respect and less attention, having failed to evolve into an integral part of the sport.

"The casual boxing fan from the United States most likely couldn't spell cruiserweight," said boxing analyst and insider Frank Stea, "let alone tell you who the best American cruiserweight is. You are more likely to find the bones of Jimmy Hoffa before you find a world-rated cruiserweight fight in this country."

The peculiar point is, if legendary heavyweight champions such as Jack Dempsey, Joe Louis and Rocky Marciano were inserted into today's fight game, they would be cruiserweights. Dempsey weighed 187 pounds the day he knocked out Jess Willard for the heavyweight title. Louis weighed 197¼ when he ended the "Cinderella Man" reign of Jim Braddock. Marciano tipped the scales at 184½ the day he flattened Jersey Joe Walcott for the heavyweight championship.

"Cruiserweight is really the premiere weight division," said former boxing promoter and manager Dave Elsberry. "If you look at the UFC (Ultimate Fighting Championship), cruiserweight is the premiere weight division. In boxing, it is the bastard division."

When the cruiserweight division turned thirty-five years old in

2014, it marked three and a half decades of fighters being disrespected because they represented a "bastard" division one notch below the most glamorous weight class in boxing. That lack of respect continued even when Evander Holyfield unified the division in 1988. His renown came later when he succeeded as a heavyweight.

"There hasn't been such a dominant cruiserweight world champion besides Evander Holyfield," said Stea. "Now there have been a couple of modern undisputed champions in the division such as O'Neil Bell and most recently David Haye. Though they should be commended for their accomplishments, both Bell and Haye beat a weak class of opposition. In no way, shape or form did they exhibit the complete dominance that Holyfield had done throughout the 1980s.

"Holyfield, though dominant at cruiserweight, reigned for less than two years as the champion before eventually moving up to heavyweight. Much like every other fighter in the past starting out at cruiserweight, it only seemed to be a springboard division for their eventual slide into the heavyweight ranks."

Frenchman Jean-Marc Mormeck became the first unified cruiserweight champ since Evander Holyfield when he decisioned previously unbeaten WBC champ Wayne "Big Truck" Braithwaite in April 2005.

Before the fight, Braithwaite understood that a unified title could give him the recognition he craved. "I want to unify the belts. I am the man in the division, and if I have to go through everybody to prove it, I will. This division needs a spark, and I am it," he said. "I am hoping that after this fight, the division will get a star and will generate a lot of excitement and a lot of money in the division." Outside of devout boxing fans, Braithwaite remained an unknown quantity.

For a division stigmatized for being disappointing, the brief history of cruiserweights reflects some pretty good offerings. Sure enough, the first great cruiserweight bouts involved the Reservation Champ, Marvin Camel, versus Mate Parlov in 1979 and 1980.

"Marvin Camel was in the wrong era in a brand new division," said Frank Stea, boxing radio host and insider. "I guess you could say that he fell victim to being in the right place at the wrong time. He was ahead of his time. There is nobody in 2013 in the cruiserweight division who can captivate people in the manner of Marvin Camel. If he were fighting today, he'd be fighting for high six-figure purses all over the world."

Sean O'Grady, who won the WBA lightweight championship in 1981 and went on to a successful career as a boxing commentator, remembered Camel: "He was awesome. My father, Pat, and I would watch Mr. Camel's fights with great interest and my father would have me try to emulate Marvin. Yes, he was great. But being a cruiserweight was hard to get noticed."

After Marvin Camel left the game, the division served up several legitimate talents (James Toney, Vassiliy Jirov, David Haye and Tomasz Adamek) and no shortage of decent fights: Toney against Jirov; Holyfield verse Dwight Qawi; and Adamek–Steve Cunningham; all Fight-of-the-Year contenders who did not get the respect they would have gotten if the guys had weighed a pound or two more.

Following the Camel-Parlov bouts, it was not until June 15, 1986, when Smokin' Bert Cooper fought Henry Tillman, that the division had another memorable bout. Cooper was a protégé of Smokin' Joe Frazier, and Tillman was the man who bounced Mike Tyson from the 1984 U.S. Olympic Trials. This was years before Cooper succumbed to drugs and bloated up to heavyweight. He was still enjoying the glow of his Olympic gold medal and had recently captured the NABF cruiserweight crown, which he attained with a first round knockout of veteran Bash Ali.

Cooper entered the fight with a record of 11–1, Tillman 10–0. Fighting out of a crouch and setting an irate pace, Cooper dropped Tillman twice early and earned a twelve-round decision for the NABF belt.

Perhaps the most eventful fight in the division took place July 12, 1986. It was Evander Holyfield's twelfth pro fight and Qawi's thirtieth. Qawi had already reigned as a champion at 175 and won his second title at cruiserweight. Two years removed from an Olympic bronze medal, Holyfield set a blistering pace. Holyfield would deliver a fertile 1,290 punches and capture a split decision over fifteen rounds.

Holyfield and Qawi have been inducted into the International Boxing Hall of Fame, the first—and perhaps only—cruiserweight match in which both participants became hall of famers.

Another memorable moment took place April 9, 1988, when Holyfield challenged Marvin Camel's old nemesis Carlos De Leon. Not a distinguished bout, but Holyfield's 8th-round TKO made him the division's first undisputed champion. At career's end, De Leon had won and lost the WBC cruiserweight title three times.

A few years later, on March 8, 1991, Bobby Czyz won a split decision over Robert Daniels to become a two-division champion. In his final significant victory, Czyz slyly outboxed Daniels to earn the belt. Czyz, who held the IBF light heavyweight and WBA cruiserweight belts during his 18-year career, is a member of both the New Jersey Boxing Hall of Fame and Mensa, a club for people with high IQ scores.

"It was a significant fight for me for a couple of reasons," said Czyz, who was raised in the slums of East Orange, New Jersey. "It validated me as a legitimate talent and because Daniels was a 4 to 1 favorite. I made six figures from it. With that said, the cruiserweight division was always a lonely division from a press and publicity standpoint."

Even though appealing fights continued to take place, the cold-shoulder of the division continued into the new millennium. In 2001, the unheralded Vassiliy Jirov was defending the cruiserweight belt, or at least one of the most prized portions of it. Jirov was the light heavyweight champion and most outstanding boxer of the 1996 Olympics. At one point he was unbeaten in 29 professional fights.

"I just did my job," said the native of Kazakhstan, who lives in Phoenix. "I didn't get frustrated. I just took it one fight at a time."

Jirov made his debut as a professional January 18, 1997, with a two-round knockout of Vince Brown in Las Vegas. He won eleven fights in his first year, all by knockout, including wins over Exum Speight and Art Jimmerson. In 1999, Jirov competed for his first world title, in front of an HBO audience, and beat IBF champion Arthur Williams by a knockout in seven rounds at Biloxi, Mississippi. "The thing about winning as a cruiserweight," said Jirov. "You never feel as if the door is open one hundred percent, or the door is open fully. Does that make sense?"

In 2008, legendary boxing trainer Angelo Dundee wrote in his memoirs that he never could "figure out what a "cruiserweight" was. "I know it's bigger than a breadbox and smaller than a battleship, but what's the weight limit?" he wrote.

While there may not be a Marciano-Louis-Dempsey talent currently competing at cruiserweight, the division is what heavyweight boxing once was: a home to some of the most athletic big men in boxing. Curiously, cruiserweight boxing has no trouble attracting interest outside of the United States. In 2013, cruiserweight titlists were a Russian, a Pole, a Cuban, even a Panamanian. But no American.

MARVIN CAMEL STOPPED WATCHING BOXING MANY YEARS AGO. He was close to the fight game when he lived in Los Angeles, but as he and Norma moved around—Torrance, Redondo Beach, and Wellington—they felt more and more detached from it. If needed, the former champ could still put on an exhibition, as one rambunctious garbage collector discovered. "The garbage man wasn't doing his job," said Norma. "He was a big, tall, six-foot five-inches, three-hundred-fifty pound black man. Marvin was trying to be polite, but the guy took a swing at Marvin, and the champ ducked and then clocked him in the jaw and solar plexus." The hyperventilating hulk was so humiliated by the much smaller man having knocked him out that he left it at that. "It was lovely," Norma said.

In 1993 Marvin and Norma married and moved to Lake County, Florida. The warm weather was a factor, and Norma's parents had wintered in Florida for years.

Camel missed boxing immensely. Even things he didn't think he would miss, he was nostalgic for: rising at 4:30 A.M., which he had been doing daily since he was a teenager; resisting the irresistible aromas wafting from kitchens; the rigors of cutting weight; having every moment of every day scripted toward a single goal. He knew such little normalcy for most of his life that when it all finally stopped and the pendulum swung, it was natural that it paused indefinitely at an aimless position. *What's next?*

Starting in 1993 Camel worked at a Circuit City warehouse near Groveland. He unloaded, separated, and reloaded heavy freight at the regional distribution center. "Don't go home until the job is done," said Camel. "When I was at Circuit City, I wanted to be one of the greatest workers ever at Circuit City."

Camel experienced a good deal of restlessness about his salary—the feeling that he was underpaid. Similar to most boxers who have gained—and lost—attractive paychecks, there was a general dissatisfaction with his deflated finances. But if he began to ruminate too strongly, he would catch himself: *The more I would have made, the more I would have lost.* His economic doubt added a kind of humbleness to his demeanor. He wasn't unhappy with his life, he only felt obscure. At times, he faced depression.

Physically, he added a few pounds and started to feel the residuals of going to war in the ring. Occasionally, his eye that suffered the detached retina became blurry. There were bad headaches.

On October 19, 1996, Henry Williams Camel passed away. He spent his last years in relative solitude. Although he had not seen his famous boxer son for decades, he did spend his last few years trying to cultivate champions of his two youngest sons—Marvin's stepbrothers.

Kenny Keene, 46, is an ex-boxer from Idaho who retired in 2006 with a 51–4 record. He fought at cruiserweight and was known as "The Emmett Eliminator." He recalled Henry as a "good, decent man." He remembered Henry and his second wife, Mildred, and their four children. He said that Henry's three sons, Zack, Bill, and J.R., boxed as a way of reconciling the cultural divide at school. "They were the only dark-skinned kids in Homedale, which was mostly or all Mormon, I think. He said he didn't want them to be vulnerable." Keene remembered that Henry had a peculiar sense of humor, often cracking about the number of children he fathered. Henry would quip, "I'm just a cigarette or two short of making a pack full of Camels," Keene said.

Marvin's mother, Alice, seemed to have retained a soft spot for Henry. "I remember Mom's face brighten up when they would yell that he was coming up the lane," said Renee Camel. "That's when I realized that she still cared for him. He didn't want to get divorced, but she was too angry. He was a womanizer, I guess. We never found anything in Mom's things of Henry's. She had letters from him that she kept close though."

Rosary services for Henry took place in Montana on Monday, October 21, and funeral services were held the next afternoon at St. Ignatius Catholic Church on the Flathead Reservation. The inside page of the mass program showed an illustration of a camel and of eagle feathers tied to a pair of boxing gloves bearing the name "Camel." Between the drawings were the words "Desert Horse."

On that day, although he did not attend the service, Marvin clutched Henry deep in his thoughts. His father's death stirred sentiments of emulation, ambition, and self-criticism. Resentment was a menace Marvin carted in his heart for Henry. In truth, no matter how unimpeded, unhurt, or strong Marvin believed that he was, he transported a soft emotion for his father. And whether he liked to acknowledge it or not, Henry's disregard for him pained him and played into his relationship with his own children. Absent father or not, those words, those instructions, that harshness, it motivated him—damn sure it did.

"Discipline" is a difficult word for most of us. It conjures up images of somebody standing over you with a stick, telling you that you're wrong. Whatever Henry was or wasn't as a parent, he definitely provided discipline—and that disciple encouraged and frightened his children into doing great things. *Nobody in the world is better than you. Nobody better than yourself, son. You'd better work. You'd better strive to be the best you can be. Get out there and show yourself. Don't turn away from the carnage. You want another shot in your ribcage, boy? Protect yourself. No self-pity. Be proud. Be strong.*

Henry and Alice had divorced when Marvin was in his late teens, but not before the elder Camel imparted the attribute of discipline that Marvin links with his success. The younger Camel absorbed the value of discipline through the seat of his pants and turned it into dedication and pragmatism. He believes it was his father's perfectionist attitude, and the resulting pressure that he placed upon his children to do everything at their best, that drove his success. "He was a slave driver," said Marvin. "I tasted that belt a lot of times. But I am who and what I am thanks to it."

In 2002 Camel was honored at the Northwest Boxing Hall of Fame in Coeur d'Alene, Idaho. Waiting to greet him at the ceremony was Chauncy Welliver, a Gros Ventres–Assiniboine with bloodlines originating in the Wolf Point and Poplar areas of Montana. Welliver began boxing professionally in 2001 and picked up several titles in more than 60 bouts. As of 2014, he stood semi-retired.

"Marvin Camel was someone that everyone looked up to," said Welliver, 31, who trained under Blackfeet heavyweight Joe Hipp. "What he did went beyond just winning a title. He made us stand out as good, not just as a bunch of drunken Indians. He proved that we could make it in athletics."

Welliver spoke with Camel, and he compared the mood of that exchange to the childlike-kick of Christmas morning. "It was such a treat," said Welliver. "He may have not meant something to the mainstream, but he meant something to us in the northwest. He did it for himself. He overcame. He accomplished so much with little opportunity. He made Native Americans proud."

20

A NEW LIFE ELSEWHERE

As human beings, we need to protect ourselves. We have to be snug. We have to feel that we're somebody. We need to believe that the dreams we followed were the right ones.

Later in his life, Marvin Camel's deepest and ultimate purpose was to look at himself and find what he saw as good. In the summer of 2005, Camel returned to Ronan to visit family and friends and to talk about his earliest dreams. There was a bottomless pit of boxing talk from Marvin—mostly highly-detailed monologues—and parleys with his brother, Kenny, about finding the next great Montana boxer. Yet even when Marvin talked about the future, of perhaps one day instructing a bright prospect in his own gym in Montana, his talk unconsciously devolved into his past—what was, what had been.

Staring at the mountains on cool nights, Marvin thought about the possibility that here was another way to live, another place to be. He had been disconnected from Montana and the reservation for so long. But in his siblings who remained on the reservation, he saw a world alien to him. He remembered the winters and their cold, isolating qualities. Outside of family, he had no intimate friends here.

In between walks and interactions with family, Camel felt adrift. He wondered if the Flathead could give him the kind of connection to life that he needed. *What are these distant things— this distant place? Who are these distant people? Where are these distant voices coming from? Where is my new direction? Is this my home? What would my ancestors want for me?* He saw the land as beautiful and green and magical. But just a few thoughts later, there would be a countervailing sense of wanting to leave.

A photo of Marvin appeared in the Salish *Char-Koosta News* on August 11, 2005. Part of the Camel clan, including Kenny and Alice Nenemay Camel, made time for a group shot with family members. A handful of Marvin's friends and kin stopped by the Valley Club Bar on a Monday night to relive Camel's legacy. Valley Club Bar owner Kenny Snyder grew up with Marvin. "I sparred with Marvin for about three seconds," joked Snyder

Friend Larry Richards, who first met Marvin in a boxing ring decades ago when Richards was fourteen, said Marvin looked good: "It was always nice to see him return. He looked like the same kid—tall and thin, in great shape—that same kid who was so difficult to hit and difficult to box so many years ago."

Memories abounded. Memories are funny—sometimes they don't reflect the truth, sometimes they leave even the most unsentimental man in a peculiar bout of maudlin. Returning to the community of his youth and upbringing touched Marvin. It made him reflect on the fragility of life. "Seems like I was a kid yesterday, now I'm 54," Camel said.

In Ronan, friends noticed how Marvin would purposely take the long way around town, hoarding all manner of greetings, smiles, backslaps, high-fives, autograph requests, before settling into his routine. Marvin still sought approbation, recognition of who he was and what he had meant, especially to the people of Flathead Nation. He wanted to feel at home. He wanted to feel the love or approval of his family, friends, and people. He wanted his life to be an inspiration for young people. But a cycle of emotion developed on such trips: once the seemingly ecstatic welcome was over, reality set in. That reality factored in profound childhood grief and ill-addressed feelings of inferiority and pain. Memories can be hidden but not the history that produced them.

Visits stirred up old wounds and sibling rivalries, and, among most strangers and youth, the novelty of the world champion was evanescent like melting snow. Life was forward. But Marvin only identified with his life when speaking and thinking in reverse.

In 2006 at the World Boxing Council's 44th annual convention, WBC President Jose Sulaiman awarded Marvin Camel and Mate Parlov honorary champion status. Held in Croatia, it provided a dignified trip for Camel. Years earlier, around the time that he and Sherry were at the height of their domestic discord, Marvin (and others) claim that she took some of the champ's boxing memorabilia into the woods and buried it. Among the gems lost: the WBC cruiserweight championship belt. Aware of the loss, the WBC presented him with a double.

Apparently a boxing fan named Robert Newman had pushed the WBC to replace the belt. Newman was an upstate New York health care worker and freelance boxing writer. Newman and Camel sealed a friendship one year earlier. He found his first meeting with the former champion to be a rendezvous with one appreciative ex-fighter.

"I've always been interested in obscure guys from the 1970s and 1980s," said Newman. "I knew that the first cruiserweight champion had a father who was half-black, was a Flathead Indian, and was a completely unique, oddball character. In 2005, I was visiting a friend who was living south of Marvin and got in touch with him. He was down-to-earth and hospitable. We spent seven hours talking and looking at chronological scrapbooks. He had clippings from Montana newspapers from when he was in the amateurs. He had giant, oversized scrapbooks of his fights in other countries and brought out a box of VHS tapes. He was so proud, so knowledgeable."

Newman wrote to the WBC and spoke with WBC president Jose Sulaiman's son, Mauricio. The WBC responded by inviting both Parlov and Camel to its next convention. Over the course of two days, Marvin found himself on planes from Florida to New

Jersey, Newark to Rome, and after a seven hour layover, Rome to Dubrovnik, Croatia.

"The WBC made me feel worthwhile," said Camel. "It was good to see Mate again. Mate was sitting around in the restaurant singing country and western songs and drinking a beer at closing time. Mate liked John Denver a lot. We shot the bull a little bit. I knew he wasn't really happy. I guess, after the fights we had he went into seclusion and felt that maybe he should have won the first fight. We had a question-and-answer session and were introduced as celebrity guests. He didn't speak very good English. We spent time discussing times gone by. We talked, and talked, and talked."

"It was great seeing the two of them together," said Newman, 50. "Parlov came in with a couple of buddies. He gestured to Marvin, and his eyes lit up. Parlov said, 'You look good.' It was in perfect English."

"My father always spoke highly of Marvin Camel," said Mauricio Sulaiman, current president of the World Boxing Council. (His father, Jose Sulaiman, died in January 2014, at age 82. Jose was elected president of the WBC in 1975 and ruled for 38 years.) "He thought that Marvin really helped the cruiserweight division go from not being accepted to a recognized division. When Camel and Parlov met, they were hugging. And it was a beautiful thing to see. Attendants from all over the world were humbled by such demonstration that both gave us as they hugged each other in tears. Marvin will always be an icon for the WBC. He set the behavior and example on how they—the boxers—should and shouldn't behave in and out of the ring."

In a shining example of the most bittersweet irony, the WBC replacement belt was embedded with images of Joe Louis and Muhammad Ali—and a pair of blurry photos bearing Camel's likeness. The WBC didn't have a better image of Marvin in their archives.

No matter. Marvin didn't take his eyes off the belt, almost as if doubting it was real. It did more than just give him back his peace of mind, it justified his existence.

"Marvin didn't take the belt off for the whole week," said Newman, who shared a room with Marvin. "He wore it around his t-shirt, his pajamas, under his suit. I think he only took it off to take a shower. If he wore it with a jacket, he parted the jacket. Every time he walked into a meeting or a room, he was beaming. No guy was prouder to wear that belt than Marvin. He slept with the belt...."

Among other belongings that have disappeared—perhaps also buried in the Montana woods—was Camel's ceremonial hand-stitched vest and his favorite Native American headdress, which he wore as symbol of tribute to his land and people.

In October 2008, Marvin Camel, 57, was located in a position that surprised virtually no one: training other boxers, this time in Lake County, Florida. In the late afternoons, Camel laced up and taped his sparring gloves from three decades ago and stepped into the ring for a little bit of action. Credence Clearwater Revival was still a mainstay as the champ taught and trained students. "As far as Credence goes," said Camel, "I have no favorite. They are all good." From the band's "Bad Moon Rising:"

I hear hurricane's a-blowing.
I know the end is coming soon.
I fear rivers overflowing.
I hear the voice of rage and ruin.
Don't go around tonight,
Well, it's bound to take your life,
There's a bad moon on the rise.

When visitors dropped in on Camel, they discovered what virtually every other person had discovered long ago, a remarkably unaffected, decent, considerate, humorous man. If one expected to find some punch-drunk, down-at-the-heels pug who could not mumble a coherent sentence, they would be mistaken.

Camel's boxing students discovered he could still box. "There's nothing they could do to surprise me," said Camel. "If they drop their hands, I'll give 'em a little shot and ask, 'What happened?'"

Camel teased his sparring partners about making a comeback. Some thought he was only kidding but Marvin's intensity suggested he was crazy enough to try it. "I never really quit," he told them. "I still got one good fight left. For all we know, it could be in the next ten minutes."

Camel and business partner Ronald Lopez opened Unique Boxing in Tavares, Florida, in the summer of 2008. They met while volunteering at Omega Zone in Eustis, Florida. Lopez, who had been around boxing for thirty years as a trainer and fan, said he was in awe of Camel.

"I know how hard it is to accomplish what he has accomplished," said Lopez. "It's an honor just to be around him. He's a legend."

The gym had students from age eight to thirty-five years old. Camel worked with as many as twenty-five students on a good day. On a bad day, he had around fifteen athletes willing to invest two-and-a-half to three hours of their day to learn how to box. The athletes paid a membership fee of $30 a month, which got them eight workouts with Camel. He hoped his work ethic and drive would whip them into condition and build character. He seemed to take great pleasure in transmitting his experiences with boxing and all of its ambient levels of misery and beauty. "I want to be in their corner because they need someone in their corner. We're going to become champions. If we don't become champions we know what we did wrong."

One of the students, Tony Benavides, 21, said he had always liked to watch boxing on television when he was younger, and he always wished he could do it. He never thought he would be getting in the ring with a champion, though. "I get a little nervous," said Benavides, "because I don't want to disappoint him. I want to show him that I'm learning."

Camel traveled with Lopez and students to amateur boxing events where the students competed against fighters from Florida, Georgia, and Alabama. "I'm looking for something," Camel said.

"I want to create an amateur champion from the state of Florida." He could see great things in the future, even though his students were "as green as grass."

He found a distinct pride in teaching boxing to a new generation of outcastes and underachievers. "I've found if you work with the underdogs they'll work right along with you," said Camel. "I think of myself as an underdog and I always want to think of myself as an underdog."

Camel enjoyed his time in the gym and reliving the role of the champion. His Omega Zone Warriors competed in local cards. He loved to display the skills reminiscent of the warrior he once was in the ring. He never sees the old, weary fighter he promised himself he would never become—but became. And why should he? He sees the champ and projects all the strength and confidence one would expect a champ to possess. At one point, he thought that retirement would devastate him. He was right. It did. But in some ways, it provided him with an overwhelming sense of relief. Glory days could now be revisited in the safety and comfort of the rearview mirror.

On July 31, 2008, Serbian President Boris Tadic sent condolences to the family of boxer Mate Parlov, who had died in Pula, Croatia, two days earlier. Parlov was a boxing legend in the former Yugoslavia and the general populace never forgot that he held two boxing matches in Belgrade, the Serbian capital. Ordinary Croatians were touched by the news of his passing.

Parlov was 60. No cause of death was immediately announced, but it was later attributed to lung cancer. Parlov was an outstanding amateur, winning Olympic Gold at light heavyweight in 1972, the European championship in 1971 and 1973. With around 300 amateur fights under his belt, he turned pro in 1975. Mate never capitalized on his tricky, southpaw style in the pros. He beat several good fighters (John Conteh, Miguel Angel Cuello, and Tony Mundine), but lost to more notables ones (Matthew Franklin and Marvin Johnson). He held the EBU light heavyweight title in 1976-77. His shining moment was fighting for the WBC cruiserweight title against Marvin Camel, fighting to a draw the first time, then losing the rematch. Losing the rematch broke Parlov physically and mentally. In 1980 he retired with a record of 24–3–2 and left boxing.

In his later years, Parlov moved back to Pula, where he owned a cafe. He didn't follow boxing at all, calling modern day pro-boxing a "circus" and deriding its countless titles. When there was a big show in Pula, Parlov didn't attend despite invitations. He did, however, accept the WBC Belt of Honor in 2007.

Camel was working at Circuit City when a friend said he was going to look up Marvin's career on Google. Camel was sitting next to his coworker watching stories about himself on the computer monitor when a story appeared about Parlov's death that very day. Marvin burst into tears. He felt dismally alone. He'd lost an opponent-turned-friend, his other half who forever linked him with the outside world.

That night Marvin went to the gym and gathered his young boxers. "We were standing around and at the end of the session I said, 'Before we all go I would like to tell you all something about a man you won't know anything about." The kids looked at him blankly. "I'd like to tell you about a gentleman who I fought by the name of Mate Parlov…," Marvin said, with his voice crumbling. The students stood and listened as he talked them through a pair of fifteen-round fights and detailed how the two rivals wound up friends.

The following morning friend Robert Newman called Marvin to deliver the bad news. "Marvin answered the phone and his very first words were, 'I know why you are calling.' He started bawling, and he was emotional and very stricken. He talked about the bond—the bond between the two fighters."

Even today, Camel's voice trembles and cracks and there are long pauses of silence when he speaks of Parlov. "What's really sad about it is that I considered him a friend of mine," said Camel. "After he lost the bout between him and I, Mate went into seclusion, bought a little bar, a gin mill, and closed himself in. He kept the world out. I feel sorry that he went into seclusion. He had a good career. He had his good days and also had his bad days. If he didn't have his bad days, I would have never been the champion. I've never set out to talk to opponents, before or after. But I called him a friend. It's a job we had to do. I don't hold grudges against opponents."

In some ways, Marvin will never be whole again: the rival who completed and defined him is no longer here. Every now and then, Marvin watches the fights against Parlov with a bittersweet sense of irony.

"I see we both did the best we could," Camel said. "The action was back and forth. He thought he won the first time, and I don't think I lost it, so they called it a draw. I felt a little let down, but then I didn't lose, so we had another fight.

"It wasn't my hometown, but I didn't lose there and I felt vindicated. But that doesn't mean the belt was just given to me. I had to fight Mate to get it. I caught him with some good shots and he was a good, tough fighter. I guess I just showed my wares better than he showed his."

On Sunday, July 25, 2010, Marvin's mother, Alice Nenemay Camel, passed away from natural causes at St. Luke's Community Hospital in Missoula. She spent most of her final months in her living room with the TV on low, accompanied by her children and comforted by the omnipresent photographs that decked the walls. Scarcely an inch of her little blue house was absent of a memory. Before she left, she said, "Do not cry for me for I am, at last, at peace." She was 90.

The Nenemay Range, a unit of land across the river from and north of Dixon, was named in honor of Alice after the Confederated Salish and Kootenai Tribes purchased the land in December 1999. According to Renee Camel, Alice was perhaps "the most fluent Pend d'Oreille speaker on the reservation."

21

HARSH WIND

A STRETCH OF NARROW BLACKTOP ROAD RUNS NORTHWEST OUT Ronan, Montana, and its image has remained in Marvin Camel's memory for decades. Whenever he sees his name in print or hears it or otherwise stumbles across the relic of his career, he remembers the road, straight and raised above flat dark fields that reached toward the horizon on either side. He would run past two-story square, weathered-gray shacks of his neighbors spotted every hundred yards or so along the road. *I need to get away. Away and away.*

Bad news on Indian reservations, it seems, is an endlessly renewable resource. Crime data put out by the United States Bureau of Justice Statistics confirms that tribal land is more violent than non-tribal land. According to the 2010 report, 4.8 million people lived on reservations or in Alaska Native villages, yet "the 1,479 suspects investigated for violent offenses in Indian country represented 23 percent of all federal investigations for violent offenses in fiscal year 2010." The number of Indian country suspects investigated by U.S. attorneys for property, drug, and other offenses increased fifty percent from 2000 to 2010. According to a Department of Justice report released in October 2012, Native American and Alaska Native women are raped at rates higher than women of any other race, and yet sexual assault is among the most under-reported crimes.

A Blackfeet Native and direct descendant of Chief Heavy Runner, Misty Upham was born on the Blackfeet reservation in Montana. She left the reservation at age 12 after a traumatic sexual assault. She ended up in California working as a housemaid, all the while focused on her dreams of Hollywood. She succeeded. Upham had a splendid year in 2013 with important roles in two major movies: *Jimmy P.: Psychotherapy of a Plains Indian* and the critically acclaimed *August: Osage County* with film icons Meryl Streep and Julia Roberts. Upham recently started an anti-rape campaign for indigenous women.

"I receive death threats all the time for speaking out," said Upham, 32. "Sometimes my people—and I can say that because I'm full-blooded—don't understand what freedom is. I feel sorry for the conditions right now on reservations, especially for young people. Anger is all that they have. I'm so lucky. But to be honest, the fear never goes away. I've tried to kill myself twice, and I constantly deal with the trauma I went through. I drink and get self-violent. While I'm here on this earth, I want to let people know that rape is violence and is a big fucking deal. But on the reservation, it's normal. I am not angry at the reservation, but just feeling extremely sorry for them. We are perpetuating our own demise and dysfunction."

Emphasizing this social chaos, in 2012 two of Marvin Camel's three sons were either in jail or facing the prospect of incarceration. On July 25, 2012, Marvin Camel, Jr., age 32, was in a Ronan court for sentencing on two separate charges: felony sexual assault and felony assault on a minor.

According to court documents, the sexual assault victim, "in her twenties," said she had been at the Pablo Bar with a friend and that they had gotten a ride with Camel. He took the friend home and was supposed to take the victim home, but according to court documents, he stopped on a secluded road. The victim stated Camel tried to kiss her. The victim pushed him away but stated she was afraid of what he would do if she resisted too much. Then, say court documents, Camel raped her.

The second case occurred a year earlier when a Flathead Tribal police officer responded to a call and found a five-year-old victim. According to court documents, the victim's mother gave a ride to Camel, who sat in the backseat with the victim. Camel started playing "very roughly" with the child, pinning the child's hands and hitting him against the window. According to court documents, Camel began choking the child. While the child was struggling to breath, the mother begged Camel to stop. Then Camel bit the child's arm. The child told police that "the defendant hurt him" and an officer "observed red scratch marks on the victim's neck and a bite mark on his arm." Camel pled guilty to the charge of assault of a minor, a felony.

The court sentenced Marvin Jr. to the Montana Department of Corrections for a period of five years—all suspended but time served. The sentences for the separate charges will run consecutively.

Why Marvin Jr. received such a light sentence is anyone's guess. "He is a deeply troubled human being who should be incarcerated," said one Ronan resident. Neighbors and relatives describe Marvin Jr., "Little Fox," as "a live wire," a fuse attached to dynamite, ready to explode. They say Little Fox's childhood has left a bitter taste in his mouth, a taste that he tried to wash away with alcohol and drugs. "The drugs and the booze have ruined his teeth and rotted out his insides," said one family member.

For Marvin Jr., having to deal with his father's considerable legacy has been a way of life. "He looks just like dad and he has his name," said brother Cass. "There is more of the expectation that he can defend himself and defend Marvin's name, and fight."

Louis Camel, three years older than Marvin Jr., has had his share of alcohol-related troubles, including at least four arrests for driving while intoxicated and for disorderly domestic situations while visiting his father in Florida. He was arrested for trespassing in Lake County, Florida, in 2003.

Cass, too, has had troubles. In his late teens he sustained traumatic brain injury from an alcohol-related car crash.

The only thing that Marvin Camel laments more than the fact that he saved little money from boxing is the toll he allowed his boxing life to take on his family. Elmer Boyce once told Marvin that the only time he wanted Marvin's mind on boxing was when he was in the gym. "You can't eat, sleep and drink boxing," Boyce told him. "It's harmful." Boyce soon realized that Marvin couldn't keep his mind off of his boxing career, to the detriment of his family life.

Marvin's relationship with his sons elicits a deeply complicated emotional response. For starters, it gnaws at him that there will never be a Camel son to wax philosophical on why he's attempting to follow his father's footsteps into the ring. But even more distressing is the likelihood that two of the sons are not biologically his. Sherry has, according to Marvin, repeatedly stated that "two of the three boys aren't mine."

Sitting in Marvin's living room in Tavares, Florida, on a beautiful spring day, he slid into the early days of that whole story, telling an anecdote about Sherry bringing him his towels and helping him with his neck exercises. He talked about the Woody Street gym in Missoula and how manager Elmer Boyce once said he was "wiry but awfully strong," and about times when, in-between skipping rope, he would dance around the room and play with two-year-old Louis. The little boy would be smiling—innocent, exuberant. Dad would be laughing, talking, and flicking punches in the air. As a dad, he said he wanted to demonstrate an example that he worked hard and showed remarkable self-discipline. Cutting him off in mid-thought, I asked Marvin: "Are your sons' difficulties at least partially your fault?"

Marvin loves to joke and can't abide much solemnity. But here was a pause. A longer pause than usual. A pause hovering on the abyss of irretrievable silence. Some truths are too difficult to hear. Others, though, can provide perspective on the unforgivable, a liberating distance through which insight may be gained.

"That's my fault—Marvin [Jr.] getting into all that trouble over and over," Marvin said. "Louis is out of that phase. Two out of three kids in trouble isn't good. Two went awry. One [Cass] got a college degree. It's my fault that they went in the wrong direction. But, you know, my parents separated when I was just fifteen, and I went on to become the champ.

"Little Fox gets into a lot of trouble because he thinks he needs to stand up and defend Marvin Camel. As a young kid he starts drinking beer, smoking cigarettes. Sherry took the kids and went to the Dakotas for ten, fifteen years; she let them get out of control. I walked out, though, so it's really my fault. She thought she was a good, strong handler of the kids. But that hasn't stopped them from getting in trouble. I think I'm a good motivator of kids, but two of them have run awry."

Could boxing have successfully deterred or redirected Marvin's sons from their troubles? The man who Boyce once referred to as "the boxingest fool you ever saw" certainly thinks so.

"I do blame myself, and I should have had them all on the ropes, in the ring. I blame myself. If they were in the boxing program, they would not have chosen to follow the path of beer, drugs, and women. It's not my lifestyle. I grew up around watching people nursing a twelve-ounce can of Olympia beer, cashing their check and buying rounds of beer. I've seen that all my life.

"If the younger generation would get into boxing, they would understand that you can't drink twenty-four beers one night and then go out and fight the next. They'd end up getting their ass kicked."

Over the years Marvin has tried to mend things with his sons. Cass has spent substantial blocks of time with his father in Florida, talking with, learning from, and listening to the man he scarcely knows. The bond that ties Cass to his father is obvious and elemental. Cass can pinpoint, more easily than most sons, the instant his dad became a mere mortal in his eyes. "I was five and saw his picture in the paper," said Cass. "I asked where he was, and he was gone." On these frequent visits, father and son re-establish, or perhaps more correctly, establish, their bond. Marvin attempts to make good on what can be mended. This is how pain, locked in a shoebox of old photos and video tapes, is freed. This is how people are saved.

"If Marvin were to return to the reservation he would fast become an old relic—kids are into MP3s and social media—and it would probably kill him," said sister Florine. At 59, she lives in the San Francisco area and hasn't seen or talked to Marvin in several years. Florine left the Flathead Reservation for Portland, Oregon, when she was 20.

"I had a vision of the city streets," said Florine. "I knew if I stayed on the reservation I would die or end up in prison. I felt as if I were a woman without a country—that's when I was a teenager. I was isolated [in Montana], and being half-black, I had to hear the taunts of Indians, who were the most racist of all. You'd get recognized as half-black if you jumped higher or ran faster. And even though that athleticism paved the way for us, you still didn't belong."

Florine returned to Montana in the 1990s during the final stages of her father's life. "I moved home and it destroyed my marriage," said Florine. "I returned hoping that it would heal my family and it only opened the wounds of the past. Here in California, I'm cycling, running, and weight training, but as soon as I got back to Ronan—to a vast state of nothingness—I wasn't taking care of myself. When I looked good or if I felt good, one of my brothers joked, 'When are you going to start looking or acting like you live in Ronan?'"

For every ugly narrative about life on the reservation, there are perhaps dozens more of men and women attempting to do something positive both internally and interpersonally. One of the many positive trajectories includes the path of actress Lily Gladstone, noted for her roles in *Winter in the Blood* and *Jimmy P: Psychotherapy of a Plains Indian.* Her first eleven years were spent primarily in Browning and East Glacier, Montana, where her family maintains a house. Instead of rattling off a litany of deep-seated problems, Gladstone speaks affectionately about her ancestral land, which she returns to occasionally.

"The reputation of Browning [on the Blackfeet Reservation] depends on who it is you talk to," said Gladstone, 28. "There are some incredibly ugly things that happen but shouldn't. But you have to look deeper into why things are the way they are. At the foundation of my life, there is community and family. There is poverty, violence, substance abuse, and unemployment everywhere. But there is so much love in that community. What unites people there is a love of family, a love of land."

Gladstone said that no matter where she lives or travels, her love begins at home. Her feet are moving, but her heart is stationary. "I love my people," said Gladstone. "What I do in life always points toward home and is done with home in mind."

Another positive story may be found in the life of Marvin's sister, sixty-two-year old Patricia Camel Kelly, who retired from the U.S. Army as a lieutenant colonel on January 1, 2012 (her birthday), after 25 years of service to America. Lt. Col. Kelly served oversees tours in Germany, Korea, and Iraq as well as numerous stateside assignments. Her awards and decorations include the Meritorious Service Medal, three times; the Army Commendation Medal, six times; and the Army Achievement Medal, three times.

Kenny Camel's learning and formal education is ongoing; his background in business administration, forestry, computer technology, and Native American art provides him with a rich foundation. After 23 professional fights, he quit boxing with a 17-3-3 record. His souvenirs are marked scars under his piercingly triangular eyebrows.

"I was tired of hitting people, tired of being hit. I had the legacy of being Marvin's younger sibling and all of the expectations were on me," said Ken. "I wanted to head out on another road."

He hopes that his love of storytelling and art will pave his road into a leadership position in his tribe. In his fifties, he struggles to find comfort on the reservation. He has held several jobs within the tribe and works as a basketball referee for the Montana Officials Association. He still grapples with anger and dependency issues, but his persistence to be a better man might finally pay off for him both financially and in personal satisfaction. He has been advocating Native management of Kerr Dam, a hydroelectric dam built on a sacred site called the Salish Falls in the early 1900s. In 2012, a water rights compact was finalized which would bring "millions to the reservation" to improve and rehabilitate the irrigation system, restore and protect wetlands, and "support unitary management of water as a resource for all." "A few non-Indians think they are being cheated and that Indians are getting more than their fair share," said one Arlee resident who requested anonymity. "In truth, Indians remain dirt poor."

Taking over ownership and operations of Kerr Dam will be both a historic and legal triumph for the Flathead Reservation. The Hellgate Treaty of 1854 was unlike many other tribal treaties in Montana because it gave the Flathead Reservation members rights to access and utilize waterways outside of their homeland. That treaty gave the tribe the legal strength to take over the dam, although it took decades of legal wrangling.

"We will finally gain managerial control of Kerr Dam after 100 years of betrayal," said Ken. "The area is flush with vegetation where camas grows readily. Its glacial till provides the perfect growing conditions for many of nature's staples—Salish people's staples."

Ken also is trying to gain recognition as an artist, and he dreams of teaching his native language. He is currently developing a language-training program that includes the use of common words and passages for those wishing to learn the "Salishian language."

His experiences since boxing included a stint as an aerial smoke jumper for the U.S. Forest Service, which gave him the surreal experience of jumping out of an airplane and feeling "like an eagle." He is now in his senior year of study at the Salish and Kootenai College to obtain a Bachelor of Science degree.

As does his brother, Ken talks of developing a program to better equip at-risk youth for society. "I want to help young people prepare for the challenges of the world and help children find themselves. If they know about Marvin Camel, they will know about the greatest boxer in the history of Montana." He wants them "to learn their heritage, culture, traditions and language."

He also wants nonmembers to be mindful of the challenges of "what it's like living on a reservation," and the "challenges and experiences being of mixed blood." A consummate storyteller, Ken shares legends and kernels of wisdom freely: "Listen to the wind, my friends. That is where the answers are."

Thousands of miles away, in the balmy coastal milieu of central Florida, Marvin Camel trolls the internet for news about the land where he was born and raised, which he still loves.

On September 10, 2012, the Associated Press announced that the Confederated Salish and Kootenai Tribe (CKST) planned to issue $10,000 checks to about 7,850 enrolled tribal members, distributing about half the $150 million it received in a national settlement over the U.S. government's long mishandling of money from tribal trust lands. (An agreement largely championed by Elouise Pepion Cobell, an enrolled member of the Blackfeet Nation in Montana. Great-granddaughter of Mountain Chief, one of the legendary Indian leaders of the West, Cobell led a 16-year momentous legal fight to get the federal government to compensate an estimated 500,000 Native Americans for mismanaging their trust accounts.)

The CSKT council disagreed as to what to do with the remainder of the $150 million. Care of the elderly, economic development, or language and culture preservation are among the projects under consideration. Some tribal members wanted all the money distributed to individual tribal members.

"I keep track of all the news—Indians getting their checks," said Camel. "I would like to go back in Montana to let the people know that you can be the greatest, whether it's at boxing or math or sports or business. If I can do it, anybody can. It's about the attitude, the will to win. All my brothers and sisters are all successful."

Marvin talks about organizing a gym in Ronan or Polson, the town where he started boxing in at age twelve. That direction, he hopes, will lead them to the taped gloves, padded posts, and knotted glove laces of the Sweet Science. Perhaps he and Kenny would do this together.

Boxing is making a slight resurgence in Montana. The H-Town Eagles Boxing Club in Helena has a slick, capable 10–1 welterweight prospect named Duran Caferro, 25, and other several amateur prospects. Other clubs are forming.

"Boxing is the only professional sport Montana can ever support or ever afford," said Todd "The Kid" Foster, 47, of Great Falls, Montana, a welterweight who fought more than 45 professional bouts between 1989 and 2001. The former C.M. Russell High School athlete earned a national Golden Gloves championship and represented Team USA at the 1988 Seoul Summer Olympics. He plans to open a boxing club for youth and adults by the end of 2014. "There's never going to be pro football or hockey, or basketball or baseball, to speak of, ever in Montana. Absolutely never. Coming from Montana you need to make your own breaks."

Camel has a similar vision. "I'd like to get some kids into the Olympics boxing," said Camel. "I spent nineteen years in the amateurs before I got my break. Boxing can touch the lives and souls of people. Not just on reservations, we can reach out to all Montana youth."

"I need to ask myself 'where do I see my future?'," Camel said. "I believe it is in moving back to my reservation. I've been so busy working I just haven't done it. I've been working 25 hours a day, eight days a week. I'm still in shape. I still run. Before moving back, though, I need to establish myself financially."

If he returns to Montana, Marvin thinks he will receive a hero's welcome. "I listen to the people who say, 'Marvin, you are from the Flathead, you might as well come back'," said Marvin. He still views himself as a "representative for the city of Ronan, the Flathead Reservation, and the state of Montana," and speaks appreciatively of Ronan boosting his popularity.

Then there is an obscure reference to a past wrong or perceived slight, "a sour deal with businessmen in Ronan" who "made a mockery of him," and alternate ebb and flow of eloquence and enigma. In quiet contemplation he adds a few words that tell the truth and require no analysis. "I didn't leave Montana to lose," he said, gesturing to a hand-painted drum bearing his name and image, given to him decades ago.

Camel's calm confidence about his roots doesn't come across as bravado. But it's hard to know whether or not his musings are outpourings of emotion or flippant whims of conversation. Clear realistic thought or an ingrained, complicated reaction? "Marvin has been saying he is coming back for years," said one friend. "Only he knows if he's ready or if he really wants to."

Transitions. That's essentially what life is all about, and it's harder than rocket science. We go from school to work to retirement to the end of the line—and we are supposed to do it without resisting too hard. Perhaps returning to Montana would only further glue Camel to the past when he should be jumping into the future.

"When you are with Marvin, you are the audience," said sister Florine. "He still has that fantasy and vision of boxing—he's not maturing. He is stuck in that time that was important to him."

22

"BOXING IS NO GOOD FOR ANYBODY."

Boxing biographies seldom end happily. Rags to riches? Perhaps briefly. But what soon follows is an even steeper reversal. Many boxers go from famous and adored to nobodies and ignored.

The only thing harder than being a fighter is being a former fighter. The manifestations are varied: dementia, drugs, debt, detention. One way or another, many of those intimate with violence are corrupted or imperiled by it. When one crosses the line from incivility to socially sanctioned savagery, it can be implausibly challenging to glide back to something requiring peace and pleasantries.

Other than showing a number of scars around his eyes, Marvin Camel, at age 63, looks more like a man in his 50s. Father Time has not knocked out Camel. There is no deep well of self-loathing, just a consuming self-regard as well as a consuming sense of what was.

Unsurprisingly, menial jobs at middle age—grappling with weeds, providing directions to the electronics aisle to seniors— lack the kind of magic you'd find in a young man's boxing auditorium. "I guess I've been trying to figure out for a long time now just what's next from Marvin Camel. What does Marvin Camel do now? How am I going to bring Marvin Camel back from the dead?"

Boxers' memories tend to get trapped in the glory of their most glorious days. That type of narcissism does not always mellow with age. "Life moves forward," said former world cruiserweight champion Vassiliy Jirov, 40. "Many who box don't see that. They don't like to move forward. Life moves forward to the next step, the next opportunity, and next possibility. My experiences in the ring are not the end of my life."

It is a delicate balance, however, as boxers must keep some connections to their pasts to maintain authenticity. "I do miss being the topic of conversation," said retired Idaho cruiserweight Kenny Keene, 46. "It's nice to walk into a place and have people recognize you and want to talk with you. It hurts to lose that."

Former WBA world lightweight champion Ray "Boom Boom" Mancini, 53, admits that he likes being remembered, even today, more than 20 years after his retirement. "My lady says that I need to have drama," Mancini told me recently. "She says that I always have to have action or stimulus going on." Mancini understands that curiosity about him will always be one of the rhythms of his presence. "The light is only there for a short period of time," said Mancini. "Then the light moves. Right now, I have the very best of both worlds. I'm asked to be around just enough to feed my ego, and not enough to disrupt my life." He realizes that change only comes through nonstop struggle, but "you've got to pace yourself in life, and there is a lot I want to accomplish."

The pendulum of ex-IBF junior lightweight champion Angel Manfredy, 39, only swings two ways these days; it sways in the present realm of the normalcy he said he so desires: youth mentorship, family, and faith. And it dangles in the glory days of fighting and the deep echoes of those past moments when he triumphed.

"During that fight against John Brown in 1998," said Manfredy, "there was a picture of me on one of the skyscrapers. There were people out there looking for autographs a block and a half long. But now nobody's watching."

Once upon a time, Matthew Saad Muhammad was the light

heavyweight champion of the world. He earned around four million dollars during his 18-year career from 1974 to 1992, maybe more—no one kept reliable count. Then he bottomed out. In June 2010, broke and with nowhere to turn, the former champion of the world walked into a homeless shelter on Ridge Avenue in North Philadelphia because he needed a place to sleep. He stayed four months.

When a Philadelphia newsman found Saad Muhammad in the shelter, the reporter kindly described him as a few pounds over his fighting weight and looking brawny across the shoulders and chest. Blessed with a deluxe knockout punch, celestial recovery powers, and enough heart to stock a brigade of Marines, Saad Muhammad was once the prototype of 1980s' sluggers. But the former champ had descended into hunger and sadness. He told the reporter: "No good, boxing. Why would anyone let himself get hit in the head?"

Few fighters got hit in the head more than Saad Muhammad. "A left-right combination drove Saad Muhammad into the ropes," reported *Sports Illustrated* about a 1982 fight against Dwight Braxton. "The unrelenting Braxton unleashed punches in great fearful volleys, hooks and straight right hands." In all, Saad Muhammad fought 58 times for a total of 397 rounds, winning 39 times and losing 16; he won by knockout 29 times and was knocked out himself eight times. But the numbers don't always disclose the whole story.

Shortly before he died in the summer of 2014 from amyotrophic lateral sclerosis, also known as Lou Gehrig's disease, I interviewed Matthew Saad Muhammad several times. "Boxing is no good for anybody," he said over and over again. "Getting hit in the head is no good. You men make your money young and then get out. Do it that way. Make your money—leave." The 57-year-old's conversation style was essentially a series of unrelated thoughts, one dissolving into another without resolution, a litany of rambling biographical excerpts that include anecdotes of punching and getting slugged. He admitted, "I still feel some of those punches." Other memories include having gobs of cash in his pockets, a gigantic entourage of sycophants sucking his bank account, a dream house, and a $275,000 Rolls-Royce.

The list of boxers who have reportedly suffered brain damage includes legends such as Joe Louis, who developed dementia symptoms, and Sugar Ray Robinson, who died of Alzheimer's disease. Experts now use a variety of terms in lieu of the old description: "punch-drunk syndrome." It's called chronic traumatic brain injury, chronic traumatic encephalopathy, boxer's encephalopathy, and *dementia pugilistica* —a medical term to describe the most severe cases.

Former WBA heavyweight champion James "Bonecrusher" Smith, 60, said that a healthy regimen among former boxers is a rarity. "I'm eating a tuna salad right now," said Smith when I interviewed him. "I'm in great shape for an old man. Sometimes when I'm out at boxing conventions, I'll see some pitiful guys. Instead of drinking water, they drink liquor. They abuse their body. Not me."

Livingstone Bramble, a West Indies-born Rastafarian, recently said that his future vitality is predicated on the wisdom of his choices today. The former WBA lightweight champion, 53, grapples with short-term memory issues and lingering soreness in his neck and shoulders.

"I have to watch it now," said Bramble, "have to stay in the gym, and I always have to do something. My destiny is to stay in shape for the rest of my life. After all those punches, you need to eat right, eat proper, and take care of your body, or you will hardly make it to 70. If you have brain damage, you can't just go and drink a vodka. You got to do it different if you were a fighter."

Like the others, Marvin Camel is concerned about the condition of former fighters. Shared bloodletting is as much a bonding agent as shared blood.

"I hope he can come out of his stupor," said Camel, shortly before Saad Muhammad's death. "His story makes me think about putting together a boxing federation fund. So many boxers get out of the sport and have nothing to look forward to. The boxing world has never had a pension operation. You leave boxing and still need to make a wage.

"Matthew Saad and I have to learn how to work at something other than boxing," Camel said. "So many guys have nothing to look forward to after boxing. Social Security is our only remuneration. We have no way to pay the bills. I never had to pay one penny for trips out of the state and country. Boxing paved the way in that regard. But I don't have a hill of beans as far as money is concerned.

"I could sit and bitch and moan, maybe I can get off my old ass and start talking to the government. I could moan, 'I need help.' But I need to help myself. Managers get thirty-three percent out of a million. Everybody wants all that money. I should have put some of that in the bank. What I made went to buying this and that. One fight kept me going until the next fight. Twenty-one fights in Las Vegas, the richest city in the world. There is a contract on the table, you need to take it or leave it. I could have held out and made more money. The more money you make, you more you lose. Would I be any different if I'd made more? Learn to live on what you got."

Indeed, Camel believed in the Spartan feeling the old fighters had toward their sport. He thought they fought as much for the love of the sport as for the money, and he admired that compulsion. Camel's misfortune was fighting in the day before cable and pay-per-view broadcasts, which can bring a monetary windfall for top fighters. Even now, Ibar Arrington (who Marvin defeated August 22, 1978) occasionally bumps into promoters he knew from years ago, "and they tell me, 'Ibar, if I had you today you'd be a multimillionaire'." The same would be true for Camel.

For some boxers, the violence in the ring is a manifestation of the violence in the soul. For most, however, the violence is a stage, and that stage has an exit door. The violent part of his life, said Arrington, 63, "stayed in the ring. There was not even a desire anymore. I still worked out after retirement. I punched a heavy bag, but that was just to stay in shape."

Religious conviction was the main reason Arrington had no longing to return to the ring. "The Bible teaches love," he said. "But when I was a boxer, I didn't love my opponents. I'd just as soon kill them as look at them. That killer instinct they say you have to have, well, I had it. There were a couple of times when I really tried my best to kill them. But now I just don't see how you can hit a man and say that it's with love. I just don't see that's God's way of doing things."

Twenty-five years after his retirement, Arrington remains remarkably intact. "I used to have people come up to me after fights and say, 'Ibar, don't those punches hurt?' And maybe with the punches I took, I should be dead. Or if not dead, maybe I should at least be brain-dead." But for Arrington, "I am," he says with a chortle, "just as crazy as I ever was."

Sean O'Grady, 55, retired at age 24 with a record of 81 wins and 5 losses, with 70 wins by coming by knockout. "I didn't want to end up like so many boxers that stayed around after their careers should have been over," said O'Grady, a former lightweight champion. "So many hang around past their prime, with an attitude of 'he can hit me all he wants, but he can't hurt me.' That's not right. You sustain more damage when you fight after your career is essentially over. You get that damage when you are still sparring. There is a point when you don't have the same reactions, and you get hit with punches you should never have been hit with. Those punches can't hurt you today, but wait 10 years and you will see the effects."

"It's not just boxers with head issues, just look at Brett Favre, just look at all of these football players," O'Grady said. "One aspect of it is, and this is something my dad would ask, what else are you doing in addition to being hit in the head? This is something my dad taught me, you need to be studying, rehearsing, learning, solving problems, reading, doing a whole bunch of other things rather than just being hit in the head."

Former heavyweight champion Pinklon Thomas retired only to succumb to the lure of false hope and legitimate paydays. Weeks after he lost to Evander Holyfield in 1989, Thomas found himself on a bar stool in Miami in the early morning hours. Slovenly, smelly, and unshaven, he had been binging on cocaine and other drugs and swigging booze for five consecutive days. He had dropped 13 pounds and worn the same clothes for a week. "That was it for me," said Thomas. "I decided to become one-hundred percent clean. I've been one-hundred percent clean since February 10, 1989. Every February 10, which is my birthday, I celebrate. There is no shame in my game."

At 56, Thomas lives in the Orlando, Florida, area and dedicates much of his time to motivating teens and at-risk youth. He founded Project P.I.N.K. (an acronym for Pride In Neighborhood Kids) as an outlet to foster youth mentorship. Thomas emphasizes shunning drugs and peer pressure, as well as the importance of setting goals and responding to mistakes and difficulties in life with aplomb. "For me, boxing is over and done," said Thomas.

It seems the most successfully transitioned boxers busy themselves with other things and feel absolutely no remorse over steering clear of the fight game.

"I can speak," said Camel. "There are guys who've had half as many fights as I have and are on Queer Street, lost their brains and are goofy. I've been very fortunate. I'm not sad. I just don't have a lot of money."

Mussolini once said that every man dies in a manner which corresponds to the way he lived his life. Those who perpetuate violence and who are applauded for it, in many cases, are themselves undone by it. Indeed, the rate of violent death among former boxers is sobering.

A recent casualty: former three-division world boxing champion Hector "Macho" Camacho, who died on November 24, 2012, in a San Juan Hospital. On November 20, the fifty-year-old Camacho was sitting in the passenger seat of a Ford Mustang parked in front of a bar in Bayamon, Puerto Rico, his hometown, when he was shot in the jaw by a gunman. The car's driver was shot and killed. Police found nine small baggies of cocaine in Camacho's pocket and an open packet inside the automobile. Two days later Camacho was declared clinically brain dead. After suffering a heart attack, he was removed from life support.

Both inside and outside the ropes, it seems that violent ends and abrupt declines will forever be embedded in boxing.

23

STILL LOOKING FOR SOMETHING

THE GREAT WAIL FROM THE PEOPLE. A STREAM OF BLOOD. SQUIRTS from the water bottle. More wails. More blood. A face bloodier than a slab of beef. Humidity of Las Vegas feeling like a Turkish bath. Punching at will. Not being able to defend against punches.

Images of the ring flash through Marvin Camel's memory every few minutes. In these flashbacks, boxing is never solely about learning to inflict and withstand harm. It is also about the bonds between trainer and boxer, family camaraderie, the jolly relationship between boxer and the boxing press, the thrill of knowing that the cameras are ready to roll.

While the passing of years is never kind to any athlete, perhaps none feel the sting quite as acutely as a boxer. Today Marvin Camel can still raise those wrists, knuckles and hands and, if he were still so inclined, deck someone with the savagery that fashioned 21 knockouts in 62 professional matches. He could still plant those gnarled hands in someone's ribs, harkening back to the kind of relentless poundings that had Mate Parlov on the ropes in front of a world-wide audience on ABC's "Wide World of Sports." He could still unleash a barrage of jabs, hooks and roundhouses, not with the same ferocity and certainly not with the stamina that once produced hundreds of punches in a 15-round fight, but enough to leave the tough guys gasping.

Camel's body and mind belie the physical and emotional toll of cramming an average man's lifetime into three decades. There may be the occasional bout of forgetfulness or absentmindedness, or the sporadic bout of ennui, but, for the most part, Camel is sharp through and through.

His eyes are another matter: the champion suffers from greatly diminished vision. Perhaps he should have walked away from boxing when the retina problem was first diagnosed, but historically boxers have demonstrated a particular stubbornness to walk away. Rare indeed is the boxer who walks away on top, championship belt in hand, faculties intact. Camel exited long after he should have—wearing no belt, enjoying no glory. But his mind was not left in the ring; it is all there.

It is one of the many ironies of Marvin Camel that he excelled in a violent, primarily urban sport, and yet he loved—and still loves—a totally peaceful, small-town life. He laughs and flirts with his wife. She frequently calls him "the Champ," which some of Marvin's siblings find a little irritating—believing that it only traps him in a distinctly immovable mindset. Marvin and Norma have a favorite set of television programs, including *Shark Tank* and *Downton Abbey*, and giggle over their large plates of strawberry and whipped cream desserts and cheap hot dogs. Norma is Marvin's balance; she is more of a homebody, loyal, dependable, and protective.

Marvin and Norma live in a retirement village called Lake Francis Estates in the county seat of Lake County, Florida. Marvin doesn't seem old enough to live there. While the rest of the graying pack zip around in their licensed golf carts and discuss the vagaries of arthritis, last wills, and death, Marvin, who hasn't even had the slightest common cold in years, appears comparatively lively. At 63, he is slim and boyish, brimming with stories and wry commentary. He engages strangers in conversation about the simpler things in life. He understands people without judging them. His mantras on life are aphoristic: treat people with respect, you will receive respect; maintain that coolness.

Marvin Camel looks for purpose. Like most men who've exerted themselves so much so early in life, it can be a challenge to find that next new conquest, the next feat to strive for. He hasn't coached local kids since he had a falling out with Ron Lopez. Some of the kids thought that Marvin was too rough with them during sparring and told Lopez. Ron took Marvin outside to talk about it. After both men aired their sharp differences of opinion, Ron said he wanted Marvin out of the gym for good, and Marvin washed his hands of the relationship. But not before he let Lopez have it verbally. "I called him every name in the book," said Camel. "Plus one." With distinctly harmonious enunciation, tinged with a slight 'Montana Native' accent, which gives piquancy to his delivery, he poured forth a flood of the most graphic word paintings. "I told that no good sonofabitch that I was trying to teach the kids boxing. There is no way you can cultivate a world champion without taking punishment."

Marvin refuses to let his life devolve into an empty grind. He mows yards and jogs wearing a black garbage bag with holes cut out for his arms: the bag retains heat which helps him sweat off the pounds and keep his desired weight. Sometimes he gets into trouble unintentionally, like the time he was bit on the knuckle of his left hand by a pygmy rattler in front of Norma's mother's house. A bite from this type of snake is occasionally fatal. "I thought that if the snake didn't do me in, then Norma's drive to the emergency room was going to," he said.

Wearing a smile as warm as the Florida sun, he jokes with—and about—his neighbors. Most days, his face is so animated—with friendly gibes, eyebrow arching, snatches of song, and sudden mimic impulses—that his rare spells of straight-face seem out of place.

Many mornings, Camel may be spotted at a local diner called The Sunrise Grill. There, above the front door, three pictures of Camel jut out as part of the wall's boxing collage. He floats through the restaurant as buoyant as a fresh helium balloon. He tips his cap and smiles politely as passersby brush in and out. He is eager to start a conversation, and he loves to sit adjacent to his photos. If customers don't notice the hat, or the sweatshirt with the boxing gloves emblem, shouldn't they recognize the similarities between the man in the photos and the one sipping coffee next to them?

When a stranger tells Marvin about their life or reflects on their past, he waits and listens and then introduces himself, "I'm Marvin Camel, two-time former cruiserweight champion of the world." Norma laughs: "Sometimes Marvin says it so fast I'm not sure people even get what it is he says. But that's okay. He's my darling."

In the retirement community, Marvin plays cards and games with the fellas. When one of them teases him about his boxing career, Camel smilingly tells the man, "If I come out of retirement, you will be my first opponent."

At one of his card games, some of the old-timers rib Marvin and make not-so-subtle remarks about his race, color, and appearance. They seem to take it a little far at times, but Marvin doesn't mind. In fact, he takes it in stride, tossing his nickels on the table while joking about Columbus' bad directions and the demise of Ira Hayes. In some ways, it's an impressive scene: a powerful man, a dangerous boxer, a former world champion, letting the wisecracks and dubious comments vanish harmlessly into thin air like a slipped punch.

Some commenters were simply ignorant. One neighbor, after eyeing the WBC belt Marvin proudly wore around his waist, told him that his accomplishment was no bigger feat than if he had won the community's horseshoe tournament.

We were in the outskirts of Orlando. Everywhere the air was full of sounds of new construction; you could almost hear the money crashing in like the big breakers rolling onto the shore. The late afternoon truck traffic was heavy, with an ambulance, its red roof light turning and its siren going, trying to get through, and in the stretches between the traffic lights, condos, and Asian massage parlors, the drivers of the passenger cars cutting back and forth between lanes.

Marvin talks incessantly about everything: the messiness of the urban cityscape, which he attributes to "goddamn foreigners," to solving the overcrowding issues facing prisons by "letting them all kill each other." He goes into a long monologue about Ira Hayes, the Indian who helped raise the American flag at Iwo Jima only to die on home soil of exposure in an irrigation ditch. "Did you know he died in nothing but a puddle? I don't want to end up like that."

There is the occasional anecdote about sex, "sacking a few ring card girls" and boxing's mantra that abstinence is the healthiest route. "I tried to lay off sex at least one and a half months before a fight."

"What did you do when you were fighting monthly?"

"I had to wait."

"You know in every single article I've ever read about you, you told people that you never chased women, right?"

"No, I never chased them," he smiles with the mischievous indication that he once went through girls like bars of soap. "Notice that I said *chase*."

Success comes with perks, perks come with temptations. Temptations come with consequences. I said to Marvin, "I interviewed someone who told me that you always had a beautiful woman on your arm."

"Better than having ugly ones, right?" retorted Marvin. "I guess whatever is printed on Marvin Camel has to be the whole story."

If life becomes a nostalgia trip, best make it a good one, rife with glittery places, championship belts, and talk of nonstop bouts of hard-fought four-rounders.

We stumble upon the Thundering Spirit Pow Wow, an annual

gathering of central Florida's native population. The air is cool and clean, the heat soft. On a whim, Camel, wearing his WBC belt, navy dress shirt, and dark blue blazer, asks the organizers if they would like to introduce "the former two-time cruiserweight champion of the world" to the crowd—and they agree. On Mount Dora's Renningers fairgrounds, Camel speaks for three impromptu minutes to a circle of families, authentic artisans, and open hearts. He talks about Montana and his home in Tavares and says he is happy to be a part of this mutual, spiritual gathering. On the way to his car, he signs a pair of boxing gloves for a muscular, twenty-something blonde-haired kid who happened upon the gloves that very morning at the adjacent flea market.

"Right now, we are respected here in the community," said Camel. "When people see me, they are proud to have a world champion living in their community. When Marvin Camel goes down to the clubhouse, in a three-piece suit, with his boxing belts, and announces that he is going to Arizona to be inducted into the 'Indian Hall of Fame'—these are the things that make me feel that my life is worthwhile."

CAMEL WAS INDUCTED INTO THE MONTANA INDIAN ATHLETIC Hall of Fame in 2007. "Boxing only has pretenders, contenders, or world champions," Camel said during the induction. "Pretenders don't train enough. Contenders can't get over the last hump. It takes 25 hours a day, eight days a week. You have to stay away from drinking, smoking, gambling, philandering, wild women. I didn't pray to become world champion. I put in the effort to become world champion."

Could the greatest of all recognition, the International Boxing Hall of Fame, be in Marvin's future?

"Marvin Camel should be considered for the International Hall of Fame," said boxing analyst and insider Frank Stea. "He could go in for being the first ever recognized world champion at cruiser-weight, for being a Native American holding the world title, and for all of the great fights he had."

The problem, Shea said, was that "people rarely saw a Marvin Camel fight on national television or grace the covers of boxing publications. There wasn't enough international fame because of those factors. That's why Marvin Camel is not in the hall."

Perhaps Marvin's fighting style also hurts his chances of getting in the IBHF. "I was at the Parlov fight when Marvin won the title," said Beau Williford, owner of the Ragin' Cajun boxing club in Lafayette, Louisiana, and longtime boxing trainer. "I can tell you that Marvin boxed perfectly that night. His problem, in my opinion, was that he was not a really exciting fighter. He had all the tools to be exciting, the publicity tools, the Indian thing. But the lack of excitement as a fighter hurts his chances."

Either way, Marvin Camel's name is forever attached to Montana.

"Other boxers, they knew he was what Montana had to offer," said former WBA lightweight champion Livingstone Bramble. "His nickname could have been 'Montana'."

"If you grew up in Montana or you were from Montana, you just knew the name Marvin Camel," said Helena-born actor Dirk Benedict, 69, most noted for his role as Templeton "Faceman" Peck on the 1980s-era TV series *The A-Team*. "Marvin was a star. He was a star. He looked like a star. I'm sure there are many, many people who've wondered what happened to him. He was there and popular and then he was like a disappearing ship. I always wanted to meet him when he was boxing."

There is still ambiguity as to just who Marvin Camel is and what he represented.

"Marvin hasn't gotten recognized in the public and by the native people as much as he should," said Browning-born former heavyweight Joe Hipp. "There is so much more media today to help people, modern people. When I was fighting, I had twenty-three or so televised fights. When Marvin fought, there wasn't as much media and television for him. There aren't enough great role models for Native Americans."

Hipp said he finally learned the details of Marvin's career only after boxing him in 1989. "It's amazing for a young native kid from a little town in Montana to win the biggest title. You know, the titles meant more back then; today, each title has about ten titles beneath it."

"To make it in athletics from Montana is a big goddamn' deal and it always will be," said Bob "Spud" McCullough, 73, who played in all of the Denver Broncos' 56 games as an offensive guard between 1962 and 1965. "Getting to the National Football League from Montana was huge then and it's still huge today. Think about it this way, Montana only had what a half a million people or so in the 1960s and 1970s. Football had scholarships and we were raised in it, and had coaches and shit. But boxing? Shit. Where do you start if you are in Montana?"

Cities such as Philadelphia and Detroit have produced epic champions, trainers, and gym wars. From Joe Frazier and Sonny Liston to Sylvester Stallone's "Rocky," the lore and culture of Philly boxing is so dense and longstanding that a volunteer-driven program even started in 2005 to place headstones on the unmarked graves of deceased fighters. In south Philly, guys have been dodging and blocking jabs and chucking uppercuts, hooks, and crosses, for generations. Coming from a state with a small population (no more than 800,000 in Camel's prime) could be viewed as a hindrance. But Marvin reworked that negativity into motivation.

"The only thing that I thought could overcome being from the state of Montana was to train and run and to train and run some more. Running for me is what made me. The hills and fresh air of Montana made Marvin Camel. It's rough terrain and I ran every mile in the state of Montana. That gave me power, endurance, and helped me knock off the excess fat. I ran that terrain for 19 years before I became a world champion."

Among many Native Americans, Camel's name still triggers a strong emotional charge. "I remember seeing a picture of him wearing a war bonnet and I thought it was cool," said Frank Kipp, 53, a third-generation boxer and trainer from Browning. Kipp, a burly former street fighter with hairline and facial scars, started the Blackfeet Nation Boxing Club to give reservation youth a safe haven. He founded the club in 2003 at the request of tribal leaders. "Marvin fought some tough guys wearing that bonnet. Boxing relies on your conditioning—and he had it. He fought at the time of the American Indian Movement and at a time when there were so many things happening among the movement of the early 1970s. We've always known of him."

Camel's name lingers in private memories even he could not be aware of. "When I drive by the building that Marvin once ran as a business, I think about him and what he meant to this community," said Robert McDonald, Tribal Communications Director of the Confederated Salish and Kootenai Tribes. "When Marvin was boxing, we as a people talked about winning and pride, talked about the excitement of his career. Today, when we get together, we generally talk about drugs or meth issues, or child endangerment or abandonment issues, or racism, or water rights, problems, and more problems. When Marvin was here, we had a champion. And now I look at that building, and Marvin is gone, and all that is left is another building on the reservation that leaks."

The hands of Marvin Camel—once instruments of punishment—are now used to mow his deceased mother-in-law's grass and fulfill pre-paid orders for landscaping services that pile up in the retirement community of 450 homes. Those hands mow seventy lawns a week; sometimes they mow all day.

Camel had worked as a security guard at Best Buy after Circuit City closed, but his shifts inexplicably dwindled to the point where it was no longer practical or cost-effective for him to continue. He concedes that taunting someone whom he apprehended stealing merchandise didn't help his job security. "They said I was rubbing his nose in it. What was I supposed to do? Pat him on the back?" So it was back to clipped grass and hot sunny labor.

"I'm pushing the mower the same way I did as a kid," Camel said. "I guess now I'm riding one, too. I've got food to eat, a place to stay, I don't have to beg. I couldn't work for anyone this day and age. So I started cutting grass. Not because I wanted to, but I had to. My first job ever started with my dad's boss, mowing grass. I hated it then. But I'm doing it now."

Camel had his name emblazoned on his favorite blue and white hat and paid for signs on his car advertising private boxing lessons. Both the hat and the signs list his claim to boxing glory: "two-time cruiserweight champ." The signs have lured in only one interested party, though ringside and public introductions are common. He understands. After speaking at the powwow, he admits, "I would say that ninety percent of the people don't know who I am, and the other ten percent don't care. But we forced it on them." He laughs.

Marvin Camel's self-image will never be threatened. He welcomes people to pry into his life for any reason or to "look him up on the computer." His pride has perhaps even strengthened a bit with age. "This is Marvin Camel, the two-time cruiserweight champion of the world," he will occasionally blurt when answering the phone. His email address includes the word 'unique' before his name.

There are times when he does not reference the past or future, when he lives for this hour and laughs at this moment, understanding that the evening sun eventually sets on each one of us. After all, many of the people involved in his boxing career—opponents, referees, managers, trainers, newspapermen—are no longer living. To further hammer home the message of life's fragility, Norma fights stage-four cancer—a disease she and Marvin believed she had defeated twenty years ago. They stay in Florida because it is close to Norma's medical care and her family; because there is steady lawn work for Marvin; and, well, because the warmth and sunshine make their world a whole lot brighter and healthier than life in Montana. A move to Montana would come with considerable financial risk, said Marvin, who received his first Social Security check in February 2013.

In May 2014, Marvin and Norma were invited to Atlantic City by the International Boxing Federation, which was recognizing its inaugural list of champions. He was awarded a plaque and in the words of friend Robert Newman, "got to ham it up." Newman, who helped organize the event, put together a few words on Marvin's behalf, strumming up the mantra about "how there can be only one first." "He was the only guy who brought the original IBF belt from 1983," said Newman. "He was opening his jacket with the belt around his waist and posing sideways. It was great to see."

But Camel is no longer a fighter, and the natural doubts about whether his life has added up to something that will be remembered occasionally comes home. He often asks himself how and why he left Montana. He questions his own drive and willingness to pack up and leave Florida to open a boxing club that can appeal to Montanans. He asks his friends on the reservation whether they would welcome him back. He second guesses the decision to say goodbye. Some days. Other days, he knows he would be just sitting on his ass in the cold winters, second guessing his decision to return. When he is reminded that years ago he told a newspaperman, "All I can do here [in Montana] is die a slow death," he is quiet. "He needs to hear that," Norma said. "He forgets."

Right now Marvin gets a lot of handshakes and lives nice. He must be forced to remember that even though he will be recognized on the streets in his home town, the fame—or the local novelty of the famous athlete, really—can disappear fast. The story of the athlete who overstays his welcome is not a new one, of course, but can one overstay their welcome with an entire people?

Would the state and my people make me feel at home? That's something that frequently floats around his mind. *Or would they treat me as if I were a busted toy? Aren't I the people's champion? Deep down in my heart, I'd like to go back.*

Mostly, Marvin Camel asks how anyone could pass judgment on him. He insists he is not escaping or living in an unsatisfactory present. He simply savors the right to enjoy the memories that still give meaning to his life. His heart beats to a dramatically different cadence, his internal clock ticking happily ever after. "I have no qualms or quarrels and I wouldn't change a thing. I don't dislike where I'm sitting."

"I see myself as successful," adds Camel. "I set out to do a job and I've seen my top potential. There's more for me still. I'm not quite sure what it is."

Why should Camel not see himself and his life in successful terms? It takes one hell of a man to handle so volatile a mix of manhood, legacy, and blood sport with such grace. His life's journey was an ambitious adventure, an obsessive need to arrive, to attain, to "make it." And he did.

Marvin Camel became the example he set out to be.

And still is.

ABOUT THE AUTHOR

BRIAN D'AMBROSIO IS A HELENA, MONTANA, WRITER, INSTRUCTOR, and media consultant. D'Ambrosio's recent articles have been published in local, regional, and national publications, including *Cowboys and Indians*, *Wisconsin Trails*, *Bark Magazine*, *Montana Magazine*, and *Backpacker Magazine*. His most recent ebook chronicled the trial and conviction of exonerated murderer Ryan Ferguson, *101 Reasons Why Ryan Ferguson Should Be Released*. D'Ambrosio is a frequent contributor to, among other internet sites, "The Huffington Post," where he profiles an eclectic assortment of people. He is currently completing a first volume of in-depth profiles of ex-entertainment wrestlers, football players, and boxers called *Life in the Trenches*. He may be reached at dambrosiobrian@hotmail.com.

INDEX